INSIDE STORIES II

SECOND EDITION

Edited by
GLEN KIRKLAND
RICHARD DAVIES

THOMSON
™
NELSON

Canadian Cataloguing in Publication Data

Main entry under title:

Inside stories II

2nd ed.
For secondary school students.
ISBN: 0-7747-0583-3
1. Short stories, Canadian (English). * 2. Short stories, American.
3. Short stories, English. I. Kirkland, Glen. II. Davies, Richard.

PN6120.2.I59 1999   823'.0108   C99-930678-2

About the Editors

Glen Kirkland
Glen is the Secondary English Consultant (Grades 7-12) for the English Catholic Schools in Edmonton, Alberta. Originally from McLennan, Alberta, Glen is well-known for his many inservices and workshops. An educator, editor, and writer, Glen leads an active life in education and communications.

Richard Davies
An English teacher at Strathcona High School for the Edmonton Public Schools, Richard is co-author of 35 publications with Glen Kirkland. Originally from Winnipeg, Manitoba, Richard combines writing, editing, and performing with his teaching career.

Project Manager: Gaynor Fitzpatrick
Editorial Assistant: Ian Nussbaum
Production Editor: Jinnean Barnard
Production Coordinator: Tanya Mossa
Copy Editor: Sharlene Weaver
Permissions Coordinator: Patricia Buckley
Permissions Editor: Emma Gorst
Photo Research: Maria DeCambra
Cover Design: Sonya V. Thursby/Opus House
Interior Design: Sonya V. Thursby/Opus House
Page Composition: Carolyn Hutchings
Cover Illustration: José Ortega/The Stock Illustration Source
Printing and Binding: Transcontinental Printing Limited
Nelson, 1120 Birchmount Road, Toronto, ON, M1K 5G4
www.nelson.com

Printed in Canada.

2 3 4 5 6 7 8   08 07 06 05

Dedicated to our remembered fathers—
William Campbell Kirkland
and Vernon Delmar Davies

G.K.
R.D.

Table of Contents

Acknowledgements

The editors and publisher gratefully acknowledge the teacher-reviewers listed below for their contribution to the development of this anthology.

Dr. Philip Allingham
Golden High School
Golden, British Columbia

Judy Ballah
English Department Head
Halifax West High School
Halifax, Nova Scotia

Susan King
English Department Head
Weston Collegiate
York City Board of Education
Toronto, Ontario

Hugh McInnon
Father Patrick Mercredi High School
Fort McMurray, Alberta

Ann Payne
St. Mary's High School
Calgary, Alberta

To the Student

Welcome to the second edition of *Inside Stories II*. This new book contains 31 selections for you to think about, discuss, and enjoy. Half the writers are Canadian (including masters such as Margaret Laurence, Alice Munro, and Sinclair Ross) and many stories are from such diverse far away corners of the globe as the Caribbean, Africa, Cuba, South America, Japan, Egypt, Pakistan, Russia, and Australia.

We have used a thematic structure of eight common literary themes including: Turning Points; Values and Choices; Conformity and Rebellion; Tradition and Change; Love, Loyalty, and Betrayal; Dreams, Illusions, and Reality; Good and Evil; and Coming of Age.

Following each story are response questions and activities for you to explore in discussion and writing. At the back of the text (starting on page 311), there is a comprehensive glossary of fiction terms to review and use as you talk and write about the stories.

We hope that, in the process of reading, reflecting on, and sharing these stories, you will discover new levels of appreciation for fiction and reading in general.

G.K.
R.D.

Turning Points

Turning points are key moments in people's lives when a new direction is either discovered or imposed through a significant change. This change is often lasting and profound, and leads to defining moments, changed perspectives, and new goals. Not surprisingly, the stories of this unit depend largely upon the fiction elements of crisis, climax, and epiphany.

In the first story, "Love Song," a boy and girl are in love, but the boy is so much a part of nature that he cannot separate himself to be truly human with his love. When he finally leaves his human self behind and faces the prospect of becoming part of nature, we know that he has achieved his destiny and inner peace. Similarly, the girl achieves a new awareness of her love, her deeper self, and the meaning of their continuing spiritual relationship.

In the second story, "Grace Period," the turning point is literally a blinding light that is going to change life on the planet for everyone including you, the reader of this short story. The main character is slow to realize what the remarkable light means, but, by the end of the story, he suddenly understands what is truly happening and how devastating change can really be.

The strange narrator of "Blue Boots" is making plans for a personal crime spree in Yellowknife. The turning point here is the move from simply planning fantasy murders to actually realizing them. The resultant glimpse into evil and its dramatic irony for victims and readers alike is truly shocking and frightening in its final effect.

Turning points in fiction, then, are meaningful shifts in the lives of individuals. The reason for the shift, what is learned from the change, and how life will be different are all elements that are worth considering because of what they reveal about our essential human nature.

"One day go to a place where the river bends, and there I shall sing for you."

Deirdre Kessler
Love Song

"A human has a human body, and walks the earth in human ways." This is what the girl tells her lover. He stares through her, not listening, and takes a handful of her hair, feels it as though it is the hair of a stranger.

The moment they saw each other, they knew in their bones they had a distance to travel. That first night they walked far into the desert, they slept under cottonwood trees by a creek. The creek sang them a song that trickled through a crack in time. And for a while, the lovers moved as one.

She knew the ways of all that grew, of all that slithered, hopped, ran, or flew. She found a place where a garden would thrive, gathered stories, explored all her desires. Someone said the sound of her name was a warm sigh at daybreak. Resting by a water hole under a bower of willows, the girl sometimes was invisible. A kit fox would drink its fill by her side. A wren would alight on her shoulder, taking a moment to preen and flutter in the watery shade.

The boy also took on the ways of wild things, moving swiftly, jumping when startled. Someone named him Coyote, and the name stuck because he was lean and tall and his hair was reddish and bushy. He let that thick hair grow down his back and wore it like a tail.

And the boy took on the habits of rock—the slow, slow ways of rock, until the mine crew felt he knew the rocks better than anyone. He worked the mines, holding with his thin strong arms the slusher that spun against the clock, burrowing into rock, slushing ore from the heart of the earth.

The men he worked with, down in those mines, came to trust him, ask him, "Is it safe today?" And though he was young enough to be the son of miners, they looked into his face and he took their question and drifted through tunnels, felt mine backs, touched cribbing and rock bolts, stopping time as he searched for an answer. Then he would give a shy, sly smile and he'd say, "Yup, it's safe today."

His mama said he was born impatient, born early, forcing his twin also to look at daylight before her time. His twin sister's eyes were weak; she could barely see. He could see too far. At four years old he took apart a broken clock and repaired it. Only, when it ran, it ran backwards. Later, his mama wondered if he had been the one to break the clock, wanting to stop time, to step aside from human habits.

Now, to the girl it is simple. A human has a human body, and walks the earth in human ways. But the boy grows more and more impatient, frustrated. He is trapped, only trapped in the skin of a human. To him it is simple: with desire a human can fly free, soar over the canyon like a red-tailed hawk, be the stratified rock with movements slow as forever. The boy sees he is everything: he is a being who slips into a form of a human, of a coyote, a bird, a rock, the wind.

What the boy does not understand is why he cannot leave his human form with the ease of a thought. Oh, in his dreams, he soars. But in the morning he wakes to the gravity of a sleeping body and pounds his fist against his thigh, his chest.

Sometimes, for days, the boy does not eat, refusing to add mass to his body, considering if he spurns it he will sooner be able to reach his ideal.

For a while, after they are lovers, the boy forgets to dream and in his sleep wraps around his lover, content with human ways. But soon his impatience returns. The girl also learns impatience. Why can't he see how simple it is to be a human?

The lovers begin to argue, to grow apart. Now there are only moments, moments when they curve to each other in the night, only moments when the boy's longing disappears.

One morning the boy awakens, tormented. He fills a skin bag with water and leaves his lover. Instead of going to the mine, he walks into the desert. Past the canyon where the river flows, past familiar barrel cactus and creosote bush, into arroyos and up onto the desert floor. He walks under the sun until the water is gone, and he walks until he stumbles and no longer can draw himself to his feet. There, he lies. He folds his boy arms around his chest and closes his eyes. He stretches out his long legs and smiles into the desert sun. Finally, the boy is able to stop time. And as night falls, he travels with planets freed from orbits. Finally and at last, he is everything.

He is everything except a certain boy in the arms of a certain girl.

That night, waves of sorrow shake the girl's body. She dreams. Inside her dream and outside it she cries. Then like a skimming hawk she floats over the ridge where her lover lies. She folds herself over him and in the shadow of wings they embrace.

"You will not mourn," he whispers, "because this, too, is life. I see how foolish I was, but only now is my wisdom sure. One day go to a place where the river bends, and there I shall sing for you."

The girl wakes from her dream. She walks across the desert, in and out of arroyos, past barrel cactus and creosote bush. She walks exactly as far as did the boy and comes to the place where he lies. She makes a travois of tamarisk branches from a nearby canyon, and drags the body of her lover to the burial place of his family.

There's a place where a river bends, a wall of rock carved smooth by water. When spring swells the river, a whirlpool sings against the canyon. A girl stands at the canyon rim and listens to the simplicity of a river carving itself to the sea. She smiles at the innocent song of water and rock, of wind and wings, of lips and breath, of death swirled into life, again and again.

RESPONDING PERSONALLY

1. Write your thoughts and feelings about this story. Share them with another student.
2. Why do you think the story is called "Love Song"? Offer classmates your interpretation based on the events of the story.

RESPONDING CRITICALLY

3. In what ways are the couple in harmony with nature? Symbolically, how is he like rock? How are the girl's images different from the boy's?
4. Why is the boy called Coyote? How does the name suit his character?
5. Poet William Wordsworth once wrote that "The Child is father of the Man." How does this quotation apply to the boy's childhood.
6. In a small group, offer your ideas about the reasons for the boy's death. How does the girl react to his passing? How do you interpret the last episode in the story?

RESPONDING CREATIVELY

7. From the point of view of the girl or the boy, write a poem expressing how she or he sees life.
8. With a partner, present a pantomime version of the couple's story.

PROBLEM-SOLVING/DECISION-MAKING

9. For paragraph writing: How would you counsel someone who was very depressed and unhappy with living? What positive advice would you give?

What's going on, you shout,
what is happening with the
atmosphere.

Will Baker
Grace Period

You notice first a difference in the quality of space. The sunlight is still golden through the dust hanging in the driveway, where your wife pulled out a few minutes ago in the Celica on a run to the mailbox, and the sky is still a regular blue, but it feels as if for an instant everything stretched just slightly, a few millimeters, then contracted again.

You shut off the electric hedge trimmers, thinking maybe vibration is affecting your inner ear. Then you are aware that the dog is whining from under the porch. On the other hand you don't hear a single bird song. A semi shifts down with a long backrap of exhaust on the state highway a quarter mile away. A few inches above one horizon an invisible jet is drawing a thin white line across the sky.

You are about to turn the trimmers on again when you have the startling sense that the earth under your feet has taken on a charge. It is not quite a trembling, but something like the deep throb of a very large dynamo at a great distance. Simultaneously there is a fluctuation of light, a tiny pulse, coming from behind the hills. In a moment another, and then another. Again and more strongly you have the absurd sense that everything inflates for a moment, then shrinks.

Your heart strikes you in the chest then, and you think instantly *aneurysm*! You are 135 over 80, and should have had a checkup two months ago. But no, the dog is howling now, and he's not alone. The neighbors' black lab is also in full cry, and in the distance a dozen others have begun yammering.

You stride into the house, not hurrying but not dawdling either, and punch in the number of a friend who lives in the city on the other side of the hills, the county seat. After the tone dance a long pause, then a busy signal. You consider for a moment, then dial the local volunteer fire chief, whom you know. Also busy.

Stretching the twenty-foot cord, you peer out the window. This time the pulse is unmistakable, a definite brightening of the sky to the west, and along with it a timber somewhere in the house creaks. You punch the Sheriff. Busy. Highway Patrol. Busy. 911. Busy. A recorded voice erupts, strident and edged with static, telling you all circuits are busy.

You look outside again and now there is a faint shimmering in the air. On the windowsill outside, against the glass, a few flakes of ash have settled. KVTX. Busy. The *Courier*. Busy. On some inexplicable frantic whim you dial out of state, to your father-in-law (Where is your wife, she should have the mail by now?), who happens to be a professor of geology on a distinguished faculty. The ringing signal this time. Once. Twice. Three times. A click.

"Physical plant."

Doctor Abendsachs, you babble, you wanted Doctor Abendsachs.

"This is physical plant, buddy. We can't connect you here."

What's going on, you shout, what is happening with the atmosphere—

He doesn't know. They are in a windowless basement. Everything fine there. It's lunchtime and they are making up the weekly football pool.

It is snowing lightly now outside, on the driveway and lawn and garage. You can see your clippers propped pathetically against the hedge. Once more, at top speed, you punch your father-in-law's number. Again a ringing. A click.

This time a recording tells you that all operators are busy and your call will be answered by the first available. The voice track ends and a burst of music begins. It is a large studio orchestra, heavy on violins, playing a version of "Hard Day's Night." At the point where the lyrics would be "sleeping like a log" the sound skips, wobbles, and skips again as if an old-fashioned needle has been bumped from a record groove.

You look out the window once more, as the house begins to shudder, and see that it is growing brighter and brighter and brighter.

RESPONDING PERSONALLY

1. Write about your thoughts and feelings as you read this story. What do you think is going on? Compare notes with a partner.
2. What associations do you have with the term *grace period*? Is there a grace period in the story? If so, identify it.

RESPONDING CRITICALLY

3. The story is told in the second person ("you"). Who is "you"? The use of "you" may be disorienting for a reader. Why do you think the author uses the second person pronoun instead of the more familiar third person ("he")?
4. Review the first impressions and first conclusion the protagonist had about what was happening. Does his first conclusion (in the fourth paragraph) make sense? Why or why not?
5. What is really going on in the story? Make a list of the details and events that support your interpretation.
6. Trying to get help in an emergency can be very frustrating. How does the story realistically portray this frustration?

RESPONDING CREATIVELY

7. As the man in the story, e-mail a message to Dr. Abendsachs.
8. Write a sequel to the story.

PROBLEM-SOLVING/DECISION-MAKING

9. In a small group, share opinions about the conventional wisdom of advice offered during emergencies such as the one described in the story. What, if anything, can an individual do?

Everybody knew me, but what
did they know?

Carol Newhouse
Blue Boots

If you live in a small town in that Victorian house set well back from
the road, where the lawn is separated by a gravel path that winds
eternally before ending at a squared area housing the rusted hulk of
a 1970 Buick, then everyone knows your name. Children fear you,
particularly if they have dared to approach on a damp Hallowe'en
night, when the wind howls, rustling the dead, dry corpses that lie
piled below the naked arms reaching menacingly from thick, wood-
en trunks.

On those infrequent occasions when you go onto Main Street,
people, old and young, peer from under hat brims then quickly look
away. Three laughing ten-year-olds grab their marbles and cower in
a doorway as the tap, tap of your walking stick resounds from the
wooden boardwalk.

No one would be surprised if unearthed skeletons of the mur-
dered point bony fingers toward your residence demanding retribu-
tion. If perchance you were found in a huddled mass at the bottom
of the stairs, ghostly culprits would be blamed amid sighs of relief. In
this mundane world, everyone has created their own story; each tale
with but one theme, and in this sameness lies its strength.

You can reach out and grapple with it, trying again and again to
diminish the whole by triumphing over each thread of the townsfolk's fantasy but this painstaking process could be a life's work. Wait!
These stories work to your advantage. As the local bugaboo you are
untouchable—free to commit dastardly deeds—particularly if your
bent, like mine, is murderous.

Of course, you may not have the luxury of owning such a man-
sion.

Apparently the per capita number of vacant houses (circa 1900)
across North America is ever dwindling. You might instead live in the

subarctic region of Canada in a city called Yellowknife, where most homes are single or double-wide trailers, the economic solution to building in an isolated rock environment where materials must be transported northward over 1500 kilometres.

Alas, creepy trees are nonexistent. No fantastic pear tree whose dead trunk can stand six steps from Landor's cottage door, nor a virtual forest of decayed trees whose leaden-hued reek can surround the House of Usher. Spindly evergreens of stunted growth are such a poor substitute they might well have rendered Edgar Allan Poe speechless.

The harsh climate militates against you too. The statistic of over two hundred days each year when the mercury dips below freezing means you cannot separate yourself through dress. Wearing the bulky parka constructed to repel temperatures of minus seventy, with the fur-lined hood and illuminating strips across the arms and back, and the knee-high Sorel boots with the double fleece liners and two-inch-thick soles, everyone looks the same. Oh yes, I forgot. Walking sticks slip on the ice. An appropriate setting does not exist. That is unfortunate. The perfect aura complements a perfect alibi and homicidal types know an appropriate person must be established before a promising career is embarked upon.

What then of our dilemma? Can a solution be found by examining the mysterious parts? The nemesis of Sherlock Holmes— Professor Moriarty—is, I fear, of little help. Genius. Philosopher. Abstract thinker. These essential elements of character are not confined to Moriarty. They may be aptly descriptive, but anyone displaying them in a city with a population of no more than twenty thousand could hardly prevail while remaining unknown. Could we, like the Professor, sheltered in a cocoon, organize and expect the populace to turn a blind ear to the droning of the agents crying forward our instructions?

Nor is there solace to be found in the crime fiction thought of as modern. Arch villains, such as Ed McBain's deaf man, may have a lifetime that exceeds one or two novels, but these wicked creations have a large metropolitan city in which to lose themselves and elude the police.

No. When you live in Yellowknife you are truly disadvantaged. I was, then, in a most dismal state, resigning myself to a fate of crimelessness as the first of eight months of winter weather commenced.

The weeks churned by and the number of daylight hours decreased as my list of potential victims increased. There seemed no end of irritating people whose names were duly inscribed in the pages of my pocket notebook. Store clerks unfamiliar with stock, office personnel operating on an agenda of hindrance, neighbours insistent upon allowing their dog to defecate on my property, telephone company employees and bank tellers—just because. Yes, all present and accounted for.

I reviewed the expanding register often in the early morning hours, repeating the names aloud. Percival Mueller. Suffocation would be a fitting end. Loretta Periwinkle. I could poison her water supply. P. Charles Endlmen, my favourite victim. Garrotting?

Each night I chortled and planned as I imagined the headlines, testaments to my macabre triumphs. But for naught. These fantasies were chimeras—mere effigies of frustration disguised as images of consolation in an otherwise ordinary existence. I could not act. My hands were tied, and all because of the constraints of my locale.

Each day, I would awaken, breakfast, then embark upon my morning dog walk planning to put aside my writing tablet once and for all. Why torment myself? The parchment could be buried under a heap of socks in an unused drawer of the bureau to lie forgotten forever.

On days of firmer resolve, the decision to destroy the notebook would direct my intentions, and my step, in rhythm with my canine friend, would grow more determined. As nightfall approached this will diminished until, like an opium addiction, the evil lure reasserted itself, and I found myself again staring at those notorious pages.

The image of my blacklist began to override all senses. At night it would appear in the midst of an otherwise banal dream; during the day I could not help visualizing it even when performing routine chores. On some occasions I would catch myself before my mental processes wound too far down the murky path. On other occasions I was not as lucky.

Even my dog regarded me with suspicion when I began uttering grisly words while fitting him with his fleecy, blue boots, a necessary preparation for an outdoor exercise session in the far North. I sought relief through physical activity and so we tramped.

With the dog alternately pulling and halting for investigative forages into the snow, my muttering of commands was interspersed with the random interjection of phrases referring, of course, to my taboo obsession. If someone drew near I would fall mute, then nod, for in a small town friend and stranger are greeted alike.

As time passed, I found more and more of my attention diverted. People stared; people waved. Changing the walk route did not erase this social obligation. Trudging the main thoroughfare meant cheerful pedestrians were replaced by cheerful motorists who followed the bizarre custom of honking their good-morning.

How could this be? What element of a habitual dog walk was generating this much interest? It was a puzzle whose solution was to elude me until a night toward November's end. On the evening in question I approached a white van, for I had been told the driver was commissioned to convey attendees of the office Christmas party back to their residence. I settled into a seat then leaned forward to provide directions to my abode.

"It's not necessary," I was advised. "I know you."

"Oh?" I frantically searched my memory but to no avail.

"Sure. I know you. You're the lady that always puts blue boots on your big dog. Everyone knows you."

"Oh."

This gave me pause.

Everyone knew me, but what did they know? I had joined no clubs and had never frequented the local drinking establishments. I rarely read the newspaper and in seven months had developed only the slightest of relationships with the neighbours. I had expressed no opinions. I was anonymous. Yet a set of blue boots on my dog had given the community all they needed to manufacture a false sense of familiarity.

I was predictable, reliable, perhaps eccentric, but definitely softhearted—at least with regard to the cold feet of animals. I had unwittingly developed a persona. I was, in a word, harmless.

I sat, that night, with my notebook open. Some preliminary weapons were assembled before me. Everything was perfect.

It was time to begin.

Responding Personally

1. Note your thoughts and feelings about the narrator of this story. Include your ideas about whether or not you find her unusual.
2. With a partner, decide why you think the author called the story "Blue Boots."

Responding Critically

3. Where do you get the first indication that the narrator is a woman? Why do you suppose it takes that long to reveal her identity?
4. Examine the motivation of the narrator. What is her problem and solution?
5. According to the narrator, what are the advantages of crime in Yellowknife? Ironically, how is the narrator regarded in the community?
6. For small group activity: Decide what is the purpose of the allusions to Hallowe'en, the House of Usher, Edgar Allan Poe, Sherlock Holmes, Moriarty, and Ed McBain.

Responding Creatively

7. Write a sequel to the story up to the point where the narrator commits her first crime.
8. For an alternative rock group, compose a song lyric entitled "Blue Boots" based on this story.

Problem-Solving/Decision-Making

9. You could say that this story mirrors the critical thinking process. How does the narrator analyze her problem? What steps does she go through that are similar to steps others go through in solving a problem?

Values and Choices

This thematic unit examines events and situations in life that reveal values as characters make choices. Reflecting on stories about values and choices gives readers a chance to reflect on their own values and choices, which may lead to a greater understanding of personal motivation and the consequences of choice.

In the first story, "Internal Monologue on a Corner in Havana," the main character is trying to survive by selling his cigarettes to feed himself. Though he is from a far-off country, we vicariously experience ourselves in his place and are hopeful for him. This street person reminds us of more difficult ways of existence and gives us some perspective for our lifestyles.

The second story, "The Museum of Vain Endeavours," offers a light satirical treatment of the history of human accomplishments. It is also a fictional record of people's futile dreams, goals, and aspirations, revealing the eternal human characteristics of hopefulness, determination, and pure folly. The two female characters of the story are a reflection of the museum—themselves being restless and somewhat unfulfilled, yet determined to keep the possibility of success open.

The last story, "North End Faust," focuses on a scientist who has an affinity for isolation chamber experiments that mask his own fears and insecurities. He enjoys spending time in isolation, until one day he finds he has unwittingly created the perfect metaphor for his unsatisfying, imperfect life. His values create a dilemma that threatens his beliefs and very existence. The story leaves readers thinking about the necessity of relationships and the long-term effects of childhood dreams.

Together, these three stories invite us to consider vicariously our own values and choices. Clearly, values and choices define who these story characters are and ultimately who we are.

Josefina de Diego
Internal Monologue on a Corner in Havana

Translated by Dick Cluster

God, I'm dying for a cigarette! If only my pension got me through the month, I wouldn't have to sell my rationed smokes. But a peso apiece, that's not bad, with that I can buy a little rice and a head of garlic every now and then. You can't do much on eighty pesos a month. Who would have thought that after twenty-plus years of work and with a university degree, I'd have to stand here on this corner selling my monthly cigarettes? And surreptitiously, because there's no way I'm getting caught in this "profit-oriented activity," as they say these days—without paying the tax on it I'd be in jail for sure. And how I love to smoke! But, in truth, I can't complain. This corner is quite entertaining, everybody's mixed up in something, more or less the same as me. Really it's a prime spot: the Farmers' Market and two kiosks of CADECA, the Houses of Hard-Currency Exchange. Such an ugly acronym, they really outdid themselves this time. There are other terrible historic ones, like CONACA or ECOA, but this is one of the worst. Sometimes I miss potential customers because I'm amusing myself by people-watching. It's comical, almost musical. You hear, "psst, psst, *change money*, listen, exchange," all the time, like a timid hawker's chant. Or else the old man who sidles up so mysteriously and tells you "I fix gas stoves" and keeps walking, and you don't know whether you really heard it or you imagined it all. The other day a lady let loose a really hair-raising yell because she thought the old guy was a thief, and then there was a hell of a fuss. The old man didn't show his face in the market for about a week. I could smoke this cigarette right now. God, how hard it is to quit! If it hadn't been for this illness, I'd still be working and things wouldn't be so tough. When they told me they were retiring me on eighty pesos for "total incapacity to work," I almost had a fit. What an absurd law, since when you get sick is when you have to spend the most. But all the letters I sent, complaining, didn't do a bit of good. That's the law. And eighty pesos, at the official rate, that's less than four dollars. So there: Improvise! Once in a while somebody with dollars drops a coin or two, which helps my budget out. The one who's even worse off than me is the guy who sells plastic bags from the *shopping*,[1] for a peso. This truly is illegal, more illegal than what I do, because at least I bought my little cigarettes myself, but those bags, where did he get them from? Whenever I can, I warn him of possible inspectors. We have a kind of unofficial union of "you scratch my back and I'll scratch yours." We're all here for the same reason, trying to get by without hurting anybody much. In fact, it doesn't seem to me we're hurting anyone at all, but I can understand how the Government can't allow it. If everybody were like us—but no, people are too much, if you give them an inch they'll take a mile and they'll end up robbing you with machine guns like in American films. Boy, how I miss my TV! A few days ago it broke on me and now I can't even

---

1 The *shopping*, pronounced "choppin," is Cuban slang for the network of hard-currency (dollar) stores, now accessible to Cubans and foreigners alike. The nickname probably comes from the bilingual ad for one such chain: *compras fáciles*, "easy shopping."

watch the soaps. Luckily just the picture went out, so at least you can hear it. 'Cause getting it fixed, forget it, it's Japanese, Sanyo, and the repairman charges in dollars. At least my nephew is an electronic technician and soon he'll be back from a mobilization in the countryside—he went with the university. The mobilizations of the sixties and seventies, they were fun. Or at least that's how I remember them. Maybe it's just the "good old days" always seeming better, I don't know. I always thought they weren't very productive, especially the Sunday morning ones. "The important thing is attitude, *compañera*," they told me when I tried to demonstrate to the leader in question that between gas, snack, depreciation on the truck tires, oil, et cetera, the cost was greater than any possible income. "Professional vices," he told me. "Be optimistic. You economists think too much." In those days to buy a pack of cigarettes over and above the ration was just a peso and sixty centavos—shocking—and now they charge ten. What I'd love to do would be to buy a jar of that coconut sweet from the guy across the way there, but for a dollar? That's what I get for a whole pack of loose cigarettes, no way. Maybe later on, if I get some "reinforcements" from my sister who lives in Venezuela. Every now and then along come a few dollars that I sure can use. If I sell all these cigarettes I'm going to treat myself to a paper cone full of banana chips, for two pesos, two cigarettes, that's not bad. You can't always live in austerity, no sir, because "Life is a Dream," as my high school literature teacher always used to say. Such a good teacher! He made us learn a few things by heart, to improve our vocabularies he said. I never thought I'd come to understand so perfectly the part about "when he turned his head/he found his answer on viewing/that another wise man was chewing/his discarded crust of bread." Around here there are tons of those wise men. But the one who's really worse off than me is the one who picks through the garbage dumpster in front of my house. The poor man, he doesn't know there's never anything of value in there—I give it a quick look every day. He ought to go to one by some embassy or near the hotels. Although it's not so easy, because the dumpsters have got their proprietors by now. If I don't sell these cigarettes soon, I'm leaving, because it looks like Noah's Flood is about to hit. And I'll end up with no banana chips. Yesterday one of my neighbors, in the building across the street, put a sign up in his porch: "Plumber—house calls." He must be dimwitted, how else can he fix plumbing except by making house calls? There's a lot of nuttiness, people are posting all kinds of signs, hilarious ones. Not to mention the names of the *paladares*.[2] Cubans have a certain nostalgia for small businesses and for advertisements different from the official ones, which sometimes makes you want to cry: "The Delights of Eden," right, and what you see are three little tables with a few homemade tablecloths. But clean, and with pleasant staff. I worked in one, and things were going really well, but then it got closed down and I was in the street again. Now it's started pouring, ugh, what do I do now? Smoke the cigarette and not buy the chips? A dilemma worse than Hamlet's! How would it go in my case, teacher? "To smoke or to eat, that is the question." That would be funny if it weren't the truth, and if it weren't for the fact that this is me instead of some latter-day tropical Hamlet. Better I should take the cigarette home and, if there's gas, make a little coffee and have my smoke. As they say in that charming English movie, "Life isn't perfect and besides, it's short." Tomorrow's another day. Who knows, maybe a few bucks from my sister will turn up.

RESPONDING PERSONALLY

1. Write your thoughts and feelings as you read this selection. OR Write an internal monologue you think a street person might be having as you walk by.
2. List the protagonist's complaints. With another student, compare lists to see how they are similar and/or different.

---

2 *Paladares*, literally "palates," are small family-run restaurants in people's homes. The popular term comes from the name of a fast-food chain started by a character in a Brazilian soap opera shown on Cuban TV.

RESPONDING CRITICALLY

3. Writing assignment: What do we learn about the narrator? Why is he living on the street? What are his goals and dreams? What do you learn about his past?

4. What is the conflict of the story? Is it resolved? Describe the man's mood at the end of the story. Is he optimistic or pessimistic?

5. What do you learn about the other street characters? How does the protagonist feel he is different from them?

6. In spite of the man's poverty, his situation is often ironic and comical. What are some humorous observations that the writer makes?

RESPONDING CREATIVELY

7. Assume that the protagonist decides to expand his business. Compose four classified ads he might run in the local newspaper.

8. With a partner, role-play a man-in-the-street interview the protagonist might have with a Canadian journalist.

PROBLEM-SOLVING/DECISION-MAKING

9. What might a local government do to make life better for the narrator and others like him? Write a letter to your newspaper, outlining suggestions for implementing positive social change on the urban poverty issue.

Leafing through one of the volumes, I came across a man who
tried for ten years to get his dog to talk.

Cristina Peri Rossi
The Museum of Vain Endeavours

Translated by Margaret Jull Costa

Every afternoon I go to the Museum of Vain Endeavours. I ask for
the catalogue and I sit down at the big wooden table. Though the
pages of the book are a little smudged I enjoy poring over them,
and I turn them as if I were turning the leaves of time. There's
never anyone else there reading and I suppose that's why the attendant lavishes so much attention on me. As I'm one of her few
visitors she tends to spoil me. No doubt she's afraid she'll lose her
job because of lack of public interest. Before going in I always
study the printed notice on the glass door. It says, *Opening hours:
Mornings 9:00–2:00. Afternoons: 5:00–8:00. Closed Mondays.*
Although I know which Vain Endeavour I want to look up I still
ask for the catalogue, just to give the girl something to do.

She politely asks me: "What year do you want?' And I reply, for
example: "The catalogue for 1922."

After a moment she reappears with a fat book bound in purple
leather and places it on the table in front of my chair. She's very
kind and if she thinks there's not enough daylight from the window, she herself switches on the bronze lamp with the green
shade and positions it so that its light falls on the pages of the
book. Sometimes when I return the catalogue I make some brief
remark. I might say, for instance: "1922 was such a busy year.
There were a tremendous number of people engaged in Vain
Endeavours. How many volumes do they fill in all?" And she'll
tell me very professionally: "Fourteen."

Then I contemplate some of the Vain Endeavours of that year.
I watch children attempting to fly, men set on making money,

complicated machinery that never worked, and innumerable couples.

"1975 was a much richer year," she says somewhat glumly. "We still haven't managed to record all the entries."

Thinking out loud, I say: "The classifiers must have an enormous amount of work to do."

"Oh, yes," she says. "Several volumes have already been published and they're only up to the letter C. And that's without the repeats."

It's really very curious how people repeat Vain Endeavours. However, their subsequent attempts aren't included in the catalogue: they'd take up too much space. One man made seven attempts to fly, each time equipped with different apparatus; several prostitutes wanted to find alternative employment; a woman wanted to paint a picture; someone struggled to lose his sense of fear; almost everyone was trying to be immortal or at least lived as if they were.

The attendant assures me that only a tiny percentage of all the Vain Endeavours undertaken actually get into the museum. Firstly, because the administration doesn't have enough money and it's almost impossible to make purchases or exchanges or get the museum's work known either at home or abroad. Secondly, because the enormous number of Vain Endeavours continually being embarked upon would require an army of staff willing to work with no prospect of recompense or of public sympathy. Sometimes, despairing of official help, they've turned to private sponsorship, but the results have been meagre and discouraging. Virginia—that's the name of the charming attendant I talk to—tells me that these private sources imposed too many conditions and were rather unsympathetic, out of the tune with the aims of the museum.

The building itself is on the outskirts of the city on a piece of waste ground full of cats and rubbish where, just below the surface, one can still turn up cannonballs from a distant war, tarnished sword hilts, or the jawbones of mules corroded by time.

"Have you got a cigarette?" Virginia asks me with an expression that ill conceals her anxiety.

I look in my pockets. I find a rather battered old key, the sharp end of a broken screwdriver, my return bus ticket, a button off my shirt, a few coins and, at last, two crumpled cigarettes. She smokes furtively, hidden amongst the thick broken-spined volumes, the grandfather clock that always shows the wrong hour, usually one just gone, and the dusty old mouldings. They say there used to be a fort on the site where the museum now stands, built in time of war. They made use of the massive stones from its base and some of the beams, and shored up the walls. The museum was inaugurated in 1946. They still have some photographs of the ceremony, with men in tails and ladies in long, dark skirts, paste jewellery and hats decked with birds and flowers. In the background you can make out an orchestra playing chamber music. The guests, captured cutting a cake tied with the official ribbon, look half solemn, half absurd.

I forgot to mention that Virginia has a slight squint. This slight defect lends a comic touch to her face that makes her seem less ingenuous. As if the refraction of her gaze were a stray witty remark, made out of context.

The Vain Endeavours are grouped by letter. When the classifiers run out of letters, they add numbers. This involves long, complicated calculations. Each one has its pigeonhole, folio number and description. Walking amongst them all with that unusual briskness of hers, Virginia could be a priestess, a virgin in some ancient cult, outside time.

Some Vain Endeavours are splendid; others sombre. We don't always agree on their classification.

Leafing through one of the volumes, I came across a man who tried for ten years to get his dog to talk. And another who spent more than twenty years wooing a woman. He brought her flowers, plants, books on butterflies, offered her trips abroad, wrote poems, invented songs, built a house, forgave all her faults, put up with her lovers, and then committed suicide.

"It was a very difficult undertaking," I say to Virginia. "But who knows, maybe he found it exciting."

281030

"Well, it's classified as 'sombre'," she replies. "The museum has a complete description of that woman. She was frivolous, talkative, fickle, lazy and sullen. She was far from tolerant and, what's worse, an egotist."

Then there are the men who made long journeys in search of non-existent places, irretrievable memories, women who died, and friends who disappeared. There are the children who undertook impossible tasks full of enthusiasm. Like the ones digging a hole that kept filling with water.

Smoking is not allowed in the museum, neither is singing. The latter prohibition seems to trouble Virginia as much as the former.

"I'd quite like to sing a song every now and then," she confesses wistfully.

There are people whose Vain Endeavour consisted in trying to reconstruct their family tree, in scratching around in a mine in search of gold, or in writing a book. Others clung to the hope of one day winning the lottery.

"I like the travellers best," Virginia tells me.

There are whole sections of the museum devoted to their journeys. We reconstruct them through the pages of the books. After a time wandering over different seas, passing through shady woods, discovering cities and markets, crossing bridges, sleeping in trains or on platform benches, they forget the reason for their journey but still continue travelling. One day they just disappear without leaving a trace, not even a memory, lost in some flood, trapped in a subway, or asleep for good in a doorway. No one claims them.

Before, Virginia tells me, there were some private researchers, enthusiasts, who provided material for the museum. She can even remember a time when it was fashionable to collect Vain Endeavour activities as others indulge in philately or embalming specimens.

"I think the sheer number of items put paid to that craze," says Virginia. "After all, it's searching for things that are in short supply that's exciting, the possibility of finding something rare."

In those days they'd come to the museum from all over, they'd ask for information, get interested in a particular case, go away with all the leaflets and come back loaded with stories that they'd write down on the forms, attaching any relevant photographs they'd found. They brought these Vain Endeavours to the museum as if they were bringing butterflies or strange insects. For example, the story of the man who spent five years trying to prevent a war only to have his head blown off by the first mortar shell. Or Lewis Carroll, who spent his life fleeing draughts and died of a cold the one time he went out without his raincoat.

I mentioned, didn't I, that Virginia has a slight squint? I often amuse myself trying to follow her gaze—I can never tell exactly which direction she's looking. When I see her cross the room, weighed down with paper and all kinds of documents, the least I can do is get up from my chair and go and help her.

Sometimes, halfway through a task, she complains a bit.

"I'm tired of all this coming and going," she says. "We'll never get it all classified. There's the newspapers too. They're just full of Vain Endeavours."

Like the story about the boxer who tried five times to recover his title only to be put out of action by a bad blow to his eye. He probably spends his time in some sleazy part of town mooching from one café to another, recalling the days when his eyes were good and his fists were deadly. Or the story about the trapeze artiste with vertigo who couldn't bear to look down. Or the one about the dwarf who wanted to grow and travelled the world looking for a doctor who could cure him.

When she gets tired of moving the books around Virginia sits down on a pile of dusty, old newspapers, smokes a cigarette— stealthily, because it's not permitted—and reflects out loud, in a tone of resignation:

"I should get another job."

Or: "I don't know when they'll pay me this month's wages."

I tried inviting her to come for a walk in the city with me, to have a coffee or to go to the cinema. But she wasn't keen. She'll only talked to me within the grey, dusty walls of the museum.

I'm so absorbed in what I'm doing in the afternoons I scarcely notice time passing, if it does pass. But Mondays are days of pain and abstinence, when I don't know what to do or how to live.

The museum closes at eight o'clock at night. Virginia herself turns the metal key in the lock, that's as far as her security measures go, after all no one's likely to burgle the place. Though she told me about a man who did break in once with the intention of removing his name from the catalogue. It seems he wanted to erase all trace of some Vain Endeavour he'd embarked on in his youth that he felt ashamed of now.

"We caught him in time," Virginia says. "But we had a really tough job dissuading him. He insisted that his endeavour was a purely private matter and wanted it returned to him. On that occasion though, I was a model of firmness and decision. Well, it was a rare piece, almost a collector's item, and it would have been a serious loss to the museum had he succeeded."

When the museum closes I leave with regret. At first, the thought of the time that has to elapse between then and the next day seemed intolerable to me. But I've learned to wait. And I've got so used to Virginia being there I can't imagine the museum without her. Evidently the Director (he's the one in the photograph with a sash of two colours across his chest) feels the same way, for he's decided to promote her. But, since there's no ladder of promotion established by law or precedent, he's invented a new post, which is in fact the same one under a different title. To emphasize the sacred nature of her mission at the portals of the museum, he has appointed her Vestal of the Temple, to guard the fleeting memory of the living.

RESPONDING PERSONALLY

1. With another student, describe a scheme or project of yours that failed. Offer explanations for why it became your own vain endeavour.
2. Does a museum of vain endeavours seem like a valid operation? What advice could you suggest to the women in the story?

RESPONDING CRITICALLY

3. Prepare a chart of five vain endeavours mentioned in the story. Give reasons why each was a vain endeavour.

4. How do the narrator and Virginia reflect the museum's theme? How is Virginia, in particular, the perfect person to work at the museum? What is the purpose of her appointment in the last paragraph of the story? Why are the contents of the narrator's pockets mentioned?

5. With a partner, discuss your ideas about the meaning of the following two incidents:
   a) the tiny percentage of vain endeavours that qualify for inclusion at the museum
   b) the break-in at the museum.

6. Despite the nature of the museum's function, there is a purpose to the story. Write your own thematic statement for the story. Compare it with ones other students have written.

RESPONDING CREATIVELY

7. Create a Web page for the museum.

8. On the Internet, locate two or more famous people who actually have succeeded in creating socially useful inventions. Write short summaries of the year, the place, and the type of products they invented.

PROBLEM-SOLVING/DECISION-MAKING

9. Describe one of your future goals. Indicate how you plan to make it work. What strategies will you use to avoid ending up with a vain endeavour?

Alex felt a chill moving along his arms and chest, panic rioting within him, the abyss opening at his feet.

Ed Kleiman
North End Faust

The sun on the horizon flashed like a nearly extinguished lantern, sending its weak crimson glow to drift bleakly among the trees and houses on Riverview Place. It was a quiet street—the Red River flowing sluggishly nearby—and rarely did an unfamiliar car pass between the rows of shiny modern storey-and-a-half houses that gleamed palely in the gathering darkness.

At eighty-thirty, having locked the doors for the night, Alex trudged downstairs to work in his basement study. Glancing at the small, narrow window to see that it was locked, he noticed that the twilight still clung to the budding branches and still shone upon the newly uncovered grass, pale from its long burial beneath the snow. Only a few weeks to go before spring would really catch hold. With a sigh, he pulled the blind down upon the indistinct Winnipeg landscape and settled into his chair. In less than half an hour, it would be dark. The voices of his wife and two children in the living room up above reached him as if from a great distance—another world.

Once he had liked this sense of isolation, the feeling of being in a cell, pitted alone against a difficult problem. Even as a child, after the initial terror of being locked in a closet by his older brother, he'd learned to welcome the darkness. When his parents had found him hours later, they'd been apprehensive, alarmed for his sake, but he'd smiled at their apprehension, as if armed by the darkness with a new secret. As he grew older, he felt nourished and strengthened by these moments of isolation. It was as if they allowed him to regroup his personal resources, look at a problem with detachment. Yet more was involved; he'd become terribly dependent on the hidden vein of strength that these moments allowed him to tap, the luminous images that would then flood into his mind.

Alone in an empty room. That was all that he'd required—the emptiness. And out of this condition he'd managed to build his whole life: a career, house, family, reputation. Others required sophisticated equipment, tools to practise their vocations, weapons with which to wage their war with life. His weapon had been his mind; and his adversary, the emptiness. Yet it had been his ally, too.

As a teenager, while some of his companions in the North End roamed along darkened streets or joined gangs that broke windows and slashed tires, he had spent his time alone—studying his way through high school and, later, through university. When the time came to declare his field of study, he found his decision already made. Nothing could have been simpler. While all his fellow students agonized and procrastinated for as long as the graduate school would let them, Alex turned as if to an old friend. His thesis was entitled: "The Effects of Isolation upon the Human Psyche."

And the results had been instantaneous. The thesis itself was published within the year; *Maclean's* ran his picture, and devoted half a page to outlining his work; and he was immediately given a temporary appointment to the Psychology Department. Then, almost at once, he'd had to ask for a two-week leave of absence. He'd been invited to New York to give a series of lectures on the probable effects of isolation in situations ranging anywhere from the industrial sphere to the kinds of space travel likely to occur in the future.

Upstairs the sound of voices and footsteps had all died away. Even the television set had been turned off. Kathy must have gone to bed shortly after the children. The silence allowed him to recall with renewed intensity his excitement that first year when one good piece of fortune after another had befallen him. All of it had come out of his ability simply to sit silently by himself, just as he was doing now. No need to be frightened because of his present difficulties: this impasse would be overcome, as had all the others.

Within months of joining the department, he'd been granted the funds to have an isolation chamber constructed in an abandoned storage room on the ground floor of the Arts Building. The room itself was eight by twelve feet and had indirect lighting. It was wired for microphones, had one-way glass so that all behavior within could be observed, and an emergency buzzer whose operation required very little explanation.

But while that door was shut, the behavior within was a closed environment, as unique as any culture growth developing behind glass. And what developed there—the unique ecology possessed by that room—was still pretty much a mystery to Alexander Markiewicz—despite what he'd written to the contrary. All he knew was that students who volunteered to enter the chamber rarely lasted more than a day. Mind you, the pay was good, and there was no lack of volunteers who promised faithfully to record every detail of their experiences. But, inevitably, after a few hours the buzzer would sound, and the terrified student had to be led, trembling, to a recovery room. One student had even refused, at first, to let go of the assistant's hands.

Alex had met his wife Kathy that way. She was from Oak Point, a town sixty miles to the northwest of Winnipeg. The thought of earning enough money in two weeks to pay a good part of her expenses for the next university term had been too attractive to resist. Alex could still recall her screams as he'd dashed into the isolation chamber. In retrospect, Alex felt disturbed when he recalled the scene and how he had led the paralyzed girl once again into the realm of familiar faces.

For days afterward, he'd questioned her about the experience. He himself could easily spend a week in the chamber without suffering unbearable strain. But for her ... The account she gave refused to settle into focus. She spoke of a sea that didn't seem to have any bound or shore. Anyone else would have thrown up his hands in despair, but Alex had responded characteristically. He'd sat down in his study and puzzled through her comments and images again and again.

To be locked up in a totally unresponsive world—wouldn't that remove one's sense of reality, dissolve all boundaries; or, to use her terms, remove the shore from the ocean? let the unconscious well up uncontrollably? Was it possible that simply perceiving everyday experience was responsible for keeping that darkness locked within bounds? And if that last restraint were to vanish, who could predict what would happen next? All historical development might reel backwards—beyond pagan practices, even beyond primordial man and his cults, back along the evolutionary scale toward an emptiness that had never known time, but consisted only of a still and endless space.

At one point, Alex had been startled by a sense of recognition when she spoke of being stared at from within the darkness of the room. He had, in fact, been haunted by the same experience, but never mentioned it to a soul. He simply hadn't felt as alarmed by the experience as Kathy. Also, his research so far had evoked almost no skepticism, and he had no intention of having his work jeopardized now because of one hysterical student.

Still he found himself strongly attracted to her; perhaps, at first, simply because she could give a voice to the emptiness that had so long intrigued him. Over the last few years, he had begun to assume—without actually formulating the thought—that one price he would have to pay for his good fortune was his own personal isolation. After all, he seemed to have embraced loneliness almost like a bride. But now that bride had taken on material form. Mind you, he hadn't even the ghost of a notion how to begin courting a pretty twenty-two year old. Nor, he realized, did Kathy herself fully understand why she was so drawn to him, though he sensed that she alone had been able to see past his loneliness and pride ... to some secret longing that he was only now aware of. So instead they spent the winter in a series of interviews during which he attempted to record every detail of her experience.

By that spring, he had gathered enough material to publish a new research paper. It had been a period of triumph. They'd each felt as if they'd broken out of their isolation cells forever. The sense of freedom lasted just long enough for them to get married. But once the children were born, Kathy no longer seemed the same. She blossomed in their presence and her days were soon caught up in their days. A new kind of tempo had been

established from which he was not excluded; but though it called
to him and he desperately longed to join it, he found he could
not. The children's lives were so different, so vibrant. Was it any
wonder that they had soon won Kathy away from him?

As Alex sat at his desk in the silent house, he puzzled where
things had gone wrong. That people should be terrified of the ex-
perimental chamber no longer surprised him. He could still recall, from years ago, the battle-hardened American marine
sergeant who had scoffed at the danger and warned that he'd
bankrupt not only the Psychology Department, but also the
University itself, perhaps even the whole province. True—he had
not pushed the button. But three and a half hours later he had to
be led from the room, his eyes staring, his limbs frozen into stillness. Nor was his case unique: some students had required psy-
chiatric help after a single experience. Others had emerged
shaken, seized their money and quickly departed.

More recently his reputation had begun to take a curious turn,
mainly as the result of the odd news item that had found its way
into the international press. Escaped political prisoners had made
it abundantly clear that totalitarian governments in Eastern
Europe had also discovered his publications—and were finding
them useful. Where physical torture was impossible to use because of adverse public opinion, psychological torture had
proven surprisingly successful—and avoided world censure in
the bargain. Later he'd heard that similar techniques had been
used in Vietnam.

Alex himself was certain that, under similar circumstances, he
would never have broken. In fact, not quite two years ago, he'd
set some sort of record by remaining in the chamber for over two
weeks. He had developed his own way of coping with the kind of
dread that lay waiting in the isolation cell. When the emptiness
welled up within him, and the walls became unreal, and he began
to suspect that the buzzer had been disconnected by a disgrun-
tled graduate student, or that his colleagues monitoring the ex-
periment behind the one-way glass had become jealous of his
reputation ... when all these doubts began to assail him and he

lost track of time, and terror began to nibble at the edges of his consciousness, he would immediately throw himself into a special psychological maneuver he'd devised to insure his self-preservation.

He was leaping from a rowboat onto an island in the far north, where he was going to build a summer cottage he had designed himself. Axe stroke by axe stroke, he cleared a path well into the interior, later chopping the logs into firewood. Painstakingly, he erected a shelter for the night and then lit a fire to cook his food. Early the next day, before dawn, he was again busy clearing brush from the site, setting out concrete foundation blocks, levelling beams. Over the next week or two, he created his own daylight and darkness, brilliant sun and wheeling stars, winds, rains, cloudy days, bent nails, and split shingles. But when everything was on the verge of completion and he had to feel that there was nothing left to do, his whole island paradise had begun to turn unreal. Not knowing what to expect next, he had pressed the buzzer.

The door had opened and there had been ... the University President himself, newspaper reporters, his colleagues, admiring students. He wasn't surprised to learn that he had established a record of sorts. More importantly, he had emerged again from that empty room with all the resources needed to bolster a reputation that was just beginning to sag.

That was his last success, he remembered, and, lately, the criticism had once more become intense. Parents of students who still felt some of the effect of their experience in the isolation chamber wrote heated letters to the Minister of Education. And just last month, he'd been totally confounded to learn of a TV interview in which an I.R.A. spokesman had denounced him for providing the occupation force in Ulster with the means of breaking the will of political prisoners. Was it his imagination or had his colleagues recently begun to look at him uneasily? And what would his parents have said if they were still living?—his parents, who'd fled to America themselves to escape persecution?

In the past, whenever faced with a threat of this kind, he had returned to the isolation chamber only to emerge with new material on which to base academic papers, and win the admiration of his colleagues. But the last time Alex had entered the chamber— about three months ago now—he'd had to press the release buzzer after only forty-five minutes. For one terrifying moment, nothing had happened. Had they all gone to coffee, certain that they wouldn't be hearing that buzzer for another week or so? But then the anxious, questioning faces had appeared at the door. "Sorry," he smiled. "I'd forgotten I still have a set of essays to mark for my Honors Class."

Alex was certain others would feel that here was proof the compelling nature of his original research was now a thing of the past. Gradually, he had grown to doubt his colleagues' respect and concern, behind which he thought he sensed an envy of his ac- complishments, perhaps even hatred. To them, everything must have seemed so easy. They thought he had paid nothing for all the honors he had won. They would know, of course, that there ought to be a price, but somehow there seemed to be no one to take an accounting.

The following week Alex busied himself with departmental work and stayed as far away from the isolation chamber as he could. He even made a point of using the doorway and stairwell at the other side of the building. Once, however, at the end of a meeting, he'd been obliged to walk right by the room housing the isolation cell. And he'd frozen. He'd had to be helped out of the building. Later, he didn't even attempt to explain what had gone wrong.

He knew he must find some way to have that isolation cham- ber dismantled. An excuse—that's what he needed. It shouldn't be too hard. His research was now complete, he'd announce, and he needed the laboratory space for a new project. Of course, there never would be any new project, and after a few years everyone in the department would realize it. So what? Let them think that he'd somehow burnt himself out. At least he would no longer be living with constant terror.

Now, as he sat at the desk in his basement study, Alex felt a chill moving along his arms and chest, panic rioting within him, the abyss opening at his feet. He had sat at his desk as often as he dared these past few months, planning ways to have that isolation chamber dismantled, even imagining himself rushing into the deserted building one night with a sledge hammer and doing the job himself. And each time, the results had been the same—chills, sweat, the barbaric darkness opening beneath and within him, and the sense of being stared at by some dark, gigantic presence. Involuntarily, Alex reached for the emergency buzzer, then looked blankly about him for a moment until he realized there was no emergency buzzer to press.

And so he did what had by now become a habit. He rushed from the house—from his wife and children—and walked quickly off into the darkness. At the corner, he turned left and set off for the city's North End—unaware of the trees, the other houses with lights in them, the passing cars, school playgrounds, passersby. He could not have been less aware of the life about him if he had been walking through an underground tunnel. When at last he turned the corner of Redwood and Main and caught sight of the bridge spanning the Red River, he felt himself gulping down the cool night air as if it were well water. He and his friends had played beneath that bridge after school, had rented rowboats and paddled beneath it on weekends.

If he could no longer dispel that inner emptiness by dreaming of a summer cottage on his own private island, then he would set his childhood memories in place of those dreams, use them to counter that endless outpouring of darkness that welled up within him constantly. His childhood memories—they were still there. Surely they would last for a while before being used up. Give him time to think. Find some way to dismantle the invisible isolation chamber that was always around him now.

He must have come here half a dozen times this spring, hoping against hope that he'd find some way out. But he could still feel those walls around him: at a departmental meeting, during a class, even at breakfast while talking to his wife and children. These everyday contacts now did not have as much reality as that vacation cottage he'd built and rebuilt on his imaginary island.

The coming of spring, the melting of snow, grass slowly turning green—he had hoped that they would relieve his awareness of those ever-present walls. Instead the quickening of life all about him had only intensified his anguish. He hadn't spoken a real word to a real person for almost the whole term. His previous record in the isolation chamber had been a little over two weeks. He'd already lasted longer than he'd ever dreamed possible, exploited and exhausted resources he didn't even know he had, survived beyond all possible limits and measures—and there was still no end in sight. No buzzer to push. Not a single human face among all those he had known that he could respond to. It was not their fault—it was his own. Long ago, he did not know exactly when or how, he had made some secret pact in the darkness. What kind of bargain was it anyway that he had unwittingly struck?

Still, there must be some way out, some hidden spring that would open a yet undiscovered door. All this pain, the constant sense of loss ... And for what? As he peered about him now, his eyes strained desperately against the darkness. Like a blind man, all his senses became more acute. What was that sound?

From beneath him, Alex heard the voices of his childhood— his companions in the rowboat—calling: "Hey, it's my turn at the oars. Watch out, will you. You're tipping us. That rock ... Pull on your left oar, stupid. The current here is too strong ... Come on, Alex, we're going to the island." They were real—he was sure of it. Not giving himself time for a second thought, Alex climbed onto the guardrail of the bridge.

Now he had only to join his companions in that final, danger- ous crossing. And then he could spring from the rowboat onto that island; then he could build that cottage. As he stepped into the darkness ... and felt the water move about him, he could sense gigantic black wings gathering and unfolding in vast sweeps that blotted out the sky. Arms flailing, he made the hammer fly in his hands as he drove nail after nail in board after board. The dark walls rose swiftly about him. Hammering. Building. He didn't dare stop. Quicker. Faster. Soon his island paradise would be complete.

RESPONDING PERSONALLY

1. In your response journal, describe how you would react to being in Alex's isolation chamber. You may choose to write your thoughts in a stream of consciousness form.
2. Look up the name *Faust* in an encyclopedia. Who was this character? Why do you think the author used this name in the story's title?

RESPONDING CRITICALLY

3. For paragraph writing: How early in life does Alex become a loner? What events lead him to make that choice? Does he resolve his childhood past at the end of the story?
4. What series of events lead to Alex's eventual breakdown? Is he obsessed, paranoid, or both? What other flaws does he have? How might he have avoided his fate?
5. How does Alex's relationship with his wife change? Why do you think he married her?
6. With another student, discuss what you think the isolation chamber symbolizes.

RESPONDING CREATIVELY

7. Write two entries about the isolation chamber that Alex might include in his journal.
8. With another student, role-play a dialogue that two of Alex's colleagues might have when they learn of his death.

PROBLEM-SOLVING/DECISION-MAKING

9. Assume you are a psychologist and that Alex has come to visit you for help. Write a report in which you explain what his problems are and what positive solutions are open to him.

UNIT THREE

Conformity and Rebellion

Whether to go along with the rest of society or to rebel and go one's own way is a common recurring conflict that humans face. Can a person live with the circumstances he or she has, or does there need to be a resistance or rebellion for things to change for the better? This question is answered thoughtfully by the three selections that follow.

In the first story, "Lenses," the protagonist fears the loss of human warmth and expressiveness which may result from the conventional surgery her friend is about to have. The surgery is a necessary act of conformity in their society with the advantage of providing clearer, more lasting sight. But leaving her friend as she is would lead, ironically, to her remaining more human for a longer period of time. The dilemma faced by the surgeon is whether to operate or to go against a standard medical procedure.

In "Ashes for the Wind," the main character and his family are pressured to leave behind their South American family home. Juan has two choices: conform and abandon his homestead, or rebel and risk his life and the lives of his wife and child. The events of this powerful story provoke us to consider two important questions: What is worth rebelling for? and What may be the price of refusing to submit to the will of others?

The third story, "Harrison Bergeron," also focuses on rebellion. In a futuristic society where everyone is made equal, the young protagonist challenges society and dramatically spurns his handicaps. This clever satire leaves us thinking about the glory and fate of rebellion in contrast to the terrible, numbing price of conformity. In Harrison's parents we see the price they pay for blindly accepting the laws of an unjust, tyrannical authority.

The decision to conform or to rebel is dependent on our own commitment to personal values in contrast with those of others. In the process of this major conflict, we learn much about ourselves and others through actions taken by these story characters.

"I'm sorry, Grusha. I have to do this. It must be done."

Leah Silverman
Lenses

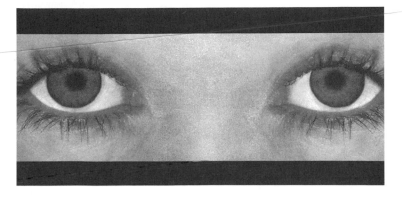

Tomorrow, I must take Grusha's eyes out. She specifically requested that I be the one to do it.

I am sitting in my room, watching the great arch of the black sky revolve around me through the clear window-wall. The stars are very large tonight, brighter than usual—perhaps we have moved closer to them. I put my hand to the wall, but I can never feel any heat through it.

I should be sleeping. It is important not to be tired when one must perform surgery.

I would not have performed this operation, except that Grusha asked me to. There are ways of getting out of doing the surgery, if you know of them. I could have said I was sick, perhaps. They know how crucial it is not to overwork their surgeons. But Grusha asked me, so I must do it.

I am twenty-eight and was born on Earth. This is unusual nowadays, I know, but my mother loved the green things of our planet and would never have survived in this world of metal and glass. I have been here for seven years. I started active duty late, compared to those born here, but I am skilled, and good surgeons are so necessary these days that there is no room to complain.

If I were to look down and to my left I would see the planet—though the soldiers on the surface are invisible from this height except to this base's sensors. We are above the planet's day-side, though it is night up here, and in a few hours the first of the day's wounded will arrive. It is hard to imagine men and women fighting and dying there. I think it's because it is such a bright yellow colour, reflecting the light of the stars. In the morning, however, the alarm bells will ring and I will rush to Level Two, as I have done every morning since I first arrived.

Level Two is where they send the patients who are the least wounded. Those who only need prosthetic limbs implanted in their already cauterized stumps, for example, or computer chips in their heads to replace destroyed parts of their brains. Recently, it has also become standard practice to replace their eyes.

Grusha is a pilot, and if I were to go to the hangar now I would find her ambulance, waiting in cold machine silence for her to return. She calls it the *Kraceevoi*, though she has never told me what it means. She is a good pilot, and very brave. I met her when I was also flying the ambulances, before it was decided that I would be more useful on Level Two.

Grusha has brown eyes, very deep, that dance with life when she laughs and flash when she is serious to echo the importance of her words. It is essential that they be replaced because of the harshness of the planet's sun. The soldiers who come back after a year there all have skins tanned a deep black, and hair bleached of almost all colour. The sun-goggles they are issued are unbearable in the heat, and in the light their eyes become useless very quickly. Without the new eyes they would all go blind. Grusha doesn't spend as much time on the planet's surface as the soldiers, but her exposed skin is a deep brown now all the same, and her score on the last eye exam was lower than her previous ones. Her new eyes will never go blind, and if a bomb or laser destroys them we can give her others.

But her new eyes will not be brown, and they will not shine with her laughter.

It is too late now to try sleeping, and I have in my hand an old photograph, one I took the last time we visited home. The photo is in black and white so that it seems old though it was only taken five years ago. If I wanted to, I could pick up the gallery box beside the other photo albums in the drawer and see all the pictures I wanted—thousands of them—flash on the screen. All in colour. Some even move.

But I like the black and white photographs. The pictures seem less real, somehow, without colour. More like an idea of what was seen, rather than the reality of it. Grusha looks back at me from the grey world of the photo I'm holding. She looks unearthly—very white against the white clouds behind her. Her hair is grey here, perhaps already starting to pale. Her eyes are darker. She is not really smiling, though her mouth curves up. Her jacket is open, and the loose sweater beneath it is a washed black. In coloured life it is red; she still has it. Her hands lightly grasp the bottom of the jacket. The fingers look lost there, somehow, where they cannot be useful.

I can imagine in my memory that moment, a second of time frozen for as long as forever is, unique from what went before or after. Did I take an instant out of her thoughts when I took that picture, just as I took the moment in time? What was she thinking at that precise moment? I never thought to ask her.

The wind in the picture is strong, and all her hair is pulled back from her forehead and to the side. Her hair was once a deeper brown than her eyes, and was always long, even after they complained to her about it.

Her eyes look like black liquid in the photo, like wells. The thoughts behind them must be serious. You can tell by the quality of her eyes, the way they glisten beneath the light. Grusha has eyes that hold you when you look into them.

If I take a picture of her again, after the operation, there will be nothing there to focus on. No more thoughts to see, no more liquid darkness. Only the eye of the camera lens will grin back at me, empty and perfectly reflected.

In ten minutes the first bell will ring, and I will have to go and help the other surgeons. Grusha will be waiting, sedated to make her calm. I do not want to see her before I do the operation. Words have always been a burden to me and I can't think of anything to say. I wonder if she is afraid. Most likely not. Grusha is far more practical than I am, and would fully understand the necessity of infallible eyes. Perhaps afterwards, when she looks into a mirror again, it will make no difference. I could never imagine her crying. I cry a lot. It is far too easy for me, even after all this time. It is not good to think of Grusha right now. It would be awful to cry so close to my duty-time.

The Pre-Op room is large and white, and smells sweet with some sort of antiseptic. The nurse hands me Grusha's final medical exam as I walk in. I have been Grusha's only doctor since I first changed from the ambulances, and I know what the small screen will list before I look at it. Grusha is in excellent health—she could not have been a pilot otherwise. Her vital signs are fine, and I force myself to stop looking for a reason not to do the operation. The nurse would have told me if there had been anything. Grusha calls out a lazy greeting, and her voice sounds loose and relaxed, her dark accent slightly more pronounced. I listen for a hint of nervousness, an edge of fear that might have slipped past the gentle mask of the sedative, but there is nothing. As I have said, Grusha is practical. And brave. And she is radiant, even in the ridiculous hospital gown. Even with far too dark hands and face and hair the colour of a winter sun. She was always very beautiful. I am glad that has not been taken from her. I am glad that she is still whole. For the moment. Thinking of that makes me want to weep. Her eyes sparkle like black water.

"Come here!" She says, she raises a deep brown hand to beckon. "Let's make this quick, *da*? I don't like this place—there are stars all around and I can't be near them. Come," she says again. She smiles, like she is the doctor and I the frightened patient who need to be reassured. I still haven't spoken, but I smile to please her. I want to say something good, befitting of my role here, but instead I only manage:

"I'm sorry, Grusha. I have to do this. It must be done." She blinks, the drugs and my words leaving her a little off-balance. Then her face becomes serious, and she nods.

"It's all right, Corinne," she says quietly. "I've accepted it. Please, don't be upset. I will be fine. Truly, I'll be fine." And then she pulls herself slowly into more of a sitting position, and embraces me, to let me share her strength.

It is two days since the operation, and though she is still sore the patches will come off and I must be there to supervise it. The few metres to her room seem like the longest distance I have ever walked. Though I was the one who put her new eyes in, I the one who sewed the muscle to the holes in the metal shell, I can barely find the courage to face what I have done. I have no words for how I felt to finally sever the optic nerve and take the globe out, though it would have been easier to carve my own heart out of my chest. I took exquisite care with the operation, to ensure that her new eyes will move as readily as the old, and will transmit perfect images to her brain. It doesn't matter. Her eyes are gone now, with two metal spheres in their place. Because of me. I think of how they looked free of their sockets—strange, lost alien things, ripped from their life and purpose. I think of the blank camera lens. My own eyes feel heavy; I am acutely aware of them. It occurs to me how easy it would be to gouge them, to take my trembling fingers and tear them out.

And now I am at her room. I announce that I am here, and the door slides open.

Grusha is sitting on the edge of the bed, impatient as the nurse checks her blood pressure. She looks no different, except for the glaring white patches on her eyes. She is nervous without her sight, and looks up quickly when she hears the door open.

"Corinne?" she asks. She is looking in my direction but not at me. I answer and she smiles. The nurse nods to me and says her blood pressure is fine. I thank him and he leaves.

"Well?" she prompts. "I'm sick of being blind and these things on my eyes are itching me!" She laughs, but it sounds tight.

I should say something to her but cannot bring the sound out of my mouth. Instead I touch her gently to make her look towards me.

"Sit still," I say finally. "This will only take a minute." She complies, her hands steady but tense on her lap, her ankles locked together. She looks suddenly like a young girl, and the image bothers me. I take the tape from the edges of the patches as quickly as possible without bothering the still-sensitive skin. They come away easily, and I have to hold her hands down to keep her from touching her slightly swollen lids. They were damaged by the operation, of course, but are not bruised because the laser cauterized the cuts. She opens her new eyes slowly, blinking a few times as if to get the feel of them.

"It's strange ..." she says slowly, shifting her gaze around the room, "I was expecting the light to hurt, but it doesn't. And everything is so clear ..." She laughs again. "My old eyes were nothing compared to these ones!" She reaches to touch them and stops. She looks at me, then and, in that instant, though I am smiling for her, I think my heart breaks.

"So," she says, her voice suddenly intent, "how do I look?" The words are flippant, but I know her, and I can see the look on her face. The idea of new eyes was easy for her, but the reality has left her shaken. Now it is I who must be the comfort.

But they are solid grey, like the pupilless eyes of a rat. The colour of the walls around us. There is no depth in them. The light reflects from them as off a mirror, jarring bright. Like she has no eyes at all.

Like my eyes. My two steel-blue eyes that were put in as soon as I left the ambulances, that magnify better than any microscope. I have long since stopped trying to tell myself that it doesn't matter that they are cold and shiny and lifeless. That these eyes have made me a better surgeon, that they have helped me save countless lives. I have seen myself too many times to still believe it.

It was with these eyes that I took the picture of her. With these eyes that I took her own out.

She looks at them now with a kind of wonder that is almost terror. Her face, her own eyes are reflected in them, and she is beginning to realize just how it will be, now, living like this for the rest of her life.

But not yet. I can still spare her that.

"You look good," I say. And I pull her close, as if I could protect her. And I try to see.

RESPONDING PERSONALLY

1. In your response journal, write about whether or not you would have metal eyes inserted if you knew it would give you perfect vision for a lifetime.
2. How important is honesty in relationships? Should Corinne have told Grusha about her misgivings? Why or why not?

RESPONDING CRITICALLY

3. List the advantages and disadvantages of the eye surgery Grusha had. In your opinion, was Grusha wise to have it done?
4. What is Corinne's dilemma? How does she feel about doing the surgery? Why does she finally do it?
5. What do we learn of life in this futuristic society? Is the lifestyle described believable? Explain.
6. From the story, give one example each of the three types of irony described in the Glossary of Fiction Terms at the end of this book.

RESPONDING CREATIVELY

7. Script the conversation between the narrator and Grusha one month after the surgery.
8. Create a rationale page from the eye surgery operation manual that Corinne consulted.

PROBLEM-SOLVING/DECISION-MAKING

9. Why does Grusha elect to have the surgery? What does she gain and lose? Would you agree to the same surgery if you were in her position? Why or why not?

Hernando Téllez
Ashes for the Wind

Translated by Harriet D. Onis

The man had a cordially sinister air. He had been trying unsuccess-
fully for at least half an hour to say what he had to say. He was seated on a thick log by the door of the house. He had not taken off his
greasy hat, a cheap brown felt, and he kept his eyes on the ground,
while he talked. Juan knew him well. He was the son of Simón
Arévalo and his wife, Laura. Even as a boy he had had a bad name,
but nobody would have dreamed that he would do what they now
said he was doing to old friends of his parents in the vicinity. Juan
had not believed it, but now…. "It would be best for you to clear
out," the man repeated without lifting his eyes from the ground.
Juan made no answer. The day had dawned lowering, and the lead-
en clouds threatened heavy rain. The air was sultry. Juan looked beyond the visitor's hat, out over the fields, green, yellow, yellow-ripe,
green again, a brighter green, and then paler. There was a good view
of the valley from where he was standing. It was a good spot from
which to see the green heads of the grain rippling in the wind.

"Who's there?" came the clear high-pitched voice of his wife
from the kitchen. He did not answer. The visitor sat on, his head
lowered. With one of his dusty shoes, he kept scuffing a little
mound of fine dust against the other shoe and then carefully
pressing it flat with the sole. "You'd better clear out," he said
again, this time lifting his face. Juan looked at him. And thought
to himself how much he looked like his father except for his eyes,
which were the colour of tobacco-leaf, like his mother's.

"Who's there?" This time his wife's voice sounded nearer. And
then Carmen was standing in the door that opened on the front

51

porch, holding the baby in her arms. The man got up from the log and mechanically rubbed one of his hands on the seat of his pants. Then he took off his hat. Thick, black, matted hair sprang up as though released from confinement. It looked as though it had not seen a comb for a long time. "Good morning, Señora Carmen," said the visitor. The baby was playing with his mother's throat, trying to bury his fingers in its softness. He was only a few months old, and he reeked of mother's milk and soiled diapers.

Juan said nothing. The man was visibly disconcerted. For a few seconds there was no sound but the silence of the countryside, and in the midst of this silence, the ever-merged, ever-latent noises of nature. The valley throbbed intact under the sullen morning. "But the sun is going to come out," Juan thought.

"Well, I'll be going," the visitor said, and the men said goodbye. Carmen was silent, her eyes on her husband. The man put on his hat again, turned his back on them, and walked slowly to the fence gate, some ten or fifteen yards from the house, and opened it carefully, the unoiled hinges giving their customary creak despite his care. Ordinary hinges made by the local blacksmith.

"They'd better clear out." Why? The son of Simón Arévalo and his dead wife, Laura, had tried to explain the reasons for nearly half an hour. But he had been so rattled. All this business of the authorities and politics was always complicated. And Simón Arévalo's son was not too clear about it in his own mind in spite of the fact that he was now hand in glove with the authorities, doing their dirty work for them. "The scoundrel," thought Juan. "He said if we weren't gone by the end of the week they'd come and put us out." "They'll have to kill us," Carmen answered. "That's what I told him," Juan replied, his face a mask of gloom. They said no more. Carmen went to the kitchen with the child clasped in her arms, and Juan remained alone, standing like a tree before his house.

The neighborhood was a poor one, and there seemed to be no good reason why the authorities should concern themselves with Juan's house and the fields around it. It was of no use to them—

a few patches of corn, some hills of potatoes, a vegetable garden with a little stream of water flowing through it, thanks be to God, as Carmen said, from the really fine, big place of the Hurtados. As for the house, it was half cabin, half house. Juan was thinking that, if the authorities took it from him, they would have to pay the balance of the money he had borrowed some years back to build the kitchen and put in the septic tank. But could it be true that they would have to clear out, as Simón Arévalo's son had told him? Sure, he had voted in the last election. So what? Who hadn't, some for one side, some for the other? And no hard feelings. There always had to be a winner and a loser. Juan let out a laugh. "He was trying to scare me." But no, that wasn't it. He recalled that when he had been in town a week before, there had been something queer. Some of the police, in addition to a gun, had carried a whip. The gun, all right, but why the whip? It puzzled him. The law with a whip in its hand frightened him. Besides, he had noticed something strange in the people. At Don Rómulo Linares' store, they had refused to sell him oil. They told him they were out of it. But the oil was there, thick and shiny, dripping from the black drum into the funnel, and from the funnel into a bottle behind the counter. He did not say anything because of the way Don Rómulo scowled at him, and he didn't like to have words with anybody. Four policemen were walking around the market place, but there were not many people. He bought a few things—a clay cooking-pot, a bar of soap, a pair of sandals. Then he went into the drugstore for a jar of perfumed vaseline and a roll of cotton. Benavides, the proprietor, asked him pleasantly but with a mysterious air: "Nothing happened out your way yet?" And as Juan was opening his mouth to answer, Benavides made him a sign to keep quiet. A policeman was walking in, and following him came Simón Arévalo's son. The policeman rapped on the wooden counter with his whip. Benavides lost color and quickly wrapped up Juan's purchases. "What's going on here?" asked the policeman. Arévalo recognized Juan, but he looked at him as though he had never seen Juan before. The policeman did not give Benavides time to answer. Turning to Juan, and switching the whip against his own pants, he said to him: "So you, too, are one of those who are resisting?" Juan must have gone pale like Benavides, for he felt his heart begin to thud. He would have liked to slap the policeman's face; just because he was a policeman he had no right to talk like that to a peaceable man buying a jar of vaseline and a roll of cotton in the drugstore and bothering nobody. Arévalo spoke up: "Yes, he's one of the Reds; he lives near here, over Tres Espigas way." Juan stood as though rooted to the floor, his eyes riveted on the short wooden whipstock with a hole at one end through which the leather thongs were strung. The knotty wood looked like a long finger whose joints were swollen with rheumatism. And the whip went on swishing against the coarse, khaki-colored cloth of the uniform. "M-hm, m-hm," growled the policeman meaningfully. "But he's one of the quiet ones, I know him," put in Arévalo. The beat of the whip against the cloth stopped. "We'll see, we'll see," and a sardonic smile creased the policeman's face. "There'll be no more haw-hawing around here, you hear, Benavides. And that goes for you, too...." They left.

Juan's mouth felt dry. He picked up the package from the counter, fished in his pocket for the forty-five centavos he owed, and said goodbye to Benavides, whose hands were still shaking and who was as pale as a person with a sudden attack of cramps.

Now the threat had taken form in the person of the son of Simón Arévalo. Juan recalled that Simón Arévalo had been his friend, and that this boy had not seemed really bad. It was just that he liked to go around shooting off his mouth about this business of politics. But what was he up to now? If he had joined the force, that would be clear. But he wasn't wearing a uniform. Ever since things had become hot, Arévalo had been hand in glove with the authorities. People in town said that he was always in the Mayor's office or drinking with the police. An informer—that's what he was, and an informer who had the advantage of knowing everybody for five, maybe ten leagues around. Why wouldn't he? He had been born right here, like Simón, his father, and like his grandfather. Why wouldn't he, when he had gone to the village school, barefooted like Juan, and like him had run all over, knowing the names of all the owners and renters and tenants and hired hands, working here and there till he was grown up, had put on shoes and a felt hat, and had settled down in the neighborhood?

The shots awakened Carmen first, then Juan; then the baby began to cry. It was getting light, and the objects in the room were clearly visible. As he jumped out of bed, Juan calculated what time it would be: about five. The shots were repeated, this time closer. He finished pulling on his pants, buckled his belt, and rushed to the door. He had been right about the time; the sky was shedding a milky light over the fields. "Yes, it's five. It's going to be a nice day," he thought without realizing it. The hinges of the fence gate announced that someone was coming in. Two men walked through. Juan recognized them at once; one was Arévalo, the other the policeman with the whip he had seen at Benavides' drugstore. Then Arévalo's warning had come true? It was twelve days since his visit. Everything had worked out just as he had said: "A week, be out of here in a week. That's the best thing you can do. Otherwise...." Now here was Arévalo again, but this time with the law.

The policeman fired another shot into the air as he approached Juan. "Sounds good, doesn't it?" he said, "and you'll hear a lot more tomorrow at this same time if you're not away from here. You understand?" He cocked his pistol again, taking aim at the slender cornstalks, just for the fun of it. Arévalo stood there with hanging head. He did not look at Juan or at Carmen, who had come running to see what was happening. "You've had fair warning. Clear out, and clear out fast." The policeman put the pistol in his holster, took Arévalo by the arm, and walked away. It was only then that Juan realized that the policeman's breath reeked of brandy.

Everyone did his duty, Arévalo and the law, Juan and Carmen and the baby. The house burned easily, with a gay crackle of dry thatch, seasoned wood, and old furniture. For two hours, or maybe three. And as a fresh breeze was blowing from the north, whipping the flames, it looked like fair-time in the village square.

A huge Roman candle. The whip-carrying policeman was having the time of his life, enjoying it much more than his four companions and Arévalo, who had come along to bear witness as to whether Juan Martinez had cleared out or put up a resistance.

When they got back to town they stopped at Linares' store. The Mayor was there, leaning lazily against the sacks of corn.

"How did things go?" "All right, your Honor," Arévalo answered briefly. "Had Martinez left?" "No," said the policeman. "The damn fool locked the doors and stayed in the house. You understand, we didn't have time to waste...."

The oil went drip-drip from the drum to the funnel and from the funnel to the bottle.

RESPONDING PERSONALLY

1. Write your thoughts and feelings as you read this selection.
2. In your opinion, is Juan a hero or a fool? Compare your ideas with a partner.

RESPONDING CRITICALLY

3. What is the central conflict of the story? What does the story reveal about the Martinez family's motivations for resisting? What do we learn about the motivation of Arévalo?
4. The narrator states that "Everyone did his duty. Arévalo and the law, Juan and Carmen and the baby." If everyone did "his duty," was any wrong done in the story? Using evidence from the story, compare your ideas with others.
5. In a well-written story, every detail contributes to the meaning. Explain the importance of the following details:
    a) Juan's continued reference to Arévalo as the "son of Simón Arévalo"
    b) Arévalo's action of scuffing and pressing flat a mound of dust
    c) the references to nature during Arévalo's first visit
    d) the whip carried by the policemen
    e) the final reference to oil.

6. What role does politics play in the lives of the community in this story? What are the different sides? What is each side interested in achieving?

RESPONDING CREATIVELY

7. Using a major newspaper, find one example of a recent news story which contains a conflict or injustice similar to that found in "Ashes for the Wind." Write your response to the article and submit it with the newspaper article to your teacher.

8. Construct a collage representing some of the images, characters, and events from this story.

PROBLEM-SOLVING/DECISION-MAKING

9. In a small group, brainstorm reasons why Juan likely stayed. Would you have done what he did? Explain.

> "I am the Emperor!" cried
> Harrison. "Do you hear? I am
> the Emperor!"

Kurt Vonnegut, Jr.
Harrison Bergeron

The year was 2081, and everybody was finally equal. They weren't only equal before God and the law. They were equal every which way. Nobody was smarter than anybody else. Nobody was better looking than anybody else. Nobody was stronger or quicker than anybody else. All this equality was due to the 211th, 212th, and 213th Amendments to the Constitution, and to the unceasing vigilance of agents of the United States Handicapper General.

Some things about living still weren't quite right, though. April, for instance, still drove people crazy by not being springtime. And it was in that clammy month that the H-G men took George and Hazel Bergeron's fourteen-year-old son, Harrison, away.

It was tragic, all right, but George and Hazel couldn't think about it very hard. Hazel had a perfectly average intelligence, which meant she couldn't think about anything except in short bursts. And George, while his intelligence was way above normal, had a little mental handicap radio in his ear. He was required by law to wear it at all times. It was tuned to a government transmitter. Every twenty seconds or so, the transmitter would send out some sharp noise to keep people like George from taking unfair advantage of their brains.

George and Hazel were watching television. There were tears on Hazel's cheeks, but she'd forgotten for the moment what they were about.

On the television screen were ballerinas.

A buzzer sounded in George's head. His thoughts fled in panic, like bandits from a burglar alarm.

"That was a real pretty dance, that dance they just did," said Hazel.

"Huh?" said George.

"That dance—it was nice," said Hazel.

"Yup," said George. He tried to think a little about the ballerinas. They weren't really very good—no better than anybody else would have been, anyway. They were burdened with sashweights and bags of birdshot, and their faces were masked, so that no one, seeing a free and graceful gesture or a pretty face, would feel like something the cat drug in. George was toying with the vague notion that maybe dancers shouldn't be handicapped. But he didn't get very far with it before another noise in his ear radio scattered his thoughts.

George winced. So did two out of the eight ballerinas.

Hazel saw him wince. Having no mental handicap herself she had to ask George what the latest sound had been.

"Sounded like somebody hitting a milk bottle with a ball-peen hammer," said George.

"I'd think it would be real interesting, hearing all the different sounds," said Hazel, a little envious. "All the things they think up."

"Um," said George.

"Only, if I was Handicapper General, you know what I would do?" said Hazel. Hazel, as matter of fact, bore a strong resemblance to the Handicapper General, a woman named Diana Moon Glampers. "If I was Diana Moon Glampers," said Hazel, "I'd have chimes on Sunday—just chimes. Kind of in honor of religion."

"I could think, if it was just chimes," said George.

"Well—maybe make 'em real loud," said Hazel. "I think I'd make a good Handicapper General."

"Good as anybody else," said George.

"Who knows better'n I do what normal is?" said Hazel.

"Right," said George. He began to think glimmeringly about his abnormal son who was now in jail, about Harrison, but a twenty-one-gun salute in his head stopped that.

"Boy!" said Hazel, "that was a doozy, wasn't it?"

It was such a doozy that George was white and trembling, and tears stood on the rims of his red eyes. Two of the eight ballerinas had collapsed to the studio floor, were holding their temples.

"All of a sudden you look so tired," said Hazel. "Why don't you stretch out on the sofa, so's you can rest your handicap bag on the pillows, honeybunch." She was referring to the forty-seven pounds of birdshot in a canvas bag, which was padlocked around George's neck. "Go on and rest the bag for a little while," she said. "I don't care if you're not equal to me for a while."

George weighed the bag with his hands. "I don't mind it," he said. "I don't notice it any more. It's just a part of me."

"You been so tired lately—kind of wore out," said Hazel. "If there was just some way we could make a little hole in the bottom of the bag, and just take out a few of them lead balls. Just a few."

"Two years in prison and two thousand dollars fine for every ball I took out," said George. "I don't call that a bargain."

"If you could just take a few out when you came home from work," said Hazel. "I mean—you don't compete with anybody around here. You just set around."

"If I tried to get away with it," said George, "then other people'd get away with it—and pretty soon we'd be right back to the dark ages again, with everybody competing against everybody else. You wouldn't like that, would you?"

"I'd hate it," said Hazel.

"There you are," said George. "The minute people start cheating on laws, what do you think happens to society?"

If Hazel hadn't been able to come up with an answer to this question, George couldn't have supplied one. A siren was going off in his head.

"Reckon it'd fall all apart," said Hazel.

"What would?" said George blankly.

"Society," said Hazel uncertainly. "Wasn't that what you just said?"

"Who knows?" said George.

The television program was suddenly interrupted for a news bulletin. It wasn't clear at first as to what the bulletin was about, since the announcer, like all announcers, had a serious speech impediment. For about half a minute, and in a state of high excitement, the announcer tried to say, "Ladies and gentlemen—"

He finally gave up, handed the bulletin to a ballerina to read.

"That's all right—" Hazel said of the announcer, "he tried. That's the big thing. He tried to do the best he could with what God gave him. He should get a nice raise for trying so hard."

"Ladies and gentlemen—" said the ballerina, reading the bulletin. She must have been extraordinarily beautiful, because the mask she wore was hideous. And it was easy to see that she was the strongest and most graceful of all the dancers, for her handicap bags were as big as those worn by two-hundred-pound men.

And she had to apologize at once for her voice, which was a very unfair voice for a woman to use. Her voice was a warm, luminous, timeless melody. "Excuse me—" she said, and she began again, making her voice absolutely uncompetitive.

"Harrison Bergeron, age fourteen," she said in a grackle squawk, "has just escaped from jail, where he was held on suspicion of plotting to overthrow the government. He is a genius and an athlete, is under-handicapped, and should be regarded as extremely dangerous."

A police photograph of Harrison Bergeron was flashed on the screen—upside down, then sideways, upside down again, then right side up. The picture showed the full length of Harrison against a background calibrated in feet and inches. He was exactly seven feet tall.

The rest of Harrison's appearance was Halloween and hardware. Nobody had ever borne heavier handicaps. He had outgrown hindrances faster than the H-G men could think them up. Instead of a little ear radio for a mental handicap, he wore a tremendous pair of earphones, and spectacles with thick, wavy lenses. The spectacles were intended to make him not only half blind, but to give him whanging headaches besides.

Scrap metal was hung all over him. Ordinarily, there was a certain symmetry, a military neatness to the handicaps issued to strong people, but Harrison looked like a walking junkyard. In the race of life, Harrison carried three hundred pounds.

And to offset his good looks, the H-G men required that he wear at all times a red rubber ball for a nose, keep his eyebrows shaved off, and cover his even white teeth with black caps at snaggle-tooth random.

"If you see this boy," said the ballerina, "do not—I repeat, do not—try to reason with him."

There was the shriek of a door being torn from its hinges.

Screams and barking cries of consternation came from the television set. The photograph of Harrison Bergeron on the screen jumped again and again, as though dancing to the tune of an earthquake.

George Bergeron correctly identified the earthquake, and well he might have—for many was the time his own home had danced to the same clashing tune. "My God—" said George, "that must be Harrison!"

The realization was blasted from his mind instantly by the sound of an automobile collision in his head.

When George could open his eyes again, the photograph of Harrison was gone. A living, breathing Harrison filled the screen.

Clanking, clownish, and huge, Harrison stood in the center of the studio. The knob of the uprooted studio door was still in his hand. Ballerinas, technicians, musicians, and announcers cowered on their knees before him, expecting to die.

"I am the Emperor!" cried Harrison. "Do you hear? I am the Emperor! Everybody must do what I say at once!" He stamped his foot and the studio shook.

"Even as I stand here—" he bellowed, "crippled, hobbled, sickened—I am a greater ruler than any man who ever lived! Now watch me become what I *can* become!"

Harrison tore the straps of his handicap harness like wet tissue paper, tore straps guaranteed to support five thousand pounds.

Harrison's scrap-iron handicaps crashed to the floor.

Harrison thrust his thumbs under the bar of the padlock that secured his head harness. The bar snapped like celery. Harrison smashed his headphones and spectacles against the wall.

He flung away his rubber-ball nose, revealed a man that would have awed Thor, the god of thunder.

"I shall now select my Empress!" he said, looking down on the cowering people. "Let the first woman who dares rise to her feet claim her mate and her throne!"

A moment passed, and then a ballerina arose, swaying like a willow.

Harrison plucked the mental handicap from her ear, snapped off her physical handicaps with marvellous delicacy. Last of all, he removed her mask.

She was blindly beautiful.

"Now—" said Harrison, taking her hand, "shall we show the people the meaning of the word dance? Music!" he commanded.

The musicians scrambled back into their chairs, and Harrison stripped them of their handicaps, too. "Play your best," he told them, "and I'll make you barons and dukes and earls."

The music began. It was normal at first—cheap, silly, false. But Harrison snatched two musicians from their chairs, waved them like batons as he sang the music as he wanted it played. He slammed them back into their chairs.

The music began again and was much improved.

Harrison and his Empress merely listened to the music for a while—listening gravely, as though synchronizing their heartbeats with it.

They shifted their weights to their toes.

Harrison placed his big hands on the girl's tiny waist, letting her sense the weightlessness that would soon be hers.

And then, in an explosion of joy and grace, into the air they sprang!

Not only were the laws of the land abandoned, but the law of gravity and the laws of motion as well.

They reeled, whirled, swivelled, flounced, capered, gambolled, and spun.

They leaped like deer on the moon.

The studio ceiling was thirty feet high, but each leap brought the dancers nearer to it.

It became their obvious intention to kiss the ceiling.

They kissed it.

And then, neutralizing gravity with love and pure will, they remained suspended in air inches below the ceiling, and they kissed each other for a long, long time.

It was then that Diana Moon Glampers, the Handicapper General, came into the studio with a double-barrelled ten-gauge shotgun. She fired twice, and the Emperor and the Empress were dead before they hit the floor.

Diana Moon Glampers loaded the gun again. She aimed it at the musicians and told them they had ten seconds to get their handicaps back on.

It was then that the Bergerons' television tube burned out.

Hazel turned to comment about the blackout to George. But George had gone out into the kitchen for a can of beer.

George came back in with the beer, paused while a handicap signal shook him up. And then he sat down again. "You been crying?" he said to Hazel.

"Yup," she sad.

"What about?" he said.

"I forget," she said. "Something real sad on television."

"What was it?" he said.

"It's all kind of mixed up in my mind," said Hazel.

"Forget sad things," said George.

"I always do," said Hazel.

"That's my girl," said George. He winced. There was the sound of a riveting gun in his head.

"Gee—I could tell that one was a doozy," said Hazel.

"You can say that again," said George.

"Gee—" said Hazel, "I could tell that one was a doozy."

RESPONDING PERSONALLY

1. Write about what it would be like to live in a society where everyone was equal in every way. Would that be possible and desirable? Explain.
2. What parts of the story do you find exaggerated? Why do you think these events are presented in this manner?

RESPONDING CRITICALLY

3. Do you think the story's opening paragraph is effective? How does it set up the conflicts?
4. What is ironic about George's comments on competition, laws, and society?
5. Describe George and Hazel's reactions at the end of the story. What do you think the author is trying to say through them?
6. Harrison Bergeron's rebellion is a failure. Given the nature of society in the story, could someone like Harrison ever have succeeded in rebelling? Explain. What point does the ending make?

RESPONDING CREATIVELY

7. Prepare a Web site for the Handicapper General.
8. With a partner, present a puppet show version of the story for preschoolers or kindergarten students.

PROBLEM-SOLVING/DECISION-MAKING

9. For discussion: What are some ways in which our society tries to make everyone equal? Are those ways effective? Support your opinions with evidence.

Tradition and Change

Tradition and change are two elements that constantly influence our lives. We are familiar with our own culture's traditions, yet we recognize that change in tradition may occur for good reasons. Tradition is primarily a comforting ritual that does not need to be questioned. Change, on the other hand, inevitably invites reflection, risk, and possibly further change.

In the first story, "The Man to Send Rain Clouds," some aboriginal people follow their traditions in burying one of their elders. A change, however, occurs involving the local priest, who is invited to sprinkle holy water on the burial site. Will the priest consent to be involved, and can the proposed change accommodate the traditions of the aboriginal people? Is it possible that two very different cultures and religions can cooperate for a common purpose? These are the larger questions the story asks.

In the second story, "A Moving Day," younger generation Japanese daughters try to understand and cope with the desire of their mother to dispose of her past in a final manner. Throughout the story, we glimpse the woman's past through stories of her life and generation, while the daughters do their best to understand the meaning of their mother's life.

Finally, in "To Set Our House in Order," we learn about a young girl's awakening to her family and the world in which she lives. The arrival of her baby brother and her deeper realizations about her grandmother and her father allow Vanessa to discover more about her imperfect but very human family. This discovery prompts Vanessa's significant epiphany and major change in her perspective on life.

As we see in these three stories, traditions are often threatened and modified by change, which may occur as a result of a crisis, new choices, or thoughtful deliberation. The task of the character having this experience is to manage the unexpected changes by focusing on the positive nature of change.

"I guess he sat down to rest in
the shade and never got up
again."

Leslie Marmon Silko
The Man to Send Rain Clouds

They found him under a big cottonwood tree. His Levi jacket and pants were faded light blue so that he had been easy to find. The big cottonwood tree stood apart from a small grove of winterbare cottonwoods which grew in the wide, sandy arroyo. He had been dead for a day or more, and the sheep had wandered and scattered up and down the arroyo. Leon and his brother-in-law, Ken, gathered the sheep and left them in the pen at the sheep camp before they returned to the cottonwood tree. Leon waited under the tree while Ken drove the truck through the deep sand to the edge of the arroyo. He squinted up at the sun and unzipped his jacket—it sure was hot for this time of year. But high and northwest the blue mountains were still in snow. Ken came sliding down the low, crumbling bank about fifty yards down, and he was bringing the red blanket.

Before they wrapped the old man, Leon took a piece of string out of his pocket and tied a small gray feather in the old man's long white hair. Ken gave him the paint. Across the brown wrinkled forehead he drew a streak of white and along the high cheekbones he drew a strip of blue paint. He paused and watched Ken throw pinches of corn meal and pollen into the wind that fluttered the small gray feather. Then Leon painted with yellow under the old man's broad nose, and finally, when he had painted green across the chin, he smiled.

"Send us rain clouds, Grandfather." They laid the bundle in the back of the pickup and covered it with a heavy tarp before they started back to the pueblo.

They turned off the highway onto the sandy pueblo road. Not long after they passed the store and post office they saw Father

Paul's car coming toward them. When he recognized their faces he slowed his car and waved for them to stop. The young priest rolled down the car window.

"Did you find old Teofilo?" he asked loudly.

Leon stopped the truck. "Good morning, Father. We were just out to the sheep camp. Everything is O.K. now."

"Thank God for that. Teofilo is a very old man. You really shouldn't allow him to stay at the sheep camp alone."

"No, he won't do that any more now."

"Well, I'm glad you understand. I hope I'll be seeing you at Mass this week—we missed you last Sunday. See if you can get old Teofilo to come with you " The priest smiled and waved at them as they drove away.

Louise and Teresa were waiting. The table was set for lunch, and the coffee was boiling on the black iron stove. Leon looked at Louise and then at Teresa.

"We found him under a cottonwood tree in the big arroyo near sheep camp. I guess he sat down to rest in the shade and never got up again." Leon walked toward the old man's bed. The red plaid shawl had been shaken and spread carefully over the bed, and a new brown flannel shirt and pair of stiff new Levi's were arranged neatly beside the pillow. Louise held the screen door open while Leon and Ken carried in the red blanket. He looked small and shriveled, and after they dressed him in the new shirt and pants he seemed more shrunken.

It was noontime now because the church bells rang the Angelus. They ate the beans with hot bread, and nobody said anything until after Teresa poured the coffee.

Ken stood up and put on his jacket. "I'll see about the gravediggers. Only the top layer of soil is frozen. I think it can be ready before dark."

Leon nodded his head and finished his coffee. After Ken had been gone for a while, the neighbors and clanspeople came quietly to embrace Teofilo's family and to leave food on the table because the gravediggers would come to eat when they were finished.

The sky in the west was full of pale yellow light. Louise stood outside with her hands in the pockets of Leon's green army jacket that was too big for her. The funeral was over, and the old men had taken their candles and medicine bags and were gone. She waited until the body was laid into the pickup before she said anything to Leon. She touched his arm, and he noticed that her hands were still dusty from the corn meal that she had sprinkled around the old man. When she spoke, Leon could not hear her.

"What did you say? I didn't hear you."

"I said that I had been thinking about something."

"About what?"

"About the priest sprinkling holy water for Grandpa. So he won't be thirsty."

Leon stared at the new moccasins that Teofilo had made for the ceremonial dances in the summer. They were nearly hidden by the red blanket. It was getting colder, and the wind pushed gray dust down the narrow pueblo road. The sun was approaching the long mesa where it disappeared during the winter. Louise stood there shivering and watching his face. Then he zipped up his jacket and opened the truck door. "I'll see if he's there."

Ken stopped the pickup at the church, and Leon got out; and then Ken drove down the hill to the graveyard where people were waiting. Leon knocked at the old carved door with its symbols of the Lamb. While he waited he looked up at the twin bells from the king of Spain with the last sunlight pouring around them in their tower.

The priest opened the door and smiled when he saw who it was. "Come in! What brings you here this evening?"

The priest walked toward the kitchen, and Leon stood with his cap in his hand, playing with the earflaps and examining the living room—the brown sofa, the green armchair, and the brass lamp that hung down from the ceiling by links of chain. The priest dragged a chair out of the kitchen and offered it to Leon.

"No thank you, Father. I only came to ask you if you would bring your holy water to the graveyard."

The priest turned away from Leon and looked out the window at the patio full of shadows and the dining-room windows of the nuns' cloister across the patio. The curtains were heavy, and the light from within faintly penetrated; it was impossible to see the nuns inside eating supper. "Why didn't you tell me he was dead? I could have brought the Last Rites anyway."

Leon smiled. "It wasn't necessary, Father."

The priest stared down at his scuffed brown loafers and the worn hem of his cassock. "For a Christian burial it was necessary."

His voice was distant, and Leon thought that his blue eyes look tired.

"It's O.K., Father, we just want him to have plenty of water."

The priest sank down into the green chair and picked up a glossy missionary magazine. He turned the colored pages full of lepers and pagans without looking at them.

"You know I can't do that, Leon. There should have been the Last Rites and a funeral Mass at the very least."

Leon put on his green cap and pulled the flaps down over his ears. "It's getting late, Father. I've got to go."

When Leon opened the door Father Paul stood up and said, "Wait." He left the room and came back wearing a long brown overcoat. He followed Leon out the door and across the dim churchyard to the adobe steps in front of the church. They both stooped to fit through the low adobe entrance. And when they started down the hill to the graveyard only half of the sun was visible above the mesa.

The priest approached the grave slowly, wondering how they had managed to dig into the frozen ground; and then he remembered that this was New Mexico, and saw the pile of cold loose sand beside the hole. The people stood close to each other with little clouds of steam puffing from their faces. The priest looked at them and saw a pile of jackets, gloves, and scarves in the yellow, dry tumbleweeds that grew in the graveyard. He looked at the red blanket, not sure that Teofilo was so small, wondering if it wasn't some perverse Indian trick—something they did in March to ensure a good harvest—wondering if maybe old Teofilo was actually at sheep camp corralling the sheep for the night. But there he was, facing into a cold dry wind and squinting at the last sunlight, ready to bury a red wool blanket while the faces of his parishioners were in shadow with the last warmth of the sun on their backs.

His fingers were stiff, and it took him a long time to twist the lid off the holy water. Drops of water fell on the red blanket and soaked into dark icy spots. He sprinkled the grave and the water disappeared almost before it touched the dim, cold sand; it reminded him of something—he tried to remember what it was, because he thought if he could remember he might understand this. He sprinkled more water; he shook the container until it was empty, and the water fell through the light from sundown like August rain that fell while the sun was still shining, almost evaporating before it touched the wilted squash flowers.

The wind pulled at the priest's brown Franciscan robe and swirled away the corn meal and pollen that had been sprinkled on the blanket. They lowered the bundle into the ground, and they didn't bother to untie the stiff pieces of new rope that were tied around the ends of the blanket. The sun was gone, and over on the highway the eastbound lane was full of headlights. The priest walked away slowly. Leon watched him climb the hill, and when he had disappeared within the tall, thick walls, Leon turned to look up at the high blue mountains in the deep snow that reflected a faint red light from the west. He felt good because it was finished, and he was happy about the sprinkling of the holy water; now the old man could send them big thunderclouds for sure.

RESPONDING PERSONALLY

1. Write your thoughts and feelings as you read this selection.
2. What is your response to the aboriginal characters' choice and the priest's decision in the story? Write your ideas in a journal entry.

LESLIE MARMON SILKO : 75

RESPONDING CRITICALLY

3. Why does Leon place a small grey feather in the old man's hair? Why does he paint the old man's face?
4. What was the old man doing when he died? What do we learn about the old man from the story?
5. Given that these aboriginal people have their own burial customs, why do they ask the priest to be involved in the funeral? Why do you think the priest agrees to participate?
6. What is the purpose of this story? What is its theme? Share your ideas with another student.

RESPONDING CREATIVELY

7. Imagine that the aboriginal characters wrote the priest a letter, encouraging him to participate in the funeral. Compose the letter they might have written.
8. Using a video camera, film one of the story's scenes with a partner.

PROBLEM-SOLVING/DECISION-MAKING

9. Writing assignment: We have all been involved in a difficult moment or challenging time such as the one presented in the story. In a paragraph, describe a predicament you once had and the strategies you used to resolve it.

The problem with children is
they can wipe out your history.

Susan Nunes
A Moving Day

Across the street, the bulldozer roars to life. Distracted, my mother looks up from the pile of embroidered linen that she has been sorting. She is seventy, tiny and fragile, the flesh burned off her shrinking frame. Her hair is gray now—she had never dyed it—and she wears it cut close to her head with the nape shaved. Her natural hairline would have been better suited to the kimono worn by women of her mother's generation. She still has a beautiful neck. In recent years she has taken a liking to jeans, cotton smocks, baggy sweaters, and running shoes. When I was a child she wouldn't have been caught dead without her nylons.

Her hands, now large-jointed with arthritis, return to the pile of linen. Her movements always had a no-nonsense quality and ever since I was a child, I have been wary of her energy because it was so often driven by suppressed anger. Now she is making two stacks, the larger one for us, the smaller for her to keep. There is a finality in the way she places things in the larger pile, as if to say that's *it*. For her, it's all over, all over but this last accounting. She does not look forward to what is coming. Strangers. Schedules. The regulated activities of those considered too old to regulate themselves. But at least, at the *very* least, she'll not be a burden. She sorts through the possession of lifetime, she and her three daughters. It's time she passed most of this on. Dreams are lumber. She can't *wait* to be rid of them.

My two sisters and I present a contrast. There is nothing purposeful or systematic about the way we move. In fact, we don't know where we're going. We know there is a message in all this activity, but we don't know what it is. Still, we search for it in the odd carton, between layers of tissue paper and silk. We open drawers, peer into the recesses of cupboards, rummage through the depths of closets. What a lot of stuff! We lift, untuck, unwrap, and set it aside. The message is there, we know. But what is it? Perhaps if we knew, then we wouldn't have to puzzle out our mother's righteous determination to shed the past.

There is a photograph of my mother taken on the porch of my grandparents' house when she was in her twenties. She is wearing a floral print dress with a square, lace-edged collar and a graceful skirt that shows off her slim body. Her shoulder-length hair has been permed. It is dark and thick and worn parted on the side to fall over her right cheek. She is very fair; "one pound powder," her friends called her. She is smiling almost reluctantly, as if she meant to appear serious but the photographer has said something amusing. One arm rests lightly on the railing, the other, which is at her side, holds a handkerchief. They were her special pleasures, handkerchiefs of hand-embroidered linen as fine as rice paper. Most were gifts (she used to say that when she was a girl, people gave one another little things—a handkerchief, a pincushion, pencils, hair ribbons), and she washed and starched them by hand, ironed them, taking care with the rolled hems, and stored them in a silk bag from Japan.

There is something expectant in her stance, as if she were waiting for something to happen. She says, your father took this photograph in 1940, before we were married. She lowers her voice confidentially and adds, now he cannot remember taking it. My father sits on the balcony, an open book on his lap, peacefully smoking his pipe. The bulldozer tears into the foundations of the Kitamura house.

What about this? My youngest sister has found a fishing boat carved of tortoise shell.

Hold it in your hand and look at it. Every plank of the hull is visible. Run your fingers along the sides, you can feel the joints. The two masts, about six inches high, are from the darkest part of the shell. I broke one of the sails many years ago. The remaining one is quite remarkable, so thin that the light comes through it in places. It is delicately ribbed to give the effect of canvas pushed gently by the wind.

My mother reaches for a sheet of tissue paper and takes the boat from my sister. She says, it was a gift from Mr. Oizumi. He bought it from an artisan in Kamakura.

Stories cling to the thing, haunt it like unrestful spirits. They are part of the object. They have been there since we were children, fascinated with her possessions. In 1932, Mr. Oizumi visits Japan. He crosses the Pacific by steamer, and when he arrives he is hosted by relatives eager to hear of his good fortune. But Mr. Oizumi soon tires of their questions. He wants to see what has become of the country. It will be arranged, he is told. Mr. Oizumi is a meticulous man. Maps are his passion. A trail of neat X's marks the steps of his journey. On his map of China, he notes each military outspot in Manchuria and appends a brief description of what he sees. Notes invade the margins, march over the blank spaces. The characters are written in a beautiful hand, precise, disciplined, orderly. Eventually, their trail leads to the back of the map. After Pearl Harbor, however, Mr. Oizumi is forced to burn his entire collection. The U.S. Army has decreed that enemy aliens caught with seditious materials will be arrested. He does it secretly in the shed behind his home, his wife standing guard. They scatter the ashes in the garden among the pumpkin vines.

My grandfather's library does not escape the flames either. After the army requisitions the Japanese school for wartime headquarters, they give my mother's parents twenty-four hours to vacate the premises, including the boarding house where they lived with about twenty students from the plantation camps outside Hilo. There is no time to save the books. Her father decides to nail wooden planks over the shelves that line the classrooms. After the army moves in, they rip open the planks, confiscate the books, and store them in the basement of the post office. Later, the authorities burn everything. Histories, children's stories, primers, biographies, language texts, everything, even a set of Encyclopaedia Britannica. My grandfather is shipped to Oahu and imprisoned on Sand Island. A few months later, he is released after three prominent Caucasians vouch for his character. It is a humiliation he doesn't speak of, ever.

All of this was part of the boat. After I broke the sail, she gathered the pieces and said, I'm not sure we can fix this. It was not a toy. Why can't you leave my things alone?

For years the broken boat sat on our bookshelf, a reminder of the brutality of the next generation.

Now she wants to give everything away. We have to beg her to keep things. Dishes from Japan, lacquerware, photographs, embroidery, letters. She says, I have no room. You take them, here, *take* them. Take them or I'll get rid of them.

They're piled around her, they fill storage chests, they fall out of open drawers and cupboards. She only wants to keep a few things—her books, some photographs, three carved wooden figures from Korea that belonged to her father, a few of her mother's dishes, perhaps one futon.

My sister holds a porcelain teapot by its bamboo handle. Four white cranes edged in black and gold fly around it. She asks, Mama, can't you hang on to this? If you keep it, I can borrow it later.

My mother shakes her head. She is adamant. And what would I do with it? I don't want any of this. Really.

My sister turns to me. She sighs. The situation is hopeless. You take it, she says. It'll only get broken at my place. The kids.

It had begun slowly, this shedding of the past, a plate here, a dish there, a handkerchief, a doily, a teacup, a few photographs, one of my grandfather's block prints. Nothing big. But then the odd gesture became a pattern; it got so we never left the house empty-handed. At first we were amused. After all, when we were children she had to fend us off her things. Threaten. We were always *at* them. She had made each one so ripe with memories that we found them impossible to resist. We snuck them outside, showed them to our friends, told and retold the stories. They bear the scars of all this handling, even her most personal possessions. A chip here, a crack there. Casualties. Like the music box her brother brought home from Italy after the war. It played a Brahms lullaby. First we broke the spring, then we lost the winding key, and for years it sat mutely on her dresser.

She would say again and again, it's impossible to keep anything nice with you children. And we'd retreat, wounded, for a while. The problem with children is they can wipe out your history. It's a miracle that anything survives this onslaught.

There's a photograph of my mother standing on the pier in Honolulu in 1932, the year she left Hawaii to attend the University of California. She's loaded to the ears with leis. She's wearing a fedora pulled smartly to the side. She's not smiling. Of my mother's two years there, my grandmother recalled that she received good grades and never wore a kimono again. My second cousin with whom my mother stayed when she first arrived, said she was surprisingly sophisticated—she liked hats. My mother said that she was homesick. Her favorite class was biology and she entertained ambitions of becoming a scientist. Her father, however, wanted her to become a teacher, and his wishes prevailed, even though he would not have forced them upon her. She was a dutiful daughter.

During her second year, she lived near campus with a mathematics professor and his wife. In exchange for room and board she cleaned house, ironed, and helped prepare meals. One of the things that survives from this period is a black composition book entitled *Recipes of California*. As a child, I read it like a book of mysteries for clues to a life which seemed both alien and familiar. Some entries she had copied by hand; others she cut out of magazines and pasted on the page, sometimes with a picture or drawing. The margins contained her cryptic comments: "Saturday bridge club," "From Mary G. Do not give away," underlined, "chopped suet by hand, wretched task, bed at 2 A.M., exhausted." I remember looking up "artichoke" in the dictionary and asking Mr. Okinaga, the vegetable vendor, if he had any edible thistles. I never ate one until I was sixteen.

That book holds part of the answer to why our family rituals didn't fit the recognized norm of either our relatives or the larger community in which we grew up. At home, we ate in fear of the glass of spilled milk, the stray elbow on the table, the boarding house reach. At my grandparents', we slurped our *chasuke*. We wore tailored dresses, white cotton pinafores, and Buster Brown shoes with white socks; however, what we longed for were the lacy, ornate dresses in the National Dollar Store that the Puerto Rican girls wore to church on Sunday. For six years, I marched to Japanese language school after my regular classes; however, we only spoke English at home. We talked too loudly and all at once, which mortified my mother, but she was always complaining about Japanese indirectness. I know that she smarted under a system which the older son is the center of the familial universe, but at thirteen I had a fit of jealous rage over her fawning attention to our only male cousin.

My sister has found a photograph of my mother, a round-faced and serious twelve or thirteen, dressed in a kimono and seated, on her knees, on the *tatami* floor. She is playing the *koto*. According to my mother, girls were expected to learn this difficult stringed instrument because it was thought to teach discipline. Of course, everything Japanese was a lesson in discipline—flower arranging, calligraphy, judo, brush painting, embroidery, everything. One summer my sister and I had to take *ikebana*, the art of flower arrangement, at Grandfather's school. The course was taught by Mrs. Oshima, a diminutive, soft-spoken, terrifying woman, and my supplies were provided by my grandmother, whose tastes ran to the oversized. I remember little of that class and its principles. What I remember most clearly is having to walk home carrying, in a delicate balancing act, one of our creations, which, more often than not, towered above our heads.

How do we choose among what we experience, what we are taught, what we run into by chance, or what is forced upon us? What is the principle of selection? My sisters and I are not bound by any of our mother's obligations, nor do we follow the rituals that seemed so important. My sister once asked, do you realize that when she's gone that's *it*? She was talking about how to make sushi, but it was a profound question nonetheless.

I remember, after we moved to Honolulu and my mother stopped teaching and began working long hours in administration, she was less vigilant about the many little things that once consumed her attention. While we didn't exactly slide into savagery, we economized in more ways than one. She would often say, there's simply no time anymore to do things right.

I didn't understand then why she looked so sad when she said it, but somehow I knew the comment applied to us. It would be terrible if centuries of culture are lost simply because there is not time.

Still, I don't understand why we carry out this fruitless search. Whatever it is we are looking for, we're not going to find it. My sister tries to lift a box filled with record albums, old seventy-eights, gives up, and sets it down again. My mother says, there are people who collect these things. Imagine.

Right, just imagine.

I think about my mother bathing me and singing, "The snow is snowing, the wind is blowing, but I will weather the storm." And I think of her story of the village boy carried by the Tengu on a fantastic flight over the cities of Japan, but who returns to a disbelieving and resistant family. So much for questions which have no answers, why we look among objects for meanings which have somehow escaped us in the growing up and growing old.

However, my mother is a determined woman. She will take nothing with her if she can help it. It is all ours. And on the balcony my father knocks the ashes of his pipe into a porcelain ashtray, and the bulldozer is finally silent.

RESPONDING PERSONALLY

1. The story's title probably reminds you of moving days when you and your family packed and unpacked while changing residences. With a partner, share one memorable moving day from your past.
2. This story covers significant past events in a person's life. Pick one memory from your past and write a personal response about it.

RESPONDING CRITICALLY

3. What is the purpose of the two references to the bulldozer and the father on the balcony?
4. How do the physical descriptions of the mother reflect her character? How has she changed from her youth? From her daughters' perspective, how has their mother changed?
5. How are the daughters different from the mother? What influence has their culture had on them?
6. For paragraph answer. What are some of the memories about Mr. Oizumi? What hardships have been experienced by the people of the mother's generation?

RESPONDING CREATIVELY

7. Write a memoir about a grandparent or parent who has been important to you.
8. Role-play a conversation between the narrator and her mother about the fate of various objects in the household.

PROBLEM-SOLVING/DECISION-MAKING

9. In a two-column chart, list 10 personal artifacts important to you on one side. On the other side, explain why each item has importance for you.

Margaret Laurence
To Set Our House in Order

When the baby was almost ready to be born, something went wrong and my mother had go to into hospital two weeks before the expected time. I was wakened by her crying in the night, and then I heard my father's footsteps as he went downstairs to phone. I stood in the doorway of my room, shivering and listening, wanting to go to my mother but afraid to go lest there be some sight there more terrifying than I could bear.

"Hello—Paul?" my father said, and I knew he was talking to Dr. Cates. "It's Beth. The waters have broken, and the fetal position doesn't seem quite—well, I'm only thinking of what happened the last time, and another like that would be—I wish she were a little huskier, damn it—she's so—no, don't worry, I'm quite all right. Yes, I think that would be the best thing. Okay, make it as soon as you can, will you?"

He came back upstairs, looking bony and dishevelled in his pyjamas, and running his fingers through his sand-colored hair. At the top of the stairs, he came face to face with Grandmother MacLeod, who was standing there in her quilted black satin dressing gown, her slight figure held straight and poised, as though she were unaware that her hair was bound grotesquely like white-feathered wings in the snare of her coarse night-time hairnet.

"What is it, Ewen?"

"It's all right, Mother. Beth's having—a little trouble, I'm going to take her into the hospital. You go back to bed."

"I told you," Grandmother MacLeod said in her clear voice, never loud, but distinct and ringing like the tap of a sterling teaspoon on a crystal goblet, "I did tell you, Ewen, did I not, that you should have got a girl in to help her with the housework? She would have rested more."

"I couldn't afford to get anyone in," my father said. "If you thought she should've rested more, why didn't you ever—oh God, I'm out of my mind tonight—just go back to bed, Mother, please. I must get back to Beth."

When my father went down to the front door to let Dr. Cates in, my need overcame my fear and I slipped into my parents' room. My mother's black hair, so neatly pinned up during the day, was startlingly spread across the white pillowcase. I stared at her, not speaking, and then she smiled and I rushed from the doorway and buried my head upon her.

"It's all right, honey," she said. "Listen, Vanessa, the baby's just going to come a little early, that's all. You'll be all right. Grandmother MacLeod will be here."

"How can she get the meals?" I wailed, fixing on the first thing that came to mind. "She never cooks. She doesn't know how."

"Yes, she does," my mother said. "She can cook as well as anyone when she has to. She's just never had to very much, that's all. Don't worry—she'll keep everything in order, and then some."

My father and Dr. Cates came in, and I had to go, without ever saying anything I had wanted to say. I went back to my own room and lay with the shadows all around me. I listened to the night murmurings that always went on in that house, sounds which never had a source, rafters and beams contracting in the dry air, perhaps, or mice in the walls, or a sparrow that had flown into the attic through the broken skylight there. After a while, although I would not have believed it possible, I slept.

The next morning I questioned my father. I believed him to be not only the best doctor in Manawaka, but also the best doctor in the whole of Manitoba, if not in the entire world, and the fact that he was not the one who was looking after my mother seemed to have something sinister about it.

"But it's always done that way, Vanessa," he explained. "Doctors never attend members of their own family. It's because they care so much about them, you see, and—"

"And what?" I insisted, alarmed at the way he had broken off. But my father did not reply. He stood there, and then he put on that difficult smile with which adults seek to conceal pain from children. I felt terrified, and ran to him, and he held me tightly.

"She's going to be fine," he said. "Honestly she is. Nessa, don't cry—"

Grandmother MacLeod appeared beside us, steel-spined despite her apparent fragility. She was wearing a purple silk dress and her ivory pendant. She looked as though she were all ready to go out for afternoon tea.

"Ewen, you're only encouraging the child to give way," she said. "Vanessa, big girls of ten don't make such a fuss about things. Come and get your breakfast. Now, Ewen, you're not to worry. I'll see to everything."

Summer holidays were not quite over, but I did not feel like going out to play with any of the kids. I was very superstitious, and I had the feeling that if I left the house, even for a few hours, some disaster would overtake my mother. I did not, of course, mention this feeling to Grandmother MacLeod, for she did not believe in the existence of fear, or if she did, she never let on. I spent the morning morbidly, in seeking hidden places in the house. There were many of these—odd-shaped nooks under the stairs. Small and loosely nailed-up doors at the back of clothes closets, leading to dusty tunnels and forgotten recesses in the heart of the house where the only things actually to be seen were drab oil paintings stacked upon the rafters, and trunks full of outmoded clothing and old photograph albums. But the unseen presences in these secret places I knew to be those of every person, young or old, who had ever belonged to the house and had died, including Uncle Roderick who got killed on the Somme, and the baby who would have been my sister if only she had managed to come to life. Grandfather MacLeod, who had died a year after I was born, was present in the house in more tangible form. At the top of the main stairs hung the mammoth picture of a darkly uniformed man riding upon a horse whose prancing stance and dilated nostrils suggested that the battle was not yet over, that it might indeed continue until Judgment Day. The stern man was actually the Duke of Wellington, but at the time I believed him to be my Grandfather MacLeod, still keeping an eye on things.

We had moved in with Grandmother MacLeod when the Depression got bad and she could no longer afford a housekeeper, but the MacLeod house never seemed like home to me. Its dark red brick was grown over at the front with Virginia creeper that turned crimson in the fall, until you could hardly tell brick from leaves. It boasted a small tower in which Grandmother MacLeod kept a weedy collection of anemic ferns. The veranda was embellished with a profusion of wrought-iron scrolls, and the circular rose-window upstairs contained glass of many colors which permitted an outlooking eye to see the world as a place of absolute sapphire or emerald, or if one wished to look with a jaundiced eye, a hateful yellow. In Grandmother MacLeod's opinion, these features gave the house style.

Inside, a multitude of doors led to rooms where my presence, if not actually forbidden, was not encouraged. One was Grandmother MacLeod's bedroom, with its stale and old-smelling air, the dim reek of medicines and lavender sachets. Here resided her monogrammed dresser silver brush and mirror, nail-buffer and button hook and scissors, none of which must even be fingered by me now, for she meant to leave them to me in her will and intended to hand them over in the same flawless and unused condition in which they had always been kept. Here, too, were the silver-framed photographs of Uncle Roderick—as a child, as a boy, as a man in his Army uniform. The massive walnut spool bed had obviously been designed for queens or giants, and my tiny grandmother used to lie within it all day when she had migraine, contriving somehow to look like a giant queen.

The living room was another alien territory where I had to tread warily, for many valuable objects sat just-so on tables and mantelpiece, and dirt must not be tracked in upon the blue Chinese carpet with its birds in eternal motionless flight and its water-lily buds caught forever just before the point of opening. My mother was always nervous when I was in this room.

"Vanessa, honey," she would say, half apologetically, "why don't you go and play in the den, or upstairs?"

"Can't you leave her, Beth?" my father would say. "She's not doing any harm."

"I'm only thinking of the rug," my mother would say, glancing at Grandmother MacLeod, "and yesterday she nearly knocked the Dresden shepherdess off the mantel. I mean, she can't help it, Ewen, she has to run around—"

"Goddamn it, I know she can't help it," my father would growl, glaring at the smirking face of the Dresden shepherdess.

"I see no need to blaspheme, Ewen," Grandmother MacLeod would say quietly, and then my father would say he was sorry, and I would leave.

The day my mother went to the hospital, Grandmother MacLeod called me at lunch-time, and when I appeared, smudged with dust from the attic, she looked at me distastefully as though I had been a cockroach that had just crawled impertinently out of the woodwork.

"For mercy's sake, Vanessa, what have you been doing with yourself? Run and get washed this minute. Here, not that way— you use the back stairs, young lady. Get along now. Oh—your father phoned."

I swung around. "What did he say? How is she? Is the baby born?"

"Curiosity killed a cat," Grandmother MacLeod said, frowning. "I cannot understand Beth and Ewen telling you all these things, at your age. What sort of vulgar person you'll grow up to be, I dare not think. No, it's not born yet. Your mother's just the same. No change."

I looked at my grandmother, not wanting to appeal to her, but unable to stop myself. "Will she— will she be all right?"

Grandmother MacLeod straightened her already-straight back. "If I said definitely yes, Vanessa, that would be a lie, and the MacLeods do not tell lies, as I have tried to impress upon you before. What happens is God's will. The Lord giveth, and the Lord taketh away."

Appalled, I turned away so she would not see my face and my eyes. Surprisingly, I heard her sigh and felt her papery white and perfectly manicured hand upon my shoulder.

"When your Uncle Roderick got killed," she said, "I thought I would die. But I didn't die, Vanessa."

At lunch, she chatted animatedly, and I realized she was trying to cheer me in the only way she knew.

"When I married your Grandfather MacLeod," she related, "he said to me, 'Eleanor, don't think because we're going to the Prairies that I expect you to live roughly. You're used to a proper house, and you shall have one.' He was as good as his word. Before we'd been in Manawaka three years, he'd had this place built. He earned a good deal of money in his time, your grandfather. He soon had more patients than either of the other doctors. We ordered our dinner service and all our silver from Birks in Toronto. We had resident help in those days, of course, and never had less than twelve guests for dinner parties. When I had a tea, it would always be twenty or thirty. Never any less than half a dozen different kinds of cake were ever served in this house. Well, no one seems to bother much these days. Too lazy, I suppose."

"Too broke," I suggested: "That's what Dad says."

"I can't bear slang," Grandmother MacLeod said. "If you mean hard up, why don't you say so? It's mainly a question of management, anyway. My accounts were always in good order, and so was my house. No unexpected expenses that couldn't be met, no fruit cellar running out of preserves before the winter was over. Do you know what my father used to say to me when I was a girl?"

"No," I said. "What?"

"God loves Order," Grandmother MacLeod replied with emphasis. "You remember that, Vanessa. God loves Order—he wants each one of us to set our house in order. I've never forgotten those words of my father's. I was a MacInnes before I got married. The MacInnes is a very ancient clan, the lairds of Morven and the constables of the Castle of Kinlochaline. Did you finish that book I gave you?"

"Yes," I said. Then, feeling some additional comment to be called for, "It was a swell book, Grandmother."

This was somewhat short of the truth. I had been hoping for her cairngorm brooch on my tenth birthday, and had received instead the plaid-bound volume entitled *The Clans and Tartans of Scotland*. Most of it was too boring to read, but I had looked up the motto of my own family and those of some of my friends' families. *Be then a wall of brass. Learn to suffer. Consider the end. Go carefully.* I had not found any of these slogans reassuring. What with Mavis Duncan learning to suffer, and Laura Kennedy considering the end, and Patsy Drummond going carefully, and I spending my time in being a wall of brass, it did not seem to me that any of us were going to lead very interesting lives. I did not say this to Grandmother MacLeod.

"The MacInnes motto is *Pleasure Arises from Work*," I said.

"Yes," she agreed proudly. "And an excellent motto it is, too. One to bear in mind."

She rose from the table, rearranging on her bosom the looped ivory beads that held the pendant on which a full-blown ivory rose was stiffly carved.

"I hope Ewen will be pleased," she said.

"What at?"

"Didn't I tell you?" Grandmother MacLeod said. "I hired a girl this morning, for the housework. She's to start tomorrow."

When my father got home that evening, Grandmother MacLeod told him her good news. He ran one hand distractedly across his forehead.

"I'm sorry, Mother, but you'll just have to unhire her. I can't possibly pay anyone."

"It seems distinctly odd," Grandmother MacLeod snapped, "that you can afford to eat chicken four times a week."

"Those chickens," my father said in an exasperated voice, "are how people are paying their bills. The same with the eggs and the milk. The scrawny turkey that arrived yesterday was for Logan MacCardney's appendix, if you must know. We probably eat better than any family in Manawaka, except Niall Cameron's. People can't entirely dispense with doctors or undertakers. That doesn't mean to say I've got any cash. Look, Mother, I don't know what's happening with Beth. Paul thinks he may have to do a Caesarean. Can't we leave all this? Just leave the house alone. Don't touch it. What does it matter?"

"I have never lived in a messy house, Ewen," Grandmother MacLeod said, "and I don't intend to begin now."

"Oh Lord," my father said. "Well, I'll phone Edna, I guess, and see if she can give us a hand, although God knows she's got enough, with the Connor house and her parents to look after."

"I don't fancy having Edna Connor in to help," Grandmother MacLeod objected.

"Why not?" my father shouted. "She's Beth's sister, isn't she?"

"She speaks in such a slangy way," Grandmother MacLeod said. "I have never believed she was a good influence on Vanessa. And there is no need for you to raise your voice to me, Ewen, if you please."

I could barely control my rage. I thought my father would surely rise to Aunt Edna's defence. But he did not.

"It'll be all right," he soothed her. "She'd only be here for part of the day, Mother. You could stay in your room."

Aunt Edna strode in the next morning. The sight of her bobbed black hair and her grin made me feel better at once. She hauled out the carpet sweeper and the weighted polisher and got to work. I dusted while she polished and swept, and we got through the living room and front hall in next to no time.

"Where's her royal highness, kiddo?" she inquired.

"In her room," I said. "She's reading the catalogue from Robinson & Cleaver."

"Good Glory, not again?" Aunt Edna cried. "The last time she ordered three linen tea-cloths and two dozen serviettes. It came to fourteen dollars. Your mother was absolutely frantic. I guess I shouldn't be saying this."

"I knew anyway," I assured her. "She was at the lace handker-chiefs section when I took up her coffee."

"Let's hope she stays there. Heaven forbid she should get onto the banqueting cloths. Well, at least she believes the Irish are good for two things—manual labor and linen-making. She's never forgotten Father used to be a blacksmith, before he got the hardware store. Can you beat it? I wish it didn't bother Beth."

"Does it?" I asked, and immediately realized this was a wrong move, for Aunt Edna was suddenly scrutinizing me.

"We're making you grow up before your time," she said. "Don't pay any attention to me, Nessa. I must've got up on the wrong side of the bed this morning."

But I was unwilling to leave the subject.

"All the same," I said thoughtfully, "Grandmother MacLeod's family were the lairds of Morven and the constables of the Castle of Kinlochaline. I bet you didn't know that."

Aunt Edna snorted. "Castle, my foot. She was born in Ontario, just like your grandfather Connor, and her father was a horse doctor. Come on, kiddo, we'd better shut up and get down to business here."

We worked in silence for a while.

"Aunt Edna—" I said at last, "what about Mother? Why won't they let me go and see her?"

"Kids aren't allowed to visit maternity patients. It's tough for you, I know that. Look, Nessa, don't worry. If it doesn't start tonight, they're going to do the operation. She's getting the best of care."

I stood there, holding the feather duster like a dead bird in my hands. I was not aware that I was going to speak until the words came out.

"I'm scared," I said.

Aunt Edna put her arms around me, and her face looked all at once stricken and empty of defences.

"Oh, honey, I'm scared, too," she said.

It was this way that Grandmother MacLeod found us when she came stepping lightly down into the front hall with the order in her hand for two dozen lace-bordered handkerchiefs of pure Irish linen.

I could not sleep that night, and when I went downstairs, I found my father in the den. I sat down on the hassock beside his chair, and he told me about the operation my mother was to have the next morning. He kept on saying it was not serious nowadays.

"But you're worried," I put in, as though seeking to explain why I was.

"I should at least have been able to keep from burdening you with it," he said in a distant voice, as though to himself. "If only the baby hadn't got itself twisted around—"

"Will it be born dead, like the little girl?"

"I don't know," my father said. "I hope not."

"She'd be disappointed, wouldn't she, if it was?" I said bleakly, wondering why I was not enough for her.

"Yes, she would," my father replied. "She won't be able to have any more, after this. It's partly on your account that she wants this one, Nessa. She doesn't want you to grow up without a brother or sister."

"As far as I'm concerned, she didn't need to bother," I retorted angrily.

My father laughed. "Well, let's talk about something else, and then maybe you'll be able to sleep. How did you and Grandmother make out today?"

"Oh, fine, I guess. What was Grandfather MacLeod like, Dad?"

"What did she tell you about him?"

"She said he made a lot of money in his time."

"Well, he wasn't any millionaire," my father said, "but I suppose he did quite well. That's not what I associate with him, though."

He reached across to the bookshelf, took out a small leather-bound volume and opened it. On the pages were mysterious marks, like doodling, only much neater and more patterned.

"What is it?" I asked.

"Greek," my father explained. "This is a play called *Antigone*. See, here's the title in English. There's a whole stack of them on the shelves there. *Oedipus Rex. Electra. Medea.* They belonged to your Grandfather MacLeod. He used to read them often."

"Why?" I inquired, unable to understand why anyone would pore over those undecipherable signs.

MARGARET LAURENCE : 95

"He was interested in them," my father said. "He must have been a lonely man, although it never struck me that way at the time. Sometimes a thing only hits you a long time afterwards."

"Why would he be lonely?" I wanted to know.

"He's the only person in Manawaka who could read these plays in the original Greek," my father said. "I don't suppose many people, if anyone, had even read them in English translations. Maybe he would have liked to be a classical scholar—I don't know. But his father was a doctor, so that's what he was. Maybe he would have liked to talk to somebody about these plays. They must have meant a lot to him."

It seemed to me that my father was talking oddly. There was a sadness in his voice that I had never heard before, and I longed to say something that would make him feel better, but I could not, because I did not know what was the matter.

"Can you read this kind of writing?" I asked hesitantly.

My father shook his head. "Nope. I was never very intellectual, I guess. Rod was always brighter than I, in school, but even he wasn't interested in learning Greek. Perhaps he would've been later, if he'd lived. As a kid, all I ever wanted to do was go into the merchant marine."

"Why didn't you, then?"

"Oh well," my father said offhandedly, "a kid who'd never seen the sea wouldn't have made much of a sailor. I might have turned out to be the seasick type."

I had lost interest now that he was speaking once more like himself.

"Grandmother MacLeod was pretty cross today about the girl," I remarked.

"I know," my father nodded. "Well, we must be as nice as we can to her, Nessa, and after a while she'll be all right."

Suddenly I did not care what I said.

"Why can't she be nice to us for a change?" I burst out. "We're always the ones who have to be nice to her."

My father put his hand down and slowly tilted my head until I was forced to look at him.

"Vanessa," he said, "she's had troubles in her life which you really don't know much about. That's why she gets migraine sometimes and has to go to bed. It's not easy for her these days,
either—the house is still the same, so she thinks other things
should be, too. It hurts her when she finds they aren't."

"I don't see—" I began.

"Listen," my father said, "you know we were talking about what
people are interested in, like Grandfather MacLeod being interested in Greek plays? Well, your grandmother was interested in being
a lady, Nessa, and for a long time it seemed to her that she was one."

I thought of the Castle of Kinlochaline, and of horse doctors in
Ontario.

"I didn't know—" I stammered.

"That's usually the trouble with most of us," my father said.
"You go on up to bed now. I'll phone tomorrow from the hospital
as soon as the operation's over."

I did sleep at last, and in my dreams I could hear the caught
sparrow fluttering in the attic, and the sound of my mother crying, and the voices of the dead children.

My father did not phone until afternoon. Grandmother MacLeod
said I was being silly, for you could hear the phone ringing all
over the house, but nevertheless I refused to move out of the den.
I had never before examined my father's books, but now, at a loss
for something to do, I took them out one by one and read snatch-
es here and there. After I had been doing this for several hours, it
dawned on me that most of the books were of the same kind. I
looked again at the titles.

Seven-League Boots. Arabia Deserta. The Seven Pillars of Wisdom.
Travels in Tibet. Count Lucknor the Sea Devil. And a hundred more.
On a shelf by themselves were copies of the *National Geographic*
magazine, which I looked at often enough, but never before with
the puzzling compulsion which I felt now, as though I were on
the verge of some discovery, something which I had to find out
and yet did not want to know. I riffled through the picture-filled
pages. Hibiscus and wild orchids grew in a soft-petalled confu-

sion. The Himalayas stood lofty as gods, with the morning sun on their peaks of snow. Leopards snarled from the vined depths of a thousand jungles. Schooners buffetted their white sails like the wings of giant angels against the great sea winds.

"What on earth are you doing?" Grandmother MacLeod inquired waspishly, from the doorway. "You've got everything scattered all over the place. Pick it all up this minute, Vanessa, do you hear?"

So I picked up the books and magazines, and put them all neatly away, as I had been told to do.

When the telephone finally rang, I was afraid to answer it. At last I picked it up. My father sounded faraway, and the relief in this voice made it unsteady.

"It's okay, honey. Everything's fine. The boy was born alive and kicking after all. Your mother's pretty weak, but she's going to be all right."

I could hardly believe it. I did not want to talk to anyone. I wanted to be by myself, to assimilate the presence of my brother, towards whom, without ever having seen him yet, I felt such tenderness and such resentment.

That evening, Grandmother MacLeod approached my father, who, still dazed with the unexpected gift of neither life now being threatened, at first did not take her seriously when she asked what they planned to call the child.

"Oh, I don't know. Hank, maybe, or Joe. Fauntleroy, perhaps."
She ignored his levity.

"Ewen," she said, "I wish you would call him Roderick."
My father's face changed. "I'd rather not."

"I think you should," Grandmother MacLeod insisted, very quietly, but in a voice as pointed and precise as her silver nail-scissors.

"Don't you think Beth ought to decide?" my father asked.
"Beth will agree if you do."

My father did not bother to deny something that even I knew to be true. He did not say anything. Then Grandmother MacLeod's voice, astonishing, faltered a little.

"It would mean a great deal to me," she said.

I remembered what she had told me—*When Your Uncle Roderick got killed, I thought I would die. But I didn't die.* All at once, her feeling for that unknown dead man became a reality for me. And yet I held it against her, as well, for I could see that it had enabled her to win now.

"All right," my father said tiredly. "We'll call him Roderick."

Then alarmingly, he threw back his head and laughed.

"Roderick Dhu!" he cried. "That's what you'll call him, isn't it? Black Roderick. Like before. Don't you remember? As though he were a character out of Sir Walter Scott, instead of an ordinary kid who—"

He broke off, and looked at her with a kind of desolation in his face.

"God, I'm sorry, Mother," he said. "I had no right to say that."

Grandmother MacLeod did not flinch, or tremble, or indicate that she felt anything at all.

"I accept your apology, Ewen," she said.

My mother had to stay in bed for several weeks after she arrived home. The baby's cot was kept in my parents' room, and I could go in and look at the small creature who lay there with his tightly closed fists and his feathery black hair. Aunt Edna came in to help each morning, and when she had finished the housework, she would have coffee with my mother. They kept the door closed, but this did not prevent me from eavesdropping, for there was an air register in the floor of the spare room, which was linked somehow with the register in my parents' room. If you put your ear to the iron grille, it was almost like a radio.

"Did you mind very much, Beth?" Aunt Edna was saying.

"Oh, it's not the name I mind," my mother replied. "It's just the fact that Ewen felt he had to. You knew that Rod had only had the sight of one eye, didn't you?"

"Sure, I knew. So what?"

"There was only a year and a half between Ewen and Rod," my mother said, "so they often went around together when they were youngsters. It was Ewen's air-rifle that did it."

"Oh Lord," Aunt Edna said heavily. "I suppose she always blamed him?"

"No, I don't think it was so much that, really. It was how he felt himself. I think he even used to wonder sometimes if—but people shouldn't let themselves think like that, or they'd go crazy. Accidents do happen, after all. When the war came, Ewen joined up first. Rod should never have been in the Army at all, but he couldn't wait to get in. He must have lied about his eyesight. It wasn't so very noticeable unless you looked at him closely, and I don't suppose the medicals were very thorough in those days. He got in as a gunner, and Ewen applied to have him in the same company. He thought he might be able to watch out for him, I guess, Rod being—at a disadvantage. They were both only kids. Ewen was nineteen and Rod was eighteen when they went to France. And then the Somme. I don't know, Edna, I think Ewen felt that if Rod had had proper sight, or if he hadn't been in the same outfit and had been sent somewhere else—you know how people always think these things afterwards, not that it's ever a bit of use. Ewen wasn't there when Rod got hit. They'd lost each other somehow, and Ewen was looking for him, not bothering about anything else, you know, just frantically looking. Then he stumbled across him quite by chance. Rod was still alive, but—"

"Stop it, Beth," Aunt Edna said. "You're only upsetting yourself."

"Ewen never spoke of it to me," my mother went on, "until once his mother showed me the letter he'd written to her at the time. It was a peculiar letter, almost formal, saying how gallantly Rod had died, and all that. I guess I shouldn't have, but I told him she'd shown it to me. He was very angry that she had. And then, as though for some reason he were terribly ashamed, he said—*I had to write something to her, but men don't really die like that, Beth. It wasn't that way at all.* It was only after the war that he decided to come back and study medicine and go into practice with his father."

"Had Rod meant to?" Aunt Edna asked.

"I don't know," my mother said slowly. "I never felt I should ask Ewen that."

Aunt Edna was gathering up the coffee things, for I could hear the clash of cups and saucers being stacked on the tray.

"You know what I heard her say to Vanessa once, Beth? *The MacLeods never tell lies.* Those were her exact words. Even then, I didn't know whether to laugh or cry."

"Please, Edna—" my mother sounded worn-out now. "Don't."

"Oh Glory," Aunt Edna said remorsefully, "I've got all the delicacy of a two-ton truck. I didn't mean Ewen, for heaven's sake. That wasn't what I meant at all. Here, let me plump up your pillows for you."

Then the baby began to cry, so I could not hear anything more of interest. I took my bike and went out beyond Manawaka, riding aimlessly along the gravel highway. It was late summer, and the wheat had changed color, but instead of being high and bronzed in the fields, it was stunted and desiccated, for there had been no rain again this year. But in the bluff where I stopped and crawled under the barbed wire fence and lay stretched out on the grass, the plentiful poplar leaves were turning to a luminous yellow and shone like church windows in the sun. I put my head down very close to the earth and looked at what was going on there. Grasshoppers with enormous eyes ticked and twitched around me, as though the dry air were perfect for their purposes. A ladybird labored mightily to climb a blade of grass, fell off, and started all over again, seeming to be unaware that she possessed wings and could have flown up.

I thought of the accidents that might easily happen to a person—or, of course, might not happen, might happen to somebody else. I thought of the dead baby, my sister, who might as easily have been I. Would she, then, have been lying here in my place, the sharp grass making its small toothmarks on her brown arms, the sun warming her to the heart? I thought of the leatherbound volumes of Greek, and the six different kinds of iced cakes that used to be offered always in the MacLeod house, and the pictures of leopards and green seas. I thought of my brother, who had been born alive after all, and now had been given his life's name.

I could not really comprehend these things, but I sensed their strangeness, their disarray. I felt that whatever God might love in this world, it was certainly not order.

RESPONDING PERSONALLY

1. With a partner, offer your opinions about the impact of the story's ending. Do you think the conclusion is a good one? Explain.

2. Which characters do you like best and least in the story? Why?

RESPONDING CRITICALLY

3. During the events of the story, what does the narrator learn about her father, grandfather, and grandmother? Using evidence from the story, explain how Vanessa feels about what she has learned?

4. For paragraph assignment: What epiphany does Vanessa have at the end of the story? How has her world changed? How has she matured?

5. The conflict between tradition and change is central in this story. What are some of the family's favourite sayings? How do they reflect the MacLeod family values and attitudes?

6. Sometimes the setting and the past experience of characters can have a limiting effect on their lives. Explain how this statement is true for this story.

RESPONDING CREATIVELY

7. Watch the Atlantis video of this story. Compare it with the original story. Which scenes have been changed? Is the video faithful to the original? Write a review of the video.

8. Write three diary entries prepared by Vanessa that reflect the changes she observes in the household.

PROBLEM-SOLVING/DECISION-MAKING

9. Some of our decisions and changed attitudes occur through our growing awareness, as they did with Vanessa. In a paragraph, describe how you have similarly arrived at a decision or judgement about a friend or family member.

Love, Loyalty, and Betrayal

Love, loyalty, and betrayal all indicate a depth of feeling that shapes people's lives. Love and loyalty are often considered key values that most humans seek. The possibility of their attainment is frequently marred by human frailty, inconstancy, and occasionally outright betrayal.

The first story, "The Poison of the Blue Rose," reveals a tragic side of arranged marriages. The narrator has lost her true love, and now her friend is about to lose hers. Their parallel predicaments resonate movingly and make us question tradition, inviting us to re-examine individual love as something of perhaps greater value. The blue rose of the title becomes a symbol of beauty that has a destructive, deadly side.

The second story, "The Curlew's Cry," is about depth of love and loyalty in contrast to the unhappy facts of separation and death. An old man who has been loyal to his wife and son for 45 years, is contrasted with the narrator, who is uncertain that she wants to continue her own troubled relationship. Both predicaments give us much to think about in terms of the story and our personal lives.

In the final story, "Choices," we see all three elements—love, loyalty, and betrayal—together. The main character loves a man, is loyal to him, and is finally betrayed by him. The quick sequence of actions prompts us to look more deeply at the range and potential in supposedly close human relationships.

Love, loyalty, and betrayal are powerful, recurring forces in people's lives. In these three stories, we gain insight into the difficulty of maintaining love and loyalty in the context of the unpredictability of life.

"How can I be married to Rafiq.
My parents have already betrothed me ..."

Yasmin Marri
The Poison of the Blue Rose

Translated by Samina Rahman

This is my house and this is my room in it. Hardly a room, more
like a blind well, although high-powered electric bulbs struggle to
provide light. There is darkness in the midst of the light, darkness
as black as the ill-fated night. Silence. If you peer out of the window, you will see, at a slight distance, the beginnings of a whole
complex of ruins. Ruins and shrieking bats, black crows cawing
loudly. Ruins peopled by ghosts who dwell there to taunt us.

I love this house, its silence is enchanting, absorbing ... but it
is still silence. Silence is not my lone possession. I have no control over it either. The day any person possesses silence will be the
day the romance of the bloom and the nightingale will cease and
the human body will be a soulless robot and no one standing on
the platform of life will turn to look back. Platform reminds me
that sometimes I have a fleeting fancy that I'm on a platform
where trains arrive for either a few seconds or a few hours. For
these brief moments the hustle and bustle of life reaches its
zenith. People rushing to catch their trains look as if this were the
sum and purpose of life, and those who descend from trains are
anxiously calling out for porters, and each person appears to have
turned into a *Tezgam* or *Dachi*; but then in a few moments the
platform is completely silent again, like a widow's hovel in con-
gealed and frozen nights where human beings, shivering in the
cold, are restrained from screaming out, as if their screams too are
to be taxed by the government.

The silence spread in the room, a deathly hush, but whence
the silence? The sound of footsteps and then Gulab Bibi stood in

front of me. She was very sorrowful today, quiet, and I too said nothing. Yet strangely the room was not silent, as if Gulab Bibi and I stood conversing at the crossroads.

She took out a folded note from her purse and handed it to me. It was a letter from Rafiq. For the past two or three years Rafiq has been writing to Gulab Bibi. To all appearances I have no interest in the relations of Rafiq and Gulab Bibi, but even without wanting to do so I read very carefully and with great interest Rafiq's letters to her. Rafiq's letters were effusive and filled with artifice.

Gulab Bibi is my son Raju's teacher. One day I was looking at the lines on Gulab Bibi's palms.

"Gulab Bibi, you will marry Rafiq."

For a moment her face bloomed only to wilt in the next.

"How can that be!" Her face reflected the world's despair.

There were tears in her eyes but they were an inadequate reflection of her internal anguish and pain. These looming black clouds flow not in tormented streams from the eyes to rain upon the face, but gush straight from the mind into the heart and the heart, in its endless depths, never brims over. Gulab Bibi's heart is an ocean and have oceans ever filled up with tears?

"How can I be married to Rafiq. My parents have already betrothed me ..." Gulab Bibi stopped in mid-sentence. Her eyes were drowning in tears. Tears ... face ... the lines on her palms ... I was startled. Gulab Bibi's face began to harden, turning to stone before my eyes, and then like a web, lines began to appear on it. The lines of life, fate, wealth, heart, mind, marriage, and countless other lines.

Rafiq was nowhere, neither in the heart or in the mind, nor in her life or destiny. Like Ranji ... thinking of Ranji instantly a heavy stone plummeted into the well, and with its fall silence reigned. A deep hush. Then on the platform of life, I am not able to see Ranji standing behind me nor Raju and his father in front of me. I do not hear Ranji's call nor do I understand the words spoken by Raju and his father. It is as if I have entered a city where the people do not understand my language and neither am I able to decipher theirs. How compelling such a town would be, and how peaceful!

A few moments later the city dissolves into thin air and the deep silence is broken. Raju is crying bitterly.

Many months passed and Gulab Bibi did not visit my home. Although this was not in itself significant, it was unusual. Like Raju's father had become a part of my life and Raju was a part of my days, in the same way Gulab Bibi was close to me and seeing her and listening to her had become a habit with me. On making enquiries I discovered that she was absent from school on long leave.

One morning Gulab Bibi arrived unexpectedly. She took off her veil and laid it on the chair and sat down on the floor facing me. Her hands were dyed in the rich tones of henna and a gold ring was glittering on her finger.

"I am about to be married," she announced in tearful tones.

"This is very good news, but you ... are you not happy?"

"I am not marrying Rafiq." The dark kohl in her eyes looked insipid.

For a few moments there was silence.

"I'll not be able to forget him. My mother should have listened to me. To treat me like an animal ..." Gulab Bibi was sobbing uncontrollably. She kept crying and I sat there quiet as a statue. I had no words to console her.

"I don't think it will be difficult to forget Rafiq. When Raju and others like him enter your life, you will forget Rafiq completely."

Gulab Bibi stared at me, wondering how I spoke with such authority.

"Was there a Rafiq in your life as well?" The question was unexpected. Sudden. Very sudden.

"Yes."

"Have your forgotten him?" Gulab Bibi's tone softened. "It's possible that you have been able to do so, but I ... I will not forget." She was in utter despair.

"Gulab Bibi, you will leave the platform of life on which you encountered Rafiq far behind you in a few years." I stared out of the window at the rows of ruined walls, some fallen and others still erect.

"But what if, in the course of my travels, I arrive on the same platform. What will happen then?" Gulab Bibi asked, partly of herself.

I was not able to answer that, but suddenly at that moment a blue rose emerged in my mind's eye. Bitter blue rose. Symbol of poison. Laden with it. For a moment I saw it on Gulab Bibi's face as well, but the next moment I dismissed the foolish thought. A blue rose that blooms only once each century; no one knows in which corner of the globe, or when, and no one knows why the beautiful bloom gets infused with poison. It was my desire to see a blue rose. Gulab Bibi departed weeping and I began to spend my days immersed in my longing.

One day I ran into Ranji at some function. He stood before me, talking to me. His wife stood next to him. Life had travelled full circle to that platform which I had left far behind a long time ago. My mind grew numb. Silence flooded my heart and mind. I trembled at my reflection in the mirror facing me and felt the blue veins spreading all over my face. A poison flooded my face, my body, my being, and I saw this century's blue rose within me. How painful it was! I looked towards Ranji. He sat in a chair in the corner with his eyes closed. What torment there was on his face! A blue rose. Yet another blue rose. I trembled.

Gulab Bibi, Rafiq, Ranji, myself, and who knows how many countless poisoned roses … I had read somewhere that only a single blue rose blooms in a hundred years … but … but it is not so. Now it seems that in every city, every community, from this corner of the world to the other, every moment blue roses flower. In fact life itself is a blue rose, blooming only to fade, created for destruction, or perhaps life exists for death, which is its reward.

RESPONDING PERSONALLY

1. With a partner, exchange ideas about Gulab Bibi's predicament. Is it a problem for any young couples you know about?
2. Describe a person you once really liked. Are you as close now as you once were? Explain.

RESPONDING CRITICALLY

3. What is Gulab Bibi's conflict? How does the narrator respond to her conflict? Why?
4. There are several references in the story to platforms. What do these platforms represent? Share your ideas with another student.
5. The key symbol of the story is the blue rose. In a paragraph, analyze the symbolism of the last three paragraphs. Why is the blue rose poisonous? How does the poison reflect Gulab Bibi's and the narrator's situations?
6. What views of love and life are presented in the narrator's concluding epiphany? Why does she feel that way?

RESPONDING CREATIVELY

7. With a partner prepare a reading of the story and present it to the class.
8. Create a colour illustration for this story and post it for others to view.

PROBLEM-SOLVING/DECISION-MAKING

9. Describe an inner conflict you've faced in which you had to turn your back on someone you were close to or loved. How did you deal with the situation?

J. Leslie Bell
The Curlew's Cry

Sheila stretched back on the couch, lit a cigarette, and looked at the
unfinished letter to Neil which lay in the centre of the coffee table.
There was something pitiful and inadequate about her letters at the
best of times compared with Neil's. His often ran to six pages, full
of details about old university friends, his jobs in the North Sea oil
rigs, the characters he met in the Aberdeen pubs. By contrast, her
letters were niggardly and hastily written, dashed off, if she had a
minute to spare in the lounge during the mid-afternoon lull. At the
far end of the table was a cardboard box containing all the letters
Neil had written to her since she had arrived in Canada. There were
48 letters in the box, 48 neatly written reminders of his depend-
ability, his love, "the auld alliance," as he had put it. He would be
here in one month. One month! She glanced at the letter again.
There would be no point in finishing it now.

She had two days off and she was bored and hot and restless.
She lit another cigarette and listened to the music which came
from the apartment next door. The old man who lived there on his
own played his classical records all evening. She enjoyed the
music, although she only recognized one or two of the composers.
She had seen his name on his letter box in the lobby: S. Sikirski.
They had nodded to one another in the hallway but they had
never spoken, thank God. She had no desire to talk to old foreign
gentlemen about their troubles, the war, their back problems, or
whatever it was that old foreign gentlemen talked about. Still,
there was a vague feeling of security knowing that he was there.

She picked up her paperback and read a few pages and then
put it down again. She went out to the balcony and leaned on the
railing. The sun was just going down and its rays burned red on

the surface of the river which she could just see between the gap of the two buildings across the street. Below, young couples walked and cycled towards the park. A man's deep, assured laughter drifted up to her. He had his thick arm around his girl-friend's narrow, tanned shoulders, locking her into his side. Sheila threw the butt end of her cigarette down at them and watched it twisting and swooping, drifting in the downdraft away to the left, missing the couple by about twenty yards. The sun had slipped out of sight, leaving only a red haze in the sky. She stood there until it was dark, looking at the lights of the city, listening to the distant sounds of traffic until the iron railing became cold in her tight grip. Only when she went inside did she feel the pain and notice the two red horizontal welts on her palms.

The next day after lunch she walked to the park. She found an unoccupied bench under a clump of poplar trees and sat down and tried to read her book again but she couldn't concentrate. It was one of the books that Neil had recommended to her. It was by an émigré Czech author whose name she couldn't pronounce. She would finish it by the end of the month. She promised her-self that. She would even finish the letter and give it to Neil when he arrived. It was very quiet in the park, save for the occasional jogger who went by, kicking up the red gravel. The sky was cloudless. Perfect. The sky over Scotland even now would be low-ering and treacherous, with its shifting layers of grey and white and black. They had camped under that sky on Rannoch Moor; tramped under it along the banks of the Tay; sheltered from it in bothies and ruined Border keeps. Neil wrote of these things, these memories.

Remember the curlew's cry, he wrote. We lay in the tent hold-ing each other all night. Listen to the curlew's cry, you said. I'll never forget that, Sheila. Never!

There was no curlew. We never heard a curlew. We never saw one.

... and the time in Lewis when we slept in the park and watched the Northern Lights.

There were clouds. Dense clouds. The moon and stars were covered by them.

And buried somewhere in one of those letters, a whispered re-frain: "Why did you leave? Why did you leave?"

She closed her book and put it in her purse. She walked across the park, crossed the bridge, and walked down Memorial Drive and ate at one of the restaurants of Kensington Road. She had one beer and smoked five cigarettes, and then walked slow-ly home.

When she got back to her apartment Mr. S. Sikirski was wait-ing at her door. He was a very tall man with grey hair and a heavy grey moustache. In his left hand he was holding a worn leather briefcase. He stood there, very stiff and straight.

"I am very sorry to inconvenience you, Miss, Miss …"

"Laidlaw. Sheila Ladlaw."

He inclined his head slightly towards her. "I have been very foolish, I forgot my key. I have locked myself out."

"Is the caretaker not in?"

Mr. S. Sikirski shook his grey head. "I wonder if I could use your balcony. I could climb over. There is only three feet separat-ing my balcony from yours."

Sheila eyed him dubiously, expecting for some reason to see a muscle twitch on his face, or to see his hands shaking. He stood, unmoving, his eyes fixed on hers. Sheila unlocked her door. "You'd better come in." She threw her jacket and purse onto the couch and opened the French windows. "Be careful, it's twelve storeys down. You'd better leave your briefcase here. I'll hand it over to you."

For an old man Sikirski was surprisingly agile. He braced him-self with his right hand on the rail, and gripping the upper part of the window frame with his left hand, he pulled himself up. He teetered there for a moment, steadied himself, and then leapt over the three-foot gap, landing without a stumble on his own balcony. There was a glimmer of a smile on his lips when he turned around to face Sheila.

She smiled back at him. "Bravo." She handed him his briefcase.

He inclined his head again. "Thank you. You are very kind." He was about to go inside when he suddenly hesitated and turned around. "Miss Laidlaw, would you care to have a glass of wine with me and perhaps listen to some of my records?"

She was about to say no, but something about his stance checked her. It was as though he was standing in front of a firing squad, as though he had just refused the blindfold. Death or life. Yes or no. It is all the same to me, his pose seemed to suggest. She smiled again at S. Sikirski. "I'd like that very much," she said.

Mr. Sikirski's apartment, Sheila noted ruefully, was much neater than hers, but there was an unfinished quality about it, as if something was missing. In one corner stood a tall, varnished bookcase lined with thick leatherbound volumes with gold lettering on the spines. In the alcove opposite, was a cabinet full of record albums, all neatly arranged. The cream-colored walls were bare except for a simple wooden crucifix above a table with a solitary framed photograph on it. Mr. Sikirski showed Sheila to a chair and then went into his kitchen and poured out two glasses of red wine. He handed one glass to Sheila and then placed his briefcase on the table and carefully took from it several records.

He glanced at her. "I go to the library once a week. They have an excellent classical section." He took one of the records from its jacket and placed it on the turntable of his stereo and clicked the switch on. He took his glass of wine and sat across from Sheila. It was a piano solo that was playing. Sheila had to strain her ears to hear. The rippling notes sounded remote, almost as though they came from some other unseen place, imperceptibly rising and falling, then covering and moving away beyond earshot.

"It's very beautiful," said Sheila.

"Paderewski. He was my mentor." Mr. Sikirski sat very still, his head tilted to one side, his long fingers encircling his wine glass. As he spoke he did not look at Sheila. His gaze was fixed on some point over her shoulder.

He spoke quietly, distantly, like the music that was playing. He spoke as though there was no need for preliminaries, as if they had made a pact to dispense with small talk. "Before the war I taught private piano lessons. I taught in Lublin and Warsaw. I also taught here until I retired. I was never as great as Paderewski.

I knew at an early age I would never be great, but I was a good teacher. That is how I met my wife. She was one of my pupils. She gave a performance in Wawel Cathedral quite recently."

"Oh, I didn't realize. I didn't...."

"You thought I was perhaps a widower or a bachelor. No, we have been married for many years. I am waiting for her and my son." He made a motion with his left hand. "That is her photograph on the table. Her name is Maria and my son's name is Stefan."

Sheila looked at the picture. She was a young, fair-haired woman standing on a snow-covered clearing in a pine forest. Beside her was a small, fair-haired boy who was holding onto his mother's sleeve. Both their heads were turned slightly away from the camera, their smiles strained, as though they were peering into the sun.

"They will be here soon," Mr. Sikirski repeated. "Very soon. I have it on the best of authority."

"You must be very happy," said Sheila. She was looking at the photograph again. Only then did she notice that the woman wore the kind of high-shouldered coat her mother used to wear during the war. The boy wore a sailor hat with a black band around it. She could guess that there would be white lettering on the hat denoting the name of the ship.

"Yes, I am very happy," said Mr. Sikirski, touching his wine glass to his lips.

It was getting dark now and the room was in half-shadow. Sheila could barely make out his features. She couldn't take her eyes off the picture. A dying ray of sunshine touched it momentarily, illuminating the woman's fair hair, creating an aureole around her head; then the light was gone. She sensed that Mr. Sikirski was following her gaze. He answered the question that she could not ask.

"It was been forty-five years since we have met. I had to leave. There was no choice. Forty-five years, but they will be here soon. There is no doubt in my mind about that. It is a question of faith."

Sheila felt her hands suddenly trembling. She placed her glass on the floor and tried to light a cigarette, but she couldn't hold the match steady. She felt cold. Mr. Sikirski had just said something else but she hadn't heard. He was leaning forward slightly, one hand held palm upwards towards her. She did not need to see the expression on his face. She knew well enough what was there. She knew what she had to say.

"I'm sure they'll be here soon. I'd like to meet them when they arrive."

His voice was lowered to a whisper, but it was firm and assured again, merging with the music in the background. "Thank you. I knew you would understand." The chair creaked as he sat back.

He was asleep when Sheila finally left, his head slumped to one side. She took the glass from his hand and put it on the table beside the photograph of Maria and Stefan. As she passed him, she touched his shoulder but he didn't stir.

RESPONDING PERSONALLY

1. In a small group, define *true love*. Share your definition with the class.
2. Look up the word *curlew* in a dictionary if it is unfamiliar to you. What do you understand to be the purpose of the reference in the story to the curlew's cry?

RESPONDING CRITICALLY

3. What do the first two pages of the story reveal about Sheila's relationship with Neil? Do they have a good communicative relationship? Explain.
4. What is interesting about Mr. Sikirski's relationship with his family? Do you think they will be reunited? Give evidence to support your opinion.
5. Write a character sketch of either Mr. Sikirski or Sheila and share it with others.
6. How does Mr. Sikirski's relationship compare with Sheila's? How is Sheila affected by Mr. Sikirski's story? Will her relationship with Neil change? Make a prediction.

RESPONDING CREATIVELY

7. Write the next letter that Sheila sends to Neil. OR Compose the thank-you letter she writes to Mr. Sikirski.

8. With two partners, role-play Sheila and Neil appearing on "The Newlywed Game" or "The Dating Game." Decide who will be the show's host and who will play the contestants.

PROBLEM-SOLVING/DECISION-MAKING

9. For small group discussion: What should Sheila do about her relationship with Neil? What would you recommend?

"Get me out of here." Her mind
said it over and over.

Susan Kerslake
Choices

Peggy had only had a little while to make up her mind. Standing
at the window, pushing her hair out of her eyes, she watched taxi-
cabs cruise the streets. It was midnight. From time to time, she
swivelled the knob on the radio, found a weather report. Well,
rain in the country was better than rain in the city; it would mean
a different type of weekend: cozy, fires, snacks, catching up on
reading. Not what she had in mind. With variations, she could do
the same thing in her small apartment. Time in the sun, gardening, croquet, a swim were more like it. The weatherman hemmed
and hawed. Cloud, fog, onshore winds, offshore winds. The front
should move in by noon tomorrow bringing overcast skies and
rainy weather for the weekend. A factor.

Cabs honked to each other at corners and followed the fire en-
gines and ambulances. Bicycles rode by making that special titter
and thrill of gears. What she wanted to hear was a nighthawk
blitzing the narrow passageway between buildings. She turned
the radio down and slept under the country and western songs.

The phone rang at six o'clock, then again at six-twenty, but she
had stayed awake, taking a last shower, packing, boiling water for
a starter cup of coffee. Then she went downstairs and sat on the
step catching the sun coming over the building across the street.
Despite not enough sleep she was wide-awake, but she knew in a
couple of hours that missed sleep would come irresistibly, anes-
thetically. Stillness wrapped the morning.

She thought about lying on the pier, adjusting her body, her
back, just so to fit the cracks in the wood, settling her bones so her
weight was mostly on the muscle of her thighs and back. The hot
sun having found her, stretched itself over her skin, then lay down

on it, lapping, seeping through, sinking beneath. A web of heat. It took the edge off the light slap of water bumping into the piles.

Being able to close the door behind her, leaving laundry, a couple of dishes, unanswered letters, unpaid bills, phone calls to be returned and library books gave her a perversely good feeling. Surrendering to the uncommunicative wilderness, a place without. Should she die tomorrow, someone else could deal with the dirty sink.

A little after seven, Ken drove up. The passenger seat was empty, but that was all. Hampers, suitcases, buckets, baskets, bags full of essentials were stuffed into every available space in the small hatchback.

Ken got out for a moment and put the hood up. Peggy looked in with him at the still grey motor, supposing that if she could see it while the car was running she could see parts moving. As it was, it seemed an unlikely contraption: a tangle of shapes, a thick, stale smell. Some parts were clean and shiny. Most were caked with oil and dirt. She tried to see some quality, some mystique that would account for the cultish zeal of people and their cars. This little car was blue. It had been decorated with strips of chrome, grill, rubber pads to cushion bumps. The inside was black and blue, a compact arrangement of storage spaces, air vents, windows, handles, visors, a radio, knobs and numbers. On the street at fifteen miles an hour she felt safe.

There were some minor rearrangements to be made before her bundle fit so it wouldn't bounce around in case of sudden moves. She asked him to stop at a liquor store when they opened so she could pick something up for the weekend. He said, "I'm glad you decided to come."

Ken came close to her for the first time last summer. She hadn't really considered it even though he was attractive in conventional ways: tall enough for her, curly hair, a brown mist and damp, unsqueezed quality when he came out of the water, lifting himself in one swift motion, water drops shimmering on the springy ends of his hair. He had small, courageous scars on his body; she wondered why some people showed scars and others not at all.

Her own legs and arms, which must have suffered the assortment of scrapes and scratches of every normal childhood, were essentially smooth, unblemished surfaces.

On casual dates during the long winter, they used to sit and discuss the peculiar relationship built out of sand and water and sun. It surprised them both that it had endured in any form past summer. Perhaps the distance, the odd formality that allowed them to say anything in speculation, was a factor. Each lapsed into intense relationships with others. Then they met like cousins, burning up late hours with wonder and woe. Between adventures they stroked each other on the back and other places.

At a million dollars, or some such figure, a mile, they took the main highway out of the city. About ten miles out, there was an intricate intersection with overpasses and large green signs of instructions. On each side, rock, grass, and scrub spruce. There was a little more traffic, others who'd gotten off to an early start: station wagons with loads of kids, cars with U-hauls, tenting equipment, vans, and the relatively light pack of picnickers. Several campsites off the main highway hooked into some scenic view.

It was hot. Singularly bored, Peggy was torn between trying to make conversation and catching a catnap under the blanket of sun coming in the window. Leaning her face on the back of the seat, readjusting the seat belt slightly, she watched Ken through drowsy eyes. He seemed attached to the car at the small of his back. She supposed it was the pressure on the gas pedal. She stared at his lap, his legs loosely apart, one knee resting on the door, the other brushing the gear shift. One hand gripped the top of the wheel, the other, upside down letting the wheel slide back and forth through his fingers, was softly curved. He should be a doctor sitting behind a big desk, his hands nestled in each other on the bare surface in front of him.

He lifted each hand separately to push up the sleeves of his T-shirt. There were wet patches on it. At that moment his body tensed. She saw it quite clearly, his entire body arched backwards and forwards at the same time. What was happening, had he seen something, was he having a fit or a stroke? She started to move....

... Voices. Slanted through the heat. No one she knew. Not Ken, no name, but nice, human, troubled, urgent, persistently calling to her. Demanding that she answer as if she were over-sleeping or had been naughty. "Hey, hey you, can you hear me? Wake up...." As if in a dream, talking back to them with a dream voice, wondering why they kept on. Such a deep sleep, why wouldn't they let her finish it, just a few more minutes? It was dark, the middle of the night, why get up in the middle of the night? What was wrong? Who was making this kind of mistake?

Someone touched her. She couldn't be sure where. She used all her concentration but still couldn't be sure where.... A light but irritating touch like an insect crawling. Then there was more. Real pain and pressure climbing on top of the dream, coming too fast; she wanted to wake up and get away from it. Struggling, she groped around the pile of sleep in the tunnel of her conscious-ness.

A smell of scorched hair. And metal. Oil, rubber. She was too close to some machine. It must be dangerous. How had she got-ten there? Those people must still be there, why didn't they get her away from the danger? She tried to call them, her mind brought up all the right words, anyone would have understood, but they blocked up in her mouth behind her lips which were soldered shut. Pain radiated from her mouth; she wanted to touch it, cover it, protect it. Where were her hands? Concentrating, she followed a path from the point of pain across her shoulder and down. Her arms seemed to be folded and pressed close to her body but she couldn't reach them. But there was more to her. Why couldn't she feel anymore?

Light pressed on her eyelids. It wasn't night; it was morning or afternoon. She thought that if she opened her eyes she would see. No one would have to tell her anything; she would know it all. There was a strong smell of fumes. Bringing her attention back to what she could hear, she hoped to find Ken's voice. That was who it was. Where were they that she and Ken were together like this? The voices were there again but they weren't trying to wake her up. The voices were tripping over each other. She heard "reach" and "rescue." She must open her eyes. What were they talking about? Who else was there?

Suddenly her back burned, each vertebra incinerated in turn. Then it stopped. She could not move. Out of the fragments of pain came the beginnings of fear; her mind formed the word "help." She overheard herself.

The light outside her eyelids were growing stronger. It would soon want to invade. She was almost awake. Now it did not seem desirable. Opening her eyes would be the last bridge. With the light of day she would have to admit this and allow the chaos to gel around her. Ready. She tried to open her eyes. They were stuck. For a moment she feared they were burned shut, but it must be blood. Of course, blood. She wondered how much blood. With effort she got her eyelids apart enough; the dried blood crumbled off, specks fell into her eyes scratching them. For a moment she was unable to focus on anything. Then she saw, right in front of her, grey surfaces; it was impossible to tell exactly what they were. Up and down and to each side, the same tangle presented itself.

Between the grey there was light. Not much. Everything was too thick and close. Desperately she wanted a deep breath, but her body was too squeezed.

"Get me out of here." Her mind said it over and over. She put words on the tips of her fingers and played them. Each breath, each heartbeat echoed through the empty pipe that rested on her ear. She had to say it, shout it out, let them know, "I'm here. I'm here. I hurt. Find me. Hear me. See me." Working the words magically in her brain.

Whimpering leaked from her brain into her mouth. Noise was possible with her mouth closed. This discovery gave her hope. She could let them know. Taking a breath, she groaned. And waited. Weren't they listening? Were they talking to each other? Had they gone away? She did it again: a higher pitch. Waited. Maybe she was imagining it? She opened her eyes again. The grey was so close. She couldn't tell where she was or how this had happened. The air was stale and hot.

What if there wasn't enough to breathe? What if there was fire? What if her nose got burned and she couldn't open her mouth to breathe? If they never heard her. Never saw her?

She tried to move again. There were things that pressed on her, a cage of hot metal, wires and pipes. They touched her forehead, bones, skin, hair. And with a knowing that did not come from her senses, she knew that her legs were bent and held. She closed her eyes.

Pain rose and fell in tides. Around it her body began to react. In spastic waves, she shivered, bumping into the bars of her cage. Then she began to sweat through cold flesh. She tried to co-operate. Counting through the waves of pain, coloring the chills, imagining the goose bumps exploding, erupting with color, gey-sers of fluorescent sparkling pink and green. Sweat did not tick-le, her skin must be too tense with pain. She followed the pain, staying just shy of it, observing, watching, trying to sandbag bar-riers around it. It went underground, under the shallows and resurfaced.

She must stay in control. She must get on top of it. Close at-tention to minute adjustments, uprisings, migrations. She tried to analyse the type of pain, burning, sharp, dull, a pressure. Was there a centre to it? How far out did it radiate? How long did it last? It took so much energy; she wasn't sure she could keep it up. So much concentration. To surrender could be imagined; giving in to the flood of pain, drowning in it, brain-breaking pain.

"I think I heard something."

Strangers were out there, still out there, they hadn't gone away. She made more sounds full of the pain.

"Can you talk?"

"Are you awake?"

"Don't move."

"There's been an accident."

Thank god, giving her information, something to keep her sane.

"You're wedged in the car. The engine has come up into the front of the car. We're trying to figure out how to get you out."

She heard creaking, the jiggling of metal. They were starting to touch the car. "Don't!" she groaned. Something might move or fall, set off sparks or explosions. "Don't." Nausea roiled up in her throat. They must be careful of her. They couldn't make a mistake. What did they know about the situation? What could they see? She heard more voices, one was louder, giving orders.

"Move on, there's nothing to see here, folks, just keep moving...." It sounded like a TV program; the boss was there. A picture flashed in her mind of the highway, placid, empty, solid cement squirted out of a tube, lying between the gravel and grass, the sky lapping, dipping a blue tongue.

Too much was going on; she was too tired for all this information. Only one thing mattered: pain. If they could get her out and straighten her out the pain would stop, it would just run out the bottoms of her feet, the top of her head. Stream out her fingers. She was too full. There was no more room.

Why didn't they just do it? Stop talking at her, explaining what *wasn't* happening. Just do it, don't talk. It shouldn't be up to her to have to figure this out, to argue and make the plans. She had too much to do with her own body. She felt sorry for it, poor, helpless, trapped thing. Punished.

Something was dripping on the side of her face, scalding her ear and neck. She was going to have to let go. For a while she had been able to browse and form a knowledge of this territory. She could not tolerate change. The stuff dripped more slowly. If it would only stop in time; before she lost control.

When she woke and smelt the air, there was a definite change: an antiseptic odor. "Am I already saved?" she thought. Was it true? A hive of voices answered her thoughts.

"Thank god she's alive!"

What did that mean? Of course she was alive. There was even a moment when she was free of the pain.

"Look, we've got to see if that engine is loose, if it can be lifted."

The voices were tense. She found herself listening analytically, thinking about the plan. Would it work? Things were happening

very fast; there was a lot of motion just outside; it made the air move. She felt calm and trusting. Even if they killed her she wouldn't blame them. Accidents piled on accidents. Skinned knees, stubbed toes, cuts. Each time she delivered herself to someone to fix it, to make things right. Each time they had.

Once started, it went very quickly; the motor began to move. In several places the pipes were bonded to her skin. When it pulled up it tore off the flesh. Sections came apart, spilling more gas and oil on her. Pain blossomed when pressure was released and blood flowed through pinched veins. At one point she slumped helplessly to the side.

Then, for the first time, she felt human hands; someone was there to catch her. Her head fell into a bowl of hands. Many hands reached her. She thought they were making that terrible grinding noise, but then she saw the motor being lifted away. They had to hold her until a board could be slipped under to slide her out.

When the men saw her move on her own, they put her on a stretcher. The sun struck her face. An enormous space dotted with faces opened above her head, but she didn't mind. Balloons. A party. She tried to smile for all the lovely faces around her.

Close to her ear, paper wrappers were being torn. Materials were laid on her as if she were a table. They began to cut away her clothes with scissors, lifting the cloth, pulling it away from her skin. She watched the faces, the cringe of lips, narrowing of eyes. When they walked around, their shoes crunched the gravel.

"I'm going to start an IV."

"I'm going to wash your mouth."

"I'm going to give you some oxygen, you're gulping air." The mask was clear plastic. She didn't want it on her face; she didn't want anything touching her face.

The sun was right overhead, shining, hot, pushing her eyelids down, settling into the hollows on each side of her collarbones. There were no images on the insides of her eyelids; just colors, nothing frightening. But she was frightened. Where was Ken? He should be there somewhere. These were nice people but they were strangers.

Then in the ambulance, he was suddenly there, sitting across from her feet. She could see him. How peculiar to see him scrunched among the medical supplies, tubes, packets. He was far away, blurred. She could smell urine. She thought about when she used to be able to move her arms. One was strapped down with the IV, but that was just for now. Even the light in the ambulance hurt her eyes; the pupils wouldn't contract. She didn't want to have to close her eyes again. Ever again.

Something made a lot of noise. The sound was in her head, the crash and thud of metal and rubber. Now she knew just what it was. Ken was bent between his arms and legs; she knew he didn't hear it.

Calmly, she noticed that he was bald—no, what was that? A bandage on his head. He'd hit his head. Was that all? A bump on the head. She looked around; did they know that? A bump on the head! The attendant was gazing out the frosted window. Periodically he glanced at the intersection in the IV.

Flat on her back it was hard to breathe; her lungs were sliding up into her throat. Reaching across her body to adjust the oxygen, the attendant jolted her legs. She saw it. No doubt, no confusion. But she didn't feel him. Not a touch, a bump, nothing. The breath jumped in her throat.

Up in the corner was a round metal surface; something was showing; an image was captured inside. She tried to catch Ken's eye, to get him to look, but he wouldn't. His lips were wrinkled as if he'd seen something distasteful. She looked at the mirror-like thing again. It drew her eyes.

"Ken, Ken!" but it was a mumble and when she found him he was putting his hands on each side of his head, leaning forward. He looked like he was thinking. What was it? Didn't he have anything more to say? About staying with her, about his responsibilities? A hollow place began to open in her chest; cold sank in. He could get up and walk away. What if he did? He was the one who'd been through this with her. Whose idea had it been anyway? Who called whom? Out of the space in her chest came the feeling that it wouldn't be enough, that she would be disappointed. The fact that there had been a choice, that this was the matter of a choice, struck her. If she'd had to go, a line of duty, emergency.... But this. For no reason.

RESPONDING PERSONALLY

1. With another student, consider what is the meaning and relevance of the story's title.
2. In your response journal, explain your understanding of the story's last paragraph.

RESPONDING CRITICALLY

3. What is Peggy's sense of her relationship with Ken before the accident? Why does Ken act as he does in the ending? What epiphany does Peggy have about her relationship with him?
4. Internal conflict becomes a more significant element in the latter half of the story. What is the nature of this conflict? Is it resolved? Why or why not?
5. An important element in the story is atmosphere. What are three examples of images and moments that create a strong impression on you?
6. The author uses a modern fiction technique called stream of consciousness. Check the Glossary for a definition of this term and decide whether you think she uses the technique effectively.

RESPONDING CREATIVELY

7. Illustrate one scene that could be used to advertise this story to a teenage audience.
8. Write the e-mail message that Peggy sends Ken after the accident.

PROBLEM-SOLVING/DECISION-MAKING

9. In a one-page composition, describe a key choice or betrayal which significantly changed your own life or the life of someone you know.

Dreams, Illusions, and Reality

Much of what we experience in life has to do with dreams, illusions, and reality. Dreams are what keep us going and are what we strive for. They are often connected to our goals. Illusions are something we are on guard against in our daily living. We seldom like to be fooled by others or, worse, by ourselves. Reality, then, is the balancing factor that keeps our dreams honest and our illusions in check.

The first story, "Why Don't You Carve Other Animals," introduces us to two artists, one of whom carves elephants and giraffes to the exclusion of anything else. The artist has a commitment to what is symbolically meaningful for him. Though he isn't particularly skilled at what he does, he manages to make a living with his odd, repetitious carvings. The reality may be that he is limited as an artist, compared to his friend, but his dreams do sustain him and provide him with much-needed purpose and meaning.

In "The Thunderstorm," we meet the narrator, an ordinary man watching a dramatic nightstorm. His life is suddenly changed by a fantastic vision right out of mythology. Is what he sees reality or an illusion? We must ultimately decide the answer to this question for ourselves. Nevertheless, we see that one man's experience and one author's imagined story can have an uncanny reality all on their own.

The final story in this unit, "The Lamp at Noon," is a study of a couple experiencing the worst of the 1930s drought. The man clings fiercely to his illusion that the drought will someday end. His wife has to decide whether to abandon her husband and follow her dream of a better life, or to remain on the farm. This tragic story reveals the consequences of unreasonable illusions and destructive dreams in the face of a harsh, unremitting reality.

In this unit, we see that it is important and necessary for human beings to dream. The trick, as these characters learn, is to make sure our dreams can be supported or fulfilled by reality. Otherwise, our dreams may face the danger of remaining unfulfilled or, worse, may become destructive illusions.

The red elephant was his idea.

Yvonne Vera
Why Don't You Carve Other Animals

He sits outside the gates of the Africans-Only hospital, making
models out of wood. The finished products are on old newspapers on the ground around him. A painter sits to his right, his finished work leaning against the hospital fence behind them. In the
dense township, cars screech, crowds flow by, voices rise, and
ambulances speed into the emergency unit of the hospital, their
flashing orange light giving fair warning to oncoming traffic.
Through the elephants he carves, and also the giraffes, with oddly
slanting necks, the sculptor brings the jungle to the city. His animals walk on the printed newspaper sheets, but he mourns that
they have no life in them. Sometimes in a fit of anger he collects
his animals and throws them frenziedly into his cardboard box,
desiring not to see their lifeless forms against the chaotic movement of traffic which flows through the hospital gates.

"Do you want that crocodile? It's a good crocodile. Do you
want it?" A mother coaxes a little boy who has been crying after
his hospital visit. A white bandage is wrapped tight around his
right arm. The boy holds his arm with his other hand, aware of
the mother's attention, which makes him draw attention to his
temporary deformity. She kneels beside him and looks into his
eyes, pleading.

"He had an injection. You know how the children fear the needle," the mother informs the man. She buys the crocodile, and
hands it the boy. The man watches one of his animals go, carried
between the little boy's tiny fingers. His animals have no life in
them, and the man is tempted to put them back in the box. He
wonders if the child will ever see a moving crocodile, surrounded
as he is by the barren city, where the only rivers are the tarred roads.

A man in a white coat stands looking at the elephants, and at the man who continues carving. He picks a red elephant, whose tusk is carved along its body, so that it cannot raise it. A red elephant? The stranger is perplexed, and amused, and decides to buy the elephant, though it is poorly carved and cannot lift its tusk. He will place it beside the window in his office, where it can look out at the patients in line. Why are there no eyes carved on the elephant? Perhaps the paint has covered them up.

The carver suddenly curses.

"What is wrong?" the painter asks.

"Look at the neck of this giraffe."

The painter looks at the giraffe, and the two men explode into uneasy laughter. It is not easy to laugh when one sits so close to the sick.

The carver wonders if he has not carved some image of himself, or of some afflicted person who stopped and looked at his breathless animals. He looks at the cardboard box beside him and decides to place it in the shade, away from view.

"Why don't you carve other animals? Like lions and chimpanzees?" the painter asks. "You are always carving giraffes and your only crocodile has been bought!" The painter has had some influence on the work of the carver, lending him the paints to color his animals. The red elephant was his idea.

"The elephant has ruled the forest for a long time, he is older than the forest, but the giraffe extends his neck and struts above the trees, as though the forest belonged to him. He eats the topmost leaves, while the elephant spends the day rolling in the mud. Do you not find it interesting? This struggle between the elephant and the giraffe, to eat the topmost leaves in the forest?" The ambulances whiz past, into the emergency unit of the Africans-Only hospital.

The painter thinks briefly, while he puts the final touches on an image of the Victoria Falls which he paints from a memory gathered from newspapers and magazines. He has never seen the Falls. The water must be blue, to give emotion to the picture, he thinks. He has been told that when the water is shown on a map, it has to be blue, and that indeed when there is a lot of it, as in the sea, the water looks like the sky. So he is generous in his depiction, and shocking blue waves cascade unnaturally over the rocky precipice.

"The giraffe walks proudly, majestically, because of the beautiful tapestry that he carries on his back. That is what the struggle is about. Otherwise, they are equals. The elephant has his long tusk to reach the leaves and the giraffe has his long neck."

He inserts two lovers at the corner of the picture, their arms around each other as they stare their love into the blue water. He wants to make the water sing to them. So he paints a bird at the top of the painting, hovering over the falls, its beak open in song. He wishes he had painted a dove, instead of this black bird which looks like a crow.

The carver borrows some paint and puts yellow and black spots on the giraffe with the short neck. He has long accepted that he cannot carve perfect animals, but will not throw them away. Maybe someone, walking out of the Africans-Only hospital, will seek some cheer in his piece. But when he has finished applying the dots, the paint runs down the sides of the animal, and it looks a little like a zebra.

"Why do you never carve a dog or a cat? Something that city people have seen. Even a rat would be good, there are lots of rats in the township!" There is much laughter. The painter realizes that a lot of spray from the falls must be reaching the lovers, so he paints off their heads with a red umbrella. He notices suddenly that something is missing in the picture, so he extends the lovers' free hands, and gives them some yellow ice cream. The picture is now full of life.

"What is the point of carving a dog? Why do you not paint dogs and cats and mice?" The carver has never seen the elephant or the giraffe that he carves so ardently. He picks up a piece of unformed wood.

Will it be a giraffe or an elephant? His carving is also his dreaming.

RESPONDING PERSONALLY

1. Why do you suppose the painter and carver work together by the hospital? Do their artworks help others?
2. In your response journal, describe a hobby you like which gives you pleasure regardless of others' opinions about it.

RESPONDING CRITICALLY

3. What are the carver's preferred subjects? What is the painter's reaction to the carver's work?
4. What are the subjects of the painter's work? What is ironic about his subjects?
5. From what point of view is the story told? Why does that point of view work?
6. What is the relevance of this story to the theme of this unit?

RESPONDING CREATIVELY

7. Draw a four-frame cartoon of one of the story's scenes.
8. Make an illustrated children's book based on the story and its theme.

PROBLEM-SOLVING/DECISION-MAKING

9. Famous mythologist Joseph Campbell once said the best that you can do is to "follow your own bliss." Write a paragraph about a memorable moment from your own past when you followed this advice. You may wish to read your paragraph to others.

Vladimir Nabokov
The Thunderstorm

At the corner of an otherwise ordinary West Berlin street, under
the canopy of a linden in full bloom, I was enveloped by a fierce
fragrance. Masses of mist were ascending in the night sky and,
when the last star-filled hollow had been absorbed, the wind, a
blind phantom, covering his face with his sleeves, swept low
through the deserted street. In lusterless darkness, over the iron
shutter of a barbershop, its suspended shield—a gilt shaving
basin—began swinging like a pendulum.

I came home and found the wind waiting for me in the room:
it banged the casement window—and staged a prompt reflux
when I shut the door behind me. Under my window there was a
deep courtyard where, in the daytime, shirts, crucified on sun-
bright clotheslines, shone through the lilac brushes. Out of that
yard voices would rise now and then: the melancholy barking of
ragmen or empty-bottle buyers; sometimes, the wail of a crippled
violin; and, once an obese blond woman stationed herself in the
center of the yard and broke into such lovely song that maids
leaned out of all the windows, bending their bare necks. Then,
when she had finished, there was a moment of extraordinary stillness; only my landlady, a slatternly widow, was heard sobbing
and blowing her nose in the corridor.

In that yard now a stifling gloom welled, but then the blind
wind, which had helplessly slithered into its depths, once again
began reaching upward, and suddenly it regained its sight, swept
up and, in the amber apertures of the black wall opposite, the sil-
houettes of arms and disheveled heads began to dart, as escaping
windows were being caught and their frames resonantly and firmly locked. The lights went out. The next moment an avalanche of

dull sound, the sound of distant thunder, came into motion, and started tumbling through the dark-violet sky. And again all grew still as it had when the beggar woman finished her song, her hands clasped to her ample bosom.

In this silence I fell asleep, exhausted by the happiness of my day, a happiness I cannot describe in writing, and my dream was full of you.

I woke up because the night had begun crashing to pieces. A wild, pale glitter was flying across the sky like a rapid reflection of colossal spokes. One crash after another rent the sky. The rain came down in a spacious and sonorous flow.

I was intoxicated by those bluish tremors, by the keen, volatile chill. I went up to the wet window ledge and inhaled the un- earthly air, which made my heart ring like glass.

Ever nearer, ever more grandly, the prophet's chariot rumbled across the clouds. The light of madness, of piercing visions, illu- mined the nocturnal world, the metal slopes of roofs, the fleeing lilac bushes. The Thunder-god, a white-haired giant with a furious beard blown back over his shoulder by the wind, dressed in the flying folds of a dazzling raiment, stood, leaning backward, in his fiery chariot, restraining with tensed arms his tremendous, jet- black steeds, their manes a violet blaze. They had broken away from the driver's control, they scattered sparkles of crackling foam, the chariot careened, and the flustered prophet tugged at the reins in vain. His face was distorted by the blast and the strain; the whirlwind, blowing back the folds of his garment, bared a mighty knee; the steeds tossed their blazing manes and rushed on ever more violently, down, down along the clouds. Then, with thun- derous hooves, they hurtled across a shiny rooftop, the chariot lurched, Elijah staggered, and the steeds, maddened by the touch of mortal metal, sprang skyward again. The prophet was pitched out. One wheel came off. From my window I saw its enormous fiery hoop roll down the roof, teeter at the edge, and jump off into darkness, while the steeds, dragging the overturned chariot, were already speeding along the highest clouds; the rumble died down, and the stormy blaze vanished in livid chasms.

The Thunder-god, who had fallen onto the roof, rose heavily. His sandals started slipping; he broke a dormer window with his foot, grunted, and, with a sweep of his arm grasped a chimney to steady himself. He slowly turned his frowning face as his eyes searched for something—probably the wheel that had flown off its golden axle. Then he glanced upward, his fingers clutching at his ruffled beard, shook his head crossly—this was probably not the first time that it happened—and, limping slightly, began a cautious descent.

In great excitement I tore myself away from the window, hurried to put on my dressing gown, and ran down the steep staircase straight to the courtyard. The storm had blown over but a waft of rain still lingered in the air. To the east an exquisite pallor was invading the sky.

The courtyard, which from above had seemed to brim with dense darkness, contained, in fact, nothing more than a delicate, melting mist. On its central patch of turf darkened by the damp, a lean, stoop-shouldered old man in a drenched robe stood muttering something and looking around him. Upon seeing me, he blinked angrily and said, "That you, Elisha?"

I bowed. The prophet clucked his tongue, scratching the while his bald brown spot.

"Lost a wheel. Find it for me, will you?"

The rain had now ceased. Enormous flame-coloured clouds collected above the roofs. The shrubs, the fence, the glistening kennel, were floating in the bluish, drowsy air around us. We groped for a long time in various corners. The old man kept grunting, hitching up the heavy hem of his robe, splashing through the puddles with his round-toed sandals, and a bright drop hung from the tip of his large, bony nose. As I brushed aside a low branch of lilac, I noticed, on a pile of rubbish, amid broken glass, a narrow-rimmed iron wheel that must have belonged to a baby carriage. The old man exhaled warm relief above my ear. Hastily, even a little brusquely, he pushed me aside, and snatched up the rusty hoop. With a joyful wink he said, "So that's where it rolled."

Then he stared at me, his white eyebrows came together in a frown, and, as if remembering something, he said in an impressive voice, "Turn away, Elisha."

I obeyed, even shutting my eyes. I stood like that for a minute or so, and then could not control my curiosity any longer.

The courtyard was empty, except for the old, shaggy dog with its graying muzzle that had thrust its head out of the kennel and was looking up, like a person, with frightened hazel eyes. I looked up too. Elijah had scrambled onto the roof, the iron hoop glimmering behind his back. Above the black chimneys a curly auroral cloud loomed like an orange-hued mountain and, beyond it, a second and a third. The hushed dog and I watched together as the prophet, who had reached the crest of the roof, calmly and unhurriedly stepped upon the cloud and continued to climb, treading heavily on masses of mellow fire....

Sunlight shot through his wheel whereupon it became at once huge and golden, and Elijah himself now seemed robed in flame, blending with the paradisal cloud along which he walked higher and higher until he disappeared in a glorious gorge of the sky.

Only then did the decrepit dog break into a hoarse morning bark. Ripples ran across the bright surface of a rain puddle. The light breeze stirred the geraniums on the balconies. Two or three windows awakened. In my soaked bedslippers and worn dressing gown I ran out into the street to overtake the first, sleepy tramcar, and pulling the skirts of my gown around me, and laughing to myself as I ran, I imagined how, in a few moments, I would be in your house and start telling you about that night's midair accident, and the cross old prophet who fell into my yard.

RESPONDING PERSONALLY

1. Write your thoughts and feelings as you read this selection.
   OR Write a description of the most severe thunderstorm you can recall.
2. What myths and mythical characters does the story make you think of?

RESPONDING CRITICALLY

3. Describe the setting of the story. What impact does the setting and initial atmosphere have on the dramatic events that follow?
4. What is the connection between Elijah and Elisha, the Thunder-god and the narrator. How has the narrator portrayed his own role in the recovery of the wheel? Why?
5. What is the effect of the event on the narrator and his neighbourhood? What action does the narrator take after his vision?
6. What does this story contribute to your understanding of the unit theme? What does it say about the importance of dreams, illusions, and reality?

RESPONDING CREATIVELY

7. Write your own modern short story based on a famous classical myth, fairy tale, or fable.
8. Write dialogue for a telephone call to a friend in which you describe something marvellous you have seen in the night sky.

PROBLEM-SOLVING/DECISION-MAKING

9. For small group discussion: Is the narrator merely the victim of hallucination or does he really witness the vision described? Do you think he is imaginative, deluded, or mad?

"See, Paul—I stand like this all day. I just stand still—so caged!
If I could only run!"

Sinclair Ross
The Lamp at Noon

A little before noon she lit the lamp. Demented wind fled keening
past the house: a wail through the eaves that died every minute or
two. Three days now without respite it had held. The dust was
thickening to an impenetrable fog.

She lit the lamp, then for a long time stood at the window motionless. In dim, fitful outline the stable and oat granary still were
visible; beyond, obscuring fields and landmarks, the lower of dust
clouds made the farmyard seem an isolated acre, poised aloft above
a sombre void. At each blast of wind it shook, as if to topple and
spin hurtling with the dust-reel into space.

From the window she went to the door, opening it a little, and
peering toward the stable again. He was not coming yet. As she
watched there was a sudden rift overhead, and for a moment
through the tattered clouds the sun raced like a wizened orange. It
shed a soft, diffused light, dim and yellow as if it were the light from
the lamp reaching out through the open door.

She closed the door, and going to the stove tried the potatoes
with a fork. Her eyes all the while were fixed and wide with a curious immobility. It was the window. Standing at it, she had let her

forehead press against the pane until the eyes were strained apart and rigid. Wide like that they had looked out to the deepening ruin of the storm. Now she could not close them.

The baby started to cry. He was lying in a homemade crib over which she had arranged a tent of muslin. Careful not to disturb the folds of it, she knelt and tried to still him, whispering huskily in a singsong voice that he must hush and go to sleep again. She would have liked to rock him, to feel the comfort of his little body in her arms, but a fear had obsessed her that in the dust-filled air he might contact pneumonia. There was dust sifting everywhere. Her own throat was parched with it. The table had been set less than ten minutes, and already a film was gathering on the dishes. The little cry continued, and with wincing, frightened lips she glanced around as if to find a corner where the air was less oppressive. But while the lips winced the eyes maintained their wide, immobile stare. "Sleep," she whispered again. "It's too soon for you to be hungry. Daddy's coming for his dinner."

He seemed a long time. Even the clock, still a few minutes off noon, could not dispel a foreboding sense that he was longer than he should be. She went to the door again—and then recoiled slowly to stand white and breathless in the middle of the room. She mustn't. He would only despise her if she ran to the stable looking for him. There was too much grim endurance in his nature ever to let him understand the fear and weakness of a woman. She must stay quiet and wait. Nothing was wrong. At noon he would come— and perhaps after dinner stay with her awhile.

Yesterday, and again at breakfast this morning, they had quarrelled bitterly. She wanted him now, the assurance of his strength and nearness, but he would stand aloof, wary, remembering the words she had flung at him in her anger, unable to understand it was only the dust and wind that had driven her.

Tense, she fixed her eyes upon the clock, listening. There were two winds: the wind in flight, and the wind that pursued. The one sought refuge in the eaves, whimpering, in fear; the other assailed it there, and shook the eaves apart to make it flee again. Once as she listened this first wind sprang inside the room, distraught like a bird that has felt the graze of talons on its wing; while furious the other wind shook the walls, and thudded tumbleweeds against the window till its quarry glanced away again in fright. But only to return—to return and quake among the feeble eaves, as if in all this dust-mad wilderness it knew no other sanctuary.

Then Paul came. At his step she hurried to the stove, intent upon the pots and frying-pan. "The worst wind yet," he ventured, hanging up his cap and smock. "I had to light the lantern in the tool shed, too."

They looked at each other, then away. She wanted to go to him, to feel his arms supporting her, to cry a little just that he might soothe her, but because his presence made the menace of the wind seem less, she gripped herself and thought, "I'm in the right. I won't give in. For his sake, too, I won't."

He washed, hurriedly, so that a few dark welts of dust remained to indent upon his face a haggard strength. It was all she could see as she wiped the dishes and set the food before him: the strength, the grimness, the young Paul growing old and hard, buckled against a desert even grimmer than his will. "Hungry?" she asked, touched to a twinge of pity she had not intended. "There's dust in everything. It keeps coming faster than I can clean it up."

He nodded. "Tonight, though, you'll see it go down. This is the third day."

She looked at him in silence a moment, and then as if to herself muttered broodingly, "Until the next time. Until it starts again."

There was a dark resentment in her voice now that boded another quarrel. He waited, his eyes on her dubiously as she mashed a potato with her fork. The lamp between them threw strong lights and shadows on their faces. Dust and drought, earth that betrayed alike his labor and his faith, to him the struggle had given sternness, an impassive courage. Beneath the whip of sand his youth had been effaced. Youth, zest, exuberance—there remained only a harsh and clenched virility that yet became him, that seemed at the cost of more engaging qualities to be fulfilment of his inmost and essential nature. Whereas to her the same debts and poverty had brought plaintive indignation, a nervous dread of what was still to come. The eyes were hollowed, the lips pinched dry and colorless. It was the face of a woman that had aged without maturing, that had loved the little vanities of life, and lost them wistfully.

"I'm afraid, Paul," she said suddenly. "I can't stand it any longer. He cries all the time. You will go, Paul—say you will. We aren't living here—not really living—"

The pleading in her voice now, after its shrill bitterness yesterday, made him think that this was only another way to persuade him. He answered evenly, "I told you this morning, Ellen; we keep on right where we are. At least I do. It's yourself you're thinking about, not the baby."

This morning such an accusation would have stung her to rage; now, her voice swift and panting, she pressed on, "Listen, Paul— I'm thinking of all of us—you, too. Look at the sky—what's happening. Are you blind? Thistles and tumbleweeds—it's a desert. You won't have a straw this fall. You won't be able to feed a cow or a chicken. Please, Paul, say we'll go away—"

"Go where?" His voice as he answered was still remote and even, inflexibility in unison with the narrowed eyes and the great hunch of muscle-knotted shoulder. "Even as a desert it's better than sweeping out your father's store and running his errands. That's all I've got ahead of me if I do what you want."

"All here—" she faltered. "What's ahead of you here? At least we'll get enough to eat and wear when you're sweeping out his store. Look at it—look at it, you fool. Desert—the lamp lit at noon—"

"You'll see it come back. There's good wheat in it yet."

"But in the meantime—year after year—can't you understand, Paul? We'll never get them back—"

He put down his knife and fork and leaned toward her across the table. "I can't go, Ellen. Living off your people—charity—stop and think of it. This is where I belong. I can't do anything else."

"Charity!" she repeated him, letting her voice rise in derision. "And this—you call this independence! Borrowed money you can't even pay the interest on, seed from the government—grocery bills—doctor bills—"

"We'll have crops again," he persisted. "Good crops—the land will come back. It's worth waiting for."

"And while we're waiting, Paul!" It was not anger now, but a kind of sob. "Think of me—and him. It's not fair. We have our lives, too, to live."

"And you think that going home to your family—taking your husband with you—"

"I don't care—anything would be better than this. Look at the air he's breathing. He cries all the time. For his sake, Paul. What's ahead of him here, even if you do get crops?"

He clenched his lips a minute, then, with his eyes hard and contemptuous, struck back, "As much as in town, growing up a pauper. You're the one who wants to go, it's not for his sake. You think that in town you'd have a better time—not so much work—more clothes—"

"Maybe—" she dropped her head defencelessly. "I'm young still. I like pretty things."

There was silence now—a deep fastness of it enclosed by rushing wind and creaking walls. It seemed the yellow lamplight cast a hush upon them. Though the haze of dusty air the walls receded, dimmed, and came again. At last she raised her head and said listlessly, "Go on—your dinner's getting cold. Don't sit and stare at me. I've said it all."

The spent quietness in her voice was even harder to endure than her anger. It reproached him, against his will insisted that he see and understand her lot. To justify himself he tried, "I was a poor man when you married me. You said you didn't mind. Farming's never been easy, and never will be."

"I wouldn't mind the work or the skimping if there was something to look forward to. It's the hopelessness—going on—watching the land blow away."

"The land's all right," he repeated. "The dry years won't last forever."

"But it's not just dry years, Paul!" The little sob in her voice gave way suddenly to a ring of exasperation. "Will you never see? It's the land itself—the soil. You've plowed and harrowed it until there's

not a root or fibre left to hold it down. That's why the soil drifts—
that's why in a year or two there'll be nothing left but the bare clay.
If in the first place you farmers had taken care of your land—if you
hadn't been so greedy for wheat every year—"

She had taught school before she married him, and of late in her
anger there had been a kind of disdain, an attitude almost of con-
descension, as if she no longer looked upon the farmers as her
equals. He sat still, his eyes fixed on the yellow lamp flame, and
seeming to know how her words had hurt him, she went on softly,
"I want to help you, Paul. That's why I won't sit quiet while you go
on wasting your life. You're only thirty—you owe it to yourself as
well as me."

He sat staring at the lamp without answering, his mouth sullen.
It seemed indifference now, as if he were ignoring her, and stung to
anger again she cried, "Do you ever think what my life is? Two
rooms to live in—once a month to town, and nothing to spend
when I get there. I'm still young—I wasn't brought up this way."

"You're a farmer's wife now. It doesn't matter what you used to
be, or how you were brought up. You get enough to eat and wear.
Just now that's all I can do. I'm not to blame that we've been dried
out five years."

"Enough to eat!" she laughed back shrilly. "Enough salt pork—
enough potatoes and eggs. And look—" Springing to the middle of
the room she thrust out a foot for him to see the scuffed old slip-
per. "When they're completely gone I suppose you'll tell me I can
go barefoot—that I'm a farmer's wife—that it's not your fault we're
dried-out—"

"And what about these?" He pushed his chair away from the
table now to let her see what he was wearing. "Cowhide—hard as
boards—but my feet are so calloused I don't feel them any more."

Then he stood up, ashamed of having tried to match her hardships with his own. But frightened now as he reached for his smock
she pressed close to him. "Don't go yet. I brood and worry when
I'm left alone. Please, Paul—you can't work on the land anyway."

"And keep on like this? You start before I'm through the door.
Week in and week out—I've troubles enough of my own."

"Paul—please stay—" The eyes were glazed now, distended a little as if with the intensity of her dread and pleading. "We won't
quarrel any more. Hear it! I can't work—I just stand still and listen—"

The eyes frightened him, but responding to a kind of instinct
that he must withstand her, that it was his self-respect and man-
hood against the fretful weakness of a woman, he answered un-
feelingly, "In here safe and quiet—you don't know how well off you
are. If you were out in it—fighting it—swallowing it—"

"Sometimes, Paul, I wish I was. I'm so caged—if I could only
break away and run. See—I stand like this all day. I can't relax. My
throat's so tight it aches—"

With a jerk he freed his smock from her clutch. "If I stay we'll
only keep on all afternoon. Wait till tomorrow—we'll talk things
over when the wind goes down."

Then without meeting her eyes again he swung outside, and,
doubled low against the buffets of the wind, fought his way slowly
toward the stable. There was a deep hollow calm within, a vast
darkness engulfed beneath the tides of moaning wind. He stood
breathless a moment, hushed almost to a stupor by the sudden ex-
tinction of the storm and the stillness that enfolded him. It was a
long, far-reaching stillness. The first dim stalls and rafters led the
way into cavern-like obscurity, into vaults and recesses that extended far beyond the stable walls. Nor in these first quiet moments
did he forbid the illusion, the sense of release from a harsh, familiar world into one of peace and darkness. The contentious mood
that his stand against Ellen had roused him to, his tenacity and
clenched despair before the ravages of wind, it was ebbing now, losing itself in the cover of darkness. Ellen and the wheat seemed remote, unimportant. At a whinny from the bay mare, Bess, he went
forward and into her stall. She seemed grateful for his presence,
and thrust her nose deep between his arm and body. They stood a
long time motionless, comforting and assuring each other.

For soon again the first deep sense of quiet and peace was
shrunken to the battered shelter of the stable. Instead of release or
escape from the assaulting wind, the walls were but a feeble stand

against it. They creaked and sawed as if the fingers of a giant hand were tightening to collapse them; the empty loft sustained a pipelike cry that rose and fell but never ended. He saw the dust-black sky again, and his fields blown smooth with drifted soil.

But always, even while listening to the storm outside, he could feel the tense and apprehensive stillness of the stable. There was not a hoof that clumped or shifted, not a rub of halter against manger. And yet, though it had been a strange stable, he would have known, despite the darkness, that every stall was filled. They, too, were all listening.

From Bess he went to the big grey gelding, Prince. Prince was twenty years old, with rib-grooved sides, and high, protruding hip-bones. Paul ran his hand over the ribs, and felt a sudden shame, a sting of fear that Ellen might be right in what she said. For wasn't it true—nine years a farmer now on his own land, and still he couldn't even feed his horses? What, then, could he hope to do for his wife and son?

There was much he planned. And so vivid was the future of his planning, so real and constant, that often the actual present was but half felt, but half endured. Its difficulties were lessened by a confidence in what lay beyond them. A new house—land for the boy—land and still more land—or education, whatever he might want.

But all the time was he only a blind and stubborn fool? Was Ellen right? Was he trampling on her life, and throwing away his own? The five years since he married her, were they to go on repeating themselves, five, ten, twenty, until all the brave future he looked forward to was but a stark and futile past?

She looked forward to no future. She had no faith or dream with which to make the dust and poverty less real. He understood suddenly. He saw her face again as only a few minutes ago it had begged him not to leave her. The darkness round him now was as a slate on which her lonely terror limned itself. He went from Prince to the other horses, combing their manes and forelocks with his fingers, but always it was her face before him, its staring eyes and twisted suffering. "See, Paul,—I stand like this all day. I just stand still—My throat's so tight it aches—"

And always the wind, the creak of walls, the wild lipless wailing through the loft. Until at last he stood there, staring into the livid face before him, it seemed that this scream of wind was a cry from her parched and frantic lips. He knew it couldn't be, he knew that she was safe within the house, but still the wind persisted as a woman's cry. The cry of a woman with eyes like those that watched him through the dark. Eyes that were mad now—lips that even as they cried still pleaded, "See, Paul—I stand like this all day. I just stand still—so caged! If I could only run!"

He saw her running, pulled and driven headlong by the wind, but when at last he returned to the house, compelled by his anxiety, she was walking quietly back and forth with the baby in her arms. Careful, despite his concern, not to reveal a fear or weakness that she might think capitulation to her wishes, he watched a moment through the window, and then went off to the tool shed to mend harness. All afternoon he stitched and riveted. It was easier with the lantern lit and his hands occupied. There was a wind whining high past the tool shed too, but it was only wind. He remembered the arguments with which Ellen had tried to persuade him away from the farm, and one by one he defeated them. There would be rain again—next year or the next. Maybe in his ignorance he had farmed his land the wrong way, seeding wheat every year, working the soil till it was lifeless dust—but he would do better now. He would plant clover and alfalfa, breed cattle, acre by acre and year by year restore to his land its fibre and fertility. That was something to work for, a way to prove himself. It was ruthless wind, blackening the sky with his earth, but it was not his master. Out of his land it had made a wilderness. He now, out of the wilderness, would make a farm and home again.

Tonight he must talk with Ellen. Patiently, when the wind was down, and they were both quiet again. It was she who had told him to grow fibrous crops, who had called him an ignorant fool because he kept on with summer fallow and wheat. Now she might be gratified to find him acknowledging her wisdom. Perhaps she would begin to feel the power and steadfastness of the land, to take a pride in it, to understand that he was not a fool, but working for her future and their son's.

And already the wind was slackening. At four o'clock he could sense a lull. At five, straining his eyes from the tool shed doorway, he could make out a neighbor's buildings half a mile away. It was over—three days of blight and havoc like a scourge—three days so bitter and so long that for a moment he stood still, unseeing, his senses idle with a numbness of relief.

But only for a moment. Suddenly he emerged from the numbness; suddenly the fields before him struck his eyes to comprehension. They lay black, naked. Beaten and mounded smooth with dust as if a sea in gentle swell had turned to stone. And though he had tried to prepare himself for such a scene, though he had known since yesterday that not a blade would last the storm, still now, before the utter waste confronting him, he sickened and stood cold. Suddenly like the fields he was naked. Everything that had sheathed him a little from the realities of existence: vision and purpose, faith in the land, in the future, in himself—it was all rent now, stripped away. "Desert," he heard her voice begin to sob. "Desert, you fool—the lamp lit at noon!"

In the stable again, measuring out their feed to the horses, he wondered what he would say to her tonight. For so deep were his instincts of loyalty to the land that still, even with the images of his betrayal stark upon his mind, his concern was how to withstand her, how to go on again and justify himself. It had not occurred to him yet that he might or should abandon the land. He had lived with it too long. Rather was his impulse still to defend it—as a man defends against the scorn of strangers even his most worthless kin.

He fed his horses, then waited. She too would be waiting, ready to cry at him, "Look now—that crop that was to feed and clothe us! And you'll still keep on! You'll still say 'Next year—there'll be rain next year'!"

But she was gone when he reached the house. The door was open, the lamp blown out, the crib empty. The dishes from their meal at noon were still on the table. She had perhaps begun to sweep, for the broom was lying in the middle of the floor. He tried to call, but a terror clamped upon his throat. In the wan, returning light it seemed that even the deserted kitchen was straining to whisper what it had seen. The tatters of the storm still whimpered through the eaves, and in their moaning told the desolation of the miles they had traversed. On tiptoe at last he crossed to the adjoining room; then at the threshold, without even a glance inside to satisfy himself that she was really gone, he wheeled again and plunged outside.

He ran a long time—distraught and headlong as a few hours ago he had seemed to watch her run—around the farmyard, a little distance into the pasture, back again blindly to the house to see whether she had returned—and then at a stumble down the road for help.

They joined him in the search, rode away for others, spread calling across the fields in the direction she might have been carried by the wind—but nearly two hours later it was himself who came upon her. Crouched down against a drift of sand as if for shelter, her hair in matted strands around her neck and face, the child clasped tightly in her arms.

The child was quite cold. It had been her arms, perhaps, too frantic to protect him, or the smother of dust upon his throat and lungs. "Hold him," she said as he knelt beside her. "So—with his face away from the wind. Hold him until I tidy my hair."

Her eyes were still wide in an immobile stare, but with her lips she smiled at him. For a long time he knelt transfixed, trying to speak to her, touching fearfully with his fingertips the dust-grimed cheeks and eyelids of the child. At last she said, "I'll take him again. Such clumsy hands—you don't know how to hold a baby yet. See how his head falls forward on your arm."

Yet it all seemed familiar—a confirmation of what he had known since noon. He gave her the child, then, gathering them up in his arms, struggled to his feet, and turned toward home.

It was evening now. Across the fields a few spent clouds of dust still shook and fled. Beyond, as if through smoke, the sunset smoldered like a distant fire.

He walked with a long dull stride, his eyes before him, heedless of her weight. Once he glanced down and with her eyes still she was smiling. "Such strong arms, Paul—and I was so tired just carrying him...."

He tried to answer, but it seemed that now the dusk was drawn apart in breathless waiting, a finger on its lips until they passed. "You were right, Paul...." Her voice came whispering, as if she too could feel the hush. "You said tonight we'd see the storm go down. So still now, and a red sky—it means tomorrow will be fine."

RESPONDING PERSONALLY

1. For small group discussion: Explain what you already know about life on the Prairies during the Great Depression. How does this story reflect or add to your prior knowledge?
2. Look up the word *tragedy* in a dictionary. What is the tragedy of this story? What story events are tragic?

RESPONDING CRITICALLY

3. Make a chart for Ellen and Paul, listing their initial reasons for staying or leaving. In a group, decide who you think is most right.
4. For paragraph assignment: Why does Ellen finally run away? What has happened to Ellen and the baby? In your opinion, could the tragedy have been avoided? Why or why not? Is the ending optimistic or pessimistic? Explain.
5. Which of the two characters do you feel more sympathy for? Defend your choice to another student.
6. Describe the atmosphere of the story and the mood created in the characters and readers by this setting. How do the setting and atmosphere create a sense of isolation in the characters?

RESPONDING CREATIVELY

7. Write a letter that Ellen or Paul might have written to her or his parents the next morning. Share your letter with others.
8. With two other students, role-play Ellen and Paul being interviewed one week later on a television talk show.

PROBLEM-SOLVING/DECISION-MAKING

9. In a paragraph, offer advice to Paul and Ellen about what they should do next. Give reasons for them to consider.

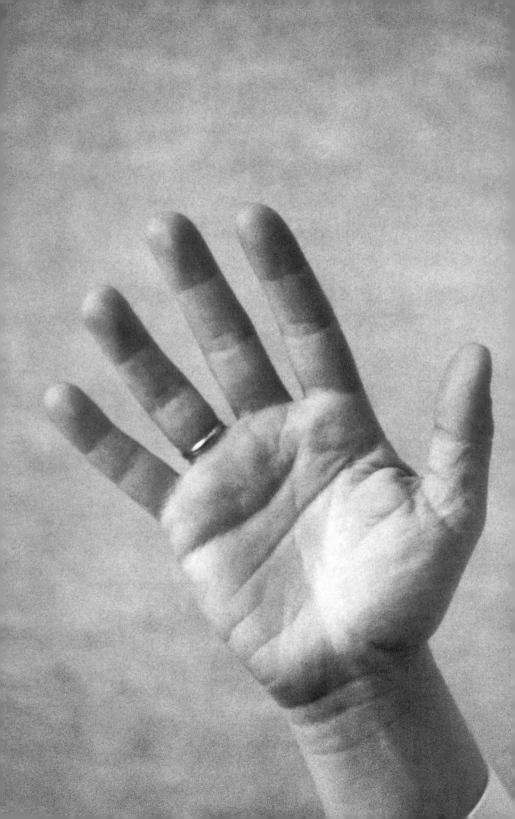

Good and Evil

One of the most basic conflicts in our lives is the struggle between good and evil. Most people see the world as a combination of these forces, often casting themselves as the "good people." But "good" and "bad" are relative terms upon which not everyone can agree. It is this relativeness of morality and its never-ending struggle between polar opposites that make the following stories engaging and challenging to read.

The first story, "The Inheritor," focuses on three characters trying to survive in the flooded Australian outback: a man, a dingo, and a ewe. In the ensuing conflict, the man becomes an agent of good quite unexpectedly and ultimately determines the fortunes of the other two characters.

The second story, "The Possibility of Evil," provides a fascinating focus on the possibility of evil in a pleasant civilized setting. Miss Strangeworth, the protagonist, is a self-appointed guardian of moral good and an enthusiastic crusader against evil. What she discovers finally is that even "good" people can be corrupted and victimized if their means of operation are intrinsically evil.

The final story, "The Portable Phonograph," presents us with four men who survive the destruction of the world. They listen to fine music and read fine books, leftover artifacts from a bygone civilized age. But there is impending violence lurking below the cordial surface, as one of the men becomes desperate with greed. In this story, we see that sometimes the lessons of good and evil can be lost on those who really should know better.

Good and evil is a popular basic theme of literature. The stories in this unit demonstrate the complexity of this essential, eternal, and recurring conflict.

"A man can be a fool," he said.

Frank Roberts
The Inheritor

The man and the ewe and the dingo and a few crows wheeling above were the only visible living creatures in all that desolation.

They were on the only high land for miles around, a peaked hill known as Lone Pine because it had one tree on it. The tree was a very ordinary eucalypt but the words Lone Pine have such an historic association, even now, half a century afterward, that any hill with one tree on it is apt to be known locally by that name.

This tree had suffered intense dry heat in its summers and withering dry cold in its winters and now, dead, its bare and gnarled and twisted branches made as good a monument as any to inland life, which is a longer war.

But the man saw it with a practical eye merely as the marker to a final refuge from the flood. The ewe and the dingo had no feelings at all about the tree, but the crows had. It was their natural roost and they had been there, conscious of the ewe cropping grass below them, and of the flood, and always prepared to wait patiently for the main chance when the dingo had appeared slinking along a low ridge, equally afraid of the rising water and of being silhouetted so plainly.

The dog scouted around the shrinking perimeter of Lone Pine, returned to the point where ridge met hillside, and stood sniffing the wind and waiting for a flash of instinct. It had come, and then he had walked up to the highest point of the hill and settled down near the tree to watch and wait.

He had seen the ewe but was not in a killing mood just then. And the crows flapped away from the tree, wheeled back to it, perched, and flapped away again. They were restless but not afraid of the dingo. He was a good provider.

But when the man appeared, walking along the ridge-top with the floodwater soaking his boots and running through the eroded dip where the ridge came to the hill, the crows left the tree and wheeled continuously.

The man leaped from the ridge to the hillside and walked up the hill. He didn't see the earth-colored dog until it snarled. Then he saw its white teeth and blazing eyes. He looked down at the ridge and then up at the branches of the tree which he could reach with a good jump. But could he pull himself up quickly enough—or would the dingo rear at the sudden movement and slash at his legs? The essential habits of dingos were not in his experience, and the flood was another factor.

Then the ewe scented the wild dog. It was unlikely that she saw him. But she turned to run downhill and found the flood in front of her and bleated and ran around the hill, and the dingo crawled a few inches, watching her.

The man felt relieved. Presently the dog would attack the ewe, and he would hoist himself into the tree. He had only to remain still, and to divert the dingo from its instinctive passion for the ewe's throat.

The sheep ran about until it lost the dog scent, and then it noticed a new patch of grass and resumed cropping, moving on and up as the flood nudged its hoofs. It was stupid, even as sheep went.

The man stayed very still, watching the dingo stir an inch every time the ewe moved, hackles up and the skin along its spine quivering.

And then, God help him, the man began to feel pity for the sheep.

He was sure that the dingo had forgotten him, closed him out, but any simple movement would restore him. That might save the ewe.

He reasoned that the dog would not attack one creature while conscious of another that might attack it. "Dingo" had become a vernacular for coward, but the wild dogs had survived from an age earlier than man by caution and cunning. Courage was a last resource. He reasoned further that the ewe was unimportant, born to be killed by dog or man, but another thought came obliquely across this reasoning. If their isolation on the hill encouraged the dingo to have its anticipation to the full, letting the flood bring the ewe to it, he might be unable to hold his motionless pose and movement might turn the impassioned dog to him. He reasoned that this was unlikely and the idea false to his interests, but it persisted.

He knew it was compassion seeking to force him into foolish action by perversion of logic, suggesting that he divert the dingo now, before its exquisite desire became madness.

All this worrying to save a sheep? Damn the sheep and damn the dingo, let them continue the drama according to their natures, and let him get into that tree.

Then he knew that he could not. It was in his nature, too, to come down from trees and be master on the ground. He felt that if he should abandon the ewe and leap to safety he would diminish his own kind on the face of the earth. He must stay on the ground while ground remained.

Besides, the only low branch was too directly above the dingo.

He realized that this kind of thinking was more than foolish, it could be fatal. Soon their island would be so small that he and the dingo inevitably would be at one another's throats.

That image needed correcting. It was too dramatic. The dingo could only attack with its jaws and its weight, probably much less than his. He had defensive and offensive power in his hands, arms, legs, and booted feet. So the dog had more to fear from him. He was afraid because it was wild, alien, capable of savagery, vicious, indomitable.

In a tight corner it might attack him and then it would fight to the death, and he would be lacerated terribly. This was really what he feared. It was still a question of the sheep or him.

The water was rising quickly and soon all three would be forced into a propinquity in which anything might happen. Unfortunately, while he could attract the dog's attention and perhaps save the ewe, he could not take the opposite line and disengage from the danger. He must act or submit to chance. This was the choice he faced.

Now he could feel pity for the ewe again, because he had made it reasonable. He felt sorry for the two inimical animals and himself, thrown together on this curious island in the flood. Only the wheeling crows were above pity. They were infinitely patient, nerveless, secure.

He realized that he had moved.

He had inclined his head and now the dingo's furious eyes were turned on him. He felt his heart respond to alarm. Then as if dismissing him as a potential danger, the dog turned back to the ewe, and he felt this was the moment. The sheep caught it, too, and stood bleating.

Even as the dog prepared for its charge to knock the ewe down and expose its throat to incisors, the man jumped and shouted. He knew it was wrong, that the whole argument had been opened again, when he had been free to jump for safety. But he was beyond reason and doing what he must.

The dingo hit the sheep and it fell over but the man was in reach before the teeth went in and booted the dog aside. It seemed to go with the kick, turning once in the air and landing on stiffened legs, facing him and snarling.

He heard the sheep scramble up and run away, and each wild bleat drew a response from the dog, a snap and snarl at the man.

He was going to kick again if it sprang at him, and he was more afraid of a dash at his legs. But suddenly the dingo swung away and ran up to the tree where it turned, hackled and savage and in command of the high ground.

Now the man knew he was where he deserved to be, with the sheep. Gradually the water would force them up toward the dog, who held all the advantages and who now recognized his prime enemy.

The man walked around the little island, looking for a stick or a stone, even searching the flood for debris, but there was nothing of the slightest value.

"A man can be a fool," he said.

His voice sounded loud and made him realize how silent everything was, particularly their common menace, the flood.

"Just a stone," he asked of the stoneless ground.

He walked around the island again, moving slowly, watching both the ground and the ewe, which might be panicked into dashing straight to the tree and its death. Now that the issue had been made, he had to protect that animal or forever be a fool.

He looked at the squatting dingo, and the tree and the crows, and the ochre flood that covered the land. He was hoping for boats, but there were none in sight and sight extended for many miles from the top of Lone Pine.

No, there were no boats. And even if there were, even if some miracle brought one, the men in it would see what against the sky? A dead tree with some crows on it and a dingo sitting under it, and they would turn away.

The man knew that he could not let the dingo maintain control of the high ground for too long. But he also knew that if he approached it now it would almost certainly fight. In a while it might become more conscious of the flood, and afraid or at least troubled enough to accept if not welcome company. He had heard or read that animals so threatened forgot all other instincts. He decided to follow his reasoning this time, and be patient.

As the flood consumed the remaining ground, the man tried to stay close to the ewe without alarming it. By moving slowly and carefully he managed to drive it around the island and keep it more aware of him than of the dog. He felt this roundabout way was better than gradual direct approach to the dingo. But nothing was better or best with this wild thing.

Stiff-legged and snarling, it turned as the man and the ewe circled, always with its hind to the tree. And as the distance between them shortened its fury increased and it snapped and snarled at both man and the ewe.

Now the sheep began to make short dashes up and down the slope, afraid of the water, terrified of the dingo, and inevitably about to sacrifice itself to one death or the other. The man was unable to stay between the two animals without danger and at any time now the dog would jump straight out at his throat.

And he had to make this happen so that he would not be surprised.

He stood in front of the dingo, almost eye to eye with it. He remained quite still, and then suddenly threw up his hands and shouted.

And the dog sprang and the man dropped to his hands and knees and sprang up again, meeting the expected midair turn and descent with the broad of his back.

He heard ground impact when he had hoped for a splash, and the dingo was back and had torn his leg while he was still turning downhill.

He kicked at it with the other foot but it danced out of his reach and in again for another slash, then aside when he kicked ahead, and in again for a tear at his flank.

And then the crazed ewe blundered into them and the dingo rolled over and the man fell on it and got both hands around its neck, lying on the dog while he strangled it.

It gagged and frothed and tried to get his wrists and dug and writhed and howled once and his hands and arms ached and his mind was torn and outraged by the act of murder. But he maintained his grim purpose.

When he stood up, perhaps a long time later, his forearms and wrists were bleeding freely and there were many gashes on his stomach and chest from the dog's paws. Both legs and one hip were badly gashed, but he had saved his hands and face.

The sheep stood a few feet away, cropping a tuft of grass under the dead tree.

It shied away when he put a hand out toward it, and ran around to the other side of the tree.

The man sat down and tore two long strips from his trouser leg. He strung them on his belt and went around one side of the tree and then doubled back quickly and caught the ewe before it could turn again. He threw it on its side and tied its legs.

Now he had only to find some way of getting it up into the tree.

He did that by going up and breaking off part of one of the gaunt limbs and using it to dig the earth around the tree, making a mound on which he was able to stand and heave the trussed ewe across the lowest fork. She struggled, bleating terribly, and nearly fell before he could clamber on to the branch and hold her in place. But once he was in the tree it was all right.

He was sighted from an Army helicopter next morning, a bloodied, injured, and demented man who refused to be taken off unless he could bring a trussed sheep with him.

"I can't do that, it's too risky, but I'll send one of the ducks to you," the pilot told him. "Can you hang on a while longer?"

"I'll hang on all right," the man said.

As they climbed away the pilot laughed and shook his head.

"That beats everything I've seen," he said to one of the rescued in the cabin. "He must be crazy about sheep."

His passenger looked down at the desolation and said, "It gets some like that, out here. That must be the only live sheep anywhere in all this."

The pilot could see that, although it had no special impact on him. He had seen all kinds of desolation. And he said, "Oh, well, I suppose that gives it some value. I guess it makes sense from his point of view."

But he couldn't help smiling again at the memory of that wild-looking man sitting astride a high branch, with his feet in the flood, and hanging on to that trussed sheep with both hands as though it had a golden fleece.

RESPONDING PERSONALLY

1. Write your thoughts and feelings as you read this story. OR Write about what you would have done in the same situation.
2. With a partner, decide who would be the inheritor at the end of the story. What has been inherited?

RESPONDING CRITICALLY

3. For paragraph answer: What is the man's reaction to his situation at the beginning of the story? Identify his dilemma. What influences him to defend the ewe against the dingo?
4. What enables the man to defeat the dingo? How is he superior to his opponent?
5. For small group discussion—Consider the following:
   a) the significance of the allusion to the golden fleece
   b) why the men in the helicopter react as they do to the stranded man
   c) whether or not the man did the right thing.
6. What implications does the man's decision have for us with regard to his response to:
   a) crime
   b) environmental problems
   c) so-called "neutral" positions in cases such as public complicity with war crimes or government wrongdoing?

RESPONDING CREATIVELY

7. With another student, create an interview between the man and a TV talk show host that might have taken place after the rescue. Present your interview to the class.
8. Create a word search using key words and details from the story. Exchange yours with a partner's and see if you can complete it.

PROBLEM-SOLVING/DECISION-MAKING

9. Debate whether the man's final decision to act was right or wrong. Offer your conclusions to the class.

Shirley Jackson
The Possibility of Evil

Miss Adela Strangeworth came daintily along Main Street on her way to the grocery. The sun was shining, the air was fresh and clear after the night's heavy rain, and everything in Miss Strangeworth's little town looked washed and bright. Miss Strangeworth took deep breaths and thought that there was nothing in the world like a fragrant summer day.

She knew everyone in town, of course; she was fond of telling strangers—tourists who sometimes passed through the town and stopped to admire Miss Strangeworth's roses—that she had never spent more than a day outside this town in all her long life. She was seventy-one, Miss Strangeworth told the tourists, with a pretty little dimple showing by her lip, and she sometimes found herself thinking that the town belonged to her. "My grandfather built the first house on Pleasant Street," she would say, opening her blue eyes wide with the wonder of it. "This house, right here. My family has lived here for better than a hundred years. My grandmother planted these roses, and my mother tended them, just as I do. I've watched my town grow; I can remember when Mr. Lewis, Senior, opened the grocery store, and the year the river flooded out the shanties on the low road, and the excitement when some young folks wanted to move the park over to the space in front of where the new post office is today. They wanted to put up a statue of Ethan Allen"—Miss Strangeworth would frown a little and sound stern—"but it should have been a statue of my grandfather. There wouldn't have been a town here at all if it hadn't been for my grandfather and the lumber mill."

Miss Strangeworth never gave away any of her roses, although the tourists often asked her. The roses belonged on Pleasant

Street, and it bothered Miss Strangeworth to think of people wanting to carry them away, to take them into strange towns and down strange streets. When the new minister came, and the ladies were gathering flowers to decorate the church, Miss Strangeworth sent over a great basket of gladioli; when she picked the roses at all, she set them in bowls and vases around the inside of the house her grandfather had built.

Walking down Main Street on a summer morning, Miss Strangeworth had to stop every minute or so to say good morning to someone or to ask after someone's health. When she came into the grocery, half a dozen people turned away from the shelves and the counters to wave at her or call out good morning.

"And good morning to you, too, Mr. Lewis," Miss Strangeworth said at last. The Lewis family had been in the town almost as long as the Strangeworths; but the day young Lewis left high school and went to work in the grocery, Miss Strangeworth had stopped calling him Tommy and started calling him Mr. Lewis, and he had stopped calling her Addie and started calling her Miss Strangeworth. They had been in high school together, and had gone to picnics together, and to high-school dances and basketball games; but now Mr. Lewis was behind the counter in the grocery, and Miss Strangeworth was living alone in the Strangeworth house on Pleasant Street.

"Good morning," Mr. Lewis said, and added politely, "Lovely day."

"It is a very nice day," Miss Strangeworth said, as though she had only just decided that it would do after all. "I would like a chop, please, Mr. Lewis, a small, lean veal chop. Are those strawberries from Arthur Parker's garden? They're early this year."

"He brought them in this morning," Mr. Lewis said.

"I shall have a box," Miss Strangeworth said. Mr. Lewis looked worried, she thought, and for a minute she hesitated, but then she decided that he surely could not be worried over the strawberries. He looked very tired indeed. He was usually so chipper, Miss Strangeworth thought, and almost commented, but it was far too personal a subject to be introduced to

Mr. Lewis, the grocer, so she only said, "and a can of cat food and, I think, a tomato."

Silently, Mr. Lewis assembled her order on the counter, and waited. Miss Strangeworth looked at him curiously and then said, "It's Tuesday, Mr. Lewis. You forgot to remind me."

"Did I? Sorry."

"Imagine your forgetting that I always buy my tea on Tuesday," Miss Strangeworth said gently. "A quarter pound of tea, please, Mr. Lewis."

"Is that all, Miss Strangeworth?"

"Yes, thank you, Mr. Lewis. Such a lovely day, isn't it?"

"Lovely," Mr. Lewis said.

Miss Strangeworth moved slightly to make room for Mrs. Harper at the counter. "Morning, Adela," Mrs. Harper said, and Miss Strangeworth said, "Good morning, Martha."

"Lovely day," Mrs. Harper said, and Miss Strangeworth said, "Yes, lovely," and Mr. Lewis, under Mrs. Harper's glance, nodded.

"Ran out of sugar for my cake frosting," Mrs. Harper explained. Her hand shook slightly as she opened her pocketbook. Miss Strangeworth wondered, glancing at her quickly, if she had been taking proper care of herself. Martha Harper was not as young as she used to be, Miss Strangeworth thought. She probably could use a good strong tonic.

"Martha," she said, "you don't look well."

"I'm perfectly all right," Mrs. Harper said shortly. She handed her money to Mr. Lewis, took her change and her sugar, and went out without speaking again. Looking after her, Miss Strangeworth shook her head slightly. Martha definitely did *not* look well.

Carrying her little bag of groceries, Miss Strangeworth came out of the store into the bright sunlight and stopped to smile down on the Crane baby. Don and Helen Crane were really the two most infatuated young parents she had ever known, she thought indulgently, looking at the delicately embroidered baby cap and the lace-edged carriage cover.

"That little girl is going to grow up expecting luxury all her life," she said to Helen Crane.

Helen laughed. "That's the way we want her to feel," she said. "Like a princess."

"A princess can see a lot of trouble sometimes," Miss Strangeworth said dryly. "How old is Her Highness now?"

"Six months next Tuesday," Helen Crane said, looking down with rapt wonder at her child. "I've been worrying, though, about her. Don't you think she ought to move around more? Try to sit up, for instance?"

"For plain and fancy worrying," Miss Strangeworth said, amused, "give me a new mother every time."

"She just seems—slow," Helen Crane said.

"Nonsense. All babies are different. Some of them develop much more quickly than others."

"That's what my mother says." Helen Crane laughed, looking a little bit ashamed.

"I suppose you've got young Don all upset about the fact that his daughter is already six months old and hasn't yet begun to learn to dance?"

"I haven't mentioned it to him. I suppose she's just so precious that I worry about her all the time."

"Well, apologize to her right now," Miss Strangeworth said. "*She* is probably worrying about why you keep jumping around all the time." Smiling to herself and shaking her old head, she went on down the sunny street, stopping once to ask little Billy Moore why he wasn't out riding in his daddy's shiny new car, and talking for a few minutes outside the library with Miss Chandler, the librarian, about the new novels to be ordered and paid for by the annual library appropriation. Miss Chandler seemed absent-minded and very much as though she were thinking about something else. Miss Strangeworth noticed that Miss Chandler had not taken much trouble with her hair that morning, and sighed. Miss Strangeworth hated sloppiness.

Many people seemed disturbed recently, Miss Strangeworth thought. Only yesterday the Stewarts' fifteen-year-old Linda had run crying down her own front walk and all the way to school, not caring who saw her. People around town thought she might have had a fight with the Harris boy, but they showed up together at the soda shop after school as usual, both of them looking grim and bleak. Trouble at home, people concluded, and sighed over the problems of trying to raise kids right these days.

From halfway down the block Miss Strangeworth could catch the heavy scent of her roses, and she moved a little more quickly. The perfume of roses meant home, and home meant the Strangeworth House on Pleasant Street. Miss Strangeworth stopped at her own front gate, as she always did, and looked with deep pleasure at her house, with the red and pink and white roses massed along the narrow lawn, and the rambler going up along the porch; and the neat, the unbelievably trim lines of the house itself, with its slimness and its washed white look. Every window sparkled, every curtain hung stiff and straight, and even the stones of the front walk were swept and clear. People around town wondered how old Miss Strangeworth managed to keep the house looking the way it did, and there was a legend about a tourist once mistaking it for the local museum and going all through the place without finding out about his mistake. But the town was proud of Miss Strangeworth and her roses and her house. They had all grown together.

Miss Strangeworth went up her front steps, unlocked her front door with her key, and went into the kitchen to put away her groceries. She debated about having a cup of tea and then decided that it was too close to midday dinnertime; she would not have the appetite for her little chop if she had tea now. Instead she went into the light, lovely sitting room, which still glowed from the hands of her mother and her grandmother, who had covered the chairs with bright chintz and hung the curtains. All the furniture was spare and shining, and the round hooked rugs on the floor had been the work of Miss Strangeworth's grandmother and her mother. Miss Strangeworth had put a bowl of her red roses on the low table before the window, and the room was full of their scent.

Miss Strangeworth went to the narrow desk in the corner and unlocked it with her key. She never knew when she might feel like writing letters, so she kept her notepaper inside and the desk locked. Miss Strangeworth's usual stationery was heavy and cream-colored, with STRANGEWORTH HOUSE engraved across the top, but, when she felt like writing her other letters, Miss Strangeworth used a pad of various-colored paper bought from the local news-paper shop. It was almost a town joke, that colored paper, layered in pink and green and blue and yellow; everyone in town bought it and used it for odd, informal notes and shopping lists. It was usual to remark, upon receiving a note written on a blue page, that so-and-so would be needing a new pad soon—here she was, down to the blue already. Everyone used the matching envelopes for tucking away recipes, or keeping odd little things in, or even to hold cookies in the school lunchboxes. Mr. Lewis sometimes gave them to the children for carrying home penny candy.

Although Miss Strangeworth's desk held a trimmed quill pen which had belonged to her grandmother, and a gold-frosted foun-tain pen which had belonged to her father, Miss Strangeworth al-ways used a dull stub of pencil when she wrote her letters, and she printed them in a childish block print. After thinking for a minute, although she had been phrasing the letter in the back of her mind all the way home, she wrote on a pink sheet: DIDN'T YOU EVER SEE AN IDIOT CHILD BEFORE? SOME PEOPLE JUST SHOULDN'T HAVE CHILDREN SHOULD THEY?

She was pleased with the letter. She was fond of doing things exactly right. When she made a mistake, as she sometimes did, or when the letters were not spaced nicely on the page, she had to take the discarded page to the kitchen stove and burn it at once. Miss Strangeworth never delayed when things had to be done.

After thinking for a minute, she decided that she would like to write another letter, perhaps to go to Mrs. Harper, to follow up the ones she had already mailed. She selected a green sheet this time and wrote quickly: HAVE YOU FOUND OUT YET WHAT THEY WERE ALL LAUGHING ABOUT AFTER YOU LEFT THE BRIDGE CLUB ON THURSDAY? OR IS THE WIFE REALLY ALWAYS THE LAST ONE TO KNOW?

Miss Strangeworth never concerned herself with facts; her let-ters all dealt with the more negotiable stuff of suspicion.

Mr. Lewis would never have imagined for a minute that his grandson might be lifting petty cash from the store register if he had not had one of Miss Strangeworth's letters. Miss Chandler, the librarian, and Linda Stewart's parents would have gone unsuspectingly ahead with their lives, never aware of possible evil lurking nearby, if Miss Strangeworth had not sent letters opening their eyes. Miss Strangeworth would have been genuinely shocked if there *had* been anything between Linda Stewart and the Harris boy, but, as long as evil existed unchecked in the world, it was Miss Strangeworth's duty to keep her town alert to it. It was far more sensible for Miss Chandler to wonder what Mr. Shelley's first wife had really died of than to take a chance on not knowing. There were so many wicked people in the world and only one Strangeworth left in the town. Besides, Miss Strangeworth liked writing her letters.

She addressed an envelope to Don Crane after a moment's thought, wondering curiously if he would show the letter to his wife, and using a pink envelope to match the pink paper. Then she addressed a second envelope, green, to Mrs. Harper. Then an idea came to her and she selected a blue sheet and wrote: YOU NEVER KNOW ABOUT DOCTORS. REMEMBER THEY'RE ONLY HUMAN AND NEED MONEY LIKE THE REST OF US. SUPPOSE THE KNIFE SLIPPED ACCIDENTALLY. WOULD DR. BURNS GET HIS FEE AND A LITTLE EXTRA FROM THAT NEPHEW OF YOURS?

She addressed the blue envelope to old Mrs. Foster, who was having an operation next month. She had thought of writing one more letter, to the head of the school board, asking how a chemistry teacher like Billy Moore's father could afford a new convertible, but, all at once, she was tired of writing letters. The three she had done would do for one day. She would write more tomorrow, it was not as though they all had to be done at once.

She had been writing her letters—sometimes two or three every day for a week, sometimes no more than one in a month—for the past year. She never got any answers, of course, because she never signed her name. If she had been asked, she would have said that her name, Adela Strangeworth, a name honored in the town for so many years, did not belong on such trash. The town where she lived had to be kept clean and sweet, but people everywhere were lustful and evil and degraded, and needed to be watched; the world was so large, and there was only one Strangeworth left in it. Miss Strangeworth sighed, locked her desk, and put the letters into her big black leather pocketbook, to be mailed when she took her evening walk.

She broiled her little chop nicely, and she had a sliced tomato and a good cup of tea ready when she sat down to her midday dinner at the table in her dining room, which could be opened to seat twenty-two, with a second table, if necessary, in the hall. Sitting in the warm sunlight that came through the tall windows of the dining room, seeing her roses massed outside, handling the heavy, old silverware and the fine, translucent china, Miss Strangeworth was pleased; she would not have cared to be doing anything else. People must live graciously, after all, she thought, and sipped her tea. Afterward, when her plate and cup and saucer were washed and dried and put back onto the shelves where they belonged, and her silverware was back in the mahogany silver chest, Miss Strangeworth went up to the graceful staircase and into her bedroom, which was the front room overlooking the roses, and had been her mother's and her grandmother's. Their Crown Derby dresser set and furs had been kept here, their fans and silver-backed brushes and their own bowls of roses; Miss Strangeworth kept a bowl of white roses on the bed table.

She drew the shades, took the rose satin spread from the bed, slipped out of her dress and her shoes, and lay down tiredly. She knew that no doorbell or phone would ring; no one in town would dare to disturb Miss Strangeworth during her afternoon nap. She slept, deep in the rich smell of roses.

After her nap she worked in her garden for a little while, sparing herself because of the heat; then she came in to her supper. She ate asparagus from her own garden, with sweet-butter sauce and a soft-boiled egg, and, while she had her supper, she listened to a late-evening news broadcast and then to a program of classical music on her small radio. After her dishes were done and her kitchen set in order, she took up her hat—Miss Strangeworth's hats were proverbial in the town; people believed that she had inherited them from her mother and her grandmother—and, locking the front door of her house behind her, set off on her evening walk, pocketbook under her arms. She nodded to Linda Stewart's father, who was washing his car in the pleasantly cool evening. She thought that he looked troubled.

There was only one place in town where she could mail her letters, and that was the new post office, shiny with red brick and silver letters. Although Miss Strangeworth had never given the matter any particular thought, she had always made a point of mailing her letters very secretly; it would, of course, not have been wise to let anyone see her mail them. Consequently, she timed her walk so she could reach the post office just as darkness was starting to dim the outlines of the trees and the shapes of people's faces, although no one could ever mistake Miss Strangeworth, with her dainty walk and her rustling skirts.

There was always a group of young people around the post office, the very youngest roller-skating upon its driveway, which went all the way around the building and was the only smooth road in town; and the slightly older ones already knowing how to gather in small groups and chatter and laugh and make great, excited plans for going across the street to the sofa shop in a minute or two. Miss Strangeworth had never had any self-consciousness before the children. She did not feel that any of them were staring at her unduly or longing to laugh at her; it would have been most reprehensible for their parents to permit their children to mock Miss Strangeworth of Pleasant Street. Most of the children stood back respectfully as Miss Strangeworth passed, silenced briefly in her presence, and some of the older children greeted her, saying soberly, "Hello, Miss Strangeworth."

Miss Strangeworth smiled at them and quickly went on. It had been a long time since she had known the name of every child in town. The mail slot was in the door of the post office. The children stood away as Miss Strangeworth approached it, seemingly surprised that anyone should want to use the post office after it had been officially closed up for the night and turned over to the children. Miss Strangeworth stood by the door, opening her black pocketbook to take out the letters, and heard a voice which she knew at once to be Linda Stewart's. Poor little Linda was crying again, and Miss Strangeworth listened carefully. This was, after all, her town, and these were her people; if one of them was in trouble she ought to know about it.

"I can't tell you, Dave," Linda was saying—so she *was* talking to the Harris boy, as Miss Strangeworth had supposed—"I just *can't*. It's just *nasty*."

"But why won't your father let me come around anymore? What on earth did I do?"

"I can't tell you. I just wouldn't tell you for *anything*. You've got to have a dirty, dirty mind for things like that."

"But something's happened. You've been crying and crying, and your father is all upset. Why can't I know about it, too? Aren't I like one of the family?"

"Not anymore, Dave, not anymore. You're not to come near our house again; my father said so. He said he'd horsewhip you. That's all I can tell you: You're not to come near our house anymore."

"But I didn't *do* anything."

"Just the same, my father said ..."

Miss Strangeworth sighed and turned away. There was so much evil in people. Even in a charming little town like this one, there was still so much evil in people.

She slipped her letters into the slot, and two of them fell inside. The third caught on the edge and fell outside, onto the ground at Miss Strangeworth's feet. She did not notice it because she was wondering whether a letter to the Harris boy's father might not be of some service in wiping out this potential badness. Wearily Miss Strangeworth turned to go home to her quiet bed in her lovely house, and never heard the Harris boy calling to her to say that she had dropped something.

"Old lady Strangeworth's getting deaf," he said, looking after her and holding in his hand the letter he had picked up.

"Well, who cares?" Linda said. "Who cares anymore, anyway?"

"It's for Don Crane," the Harris boy said, "this letter. She dropped a letter addressed to Don Crane. Might as well take it on over. We pass his house anyway." He laughed. "Maybe it's got a cheque or something in it and he'd be just as glad to get it tonight instead of tomorrow."

"Catch old lady Strangeworth sending anybody a cheque," Linda said. "Throw it in the post office. Why do anyone a favor?" She sniffled. "Doesn't seem to me anybody around here cares about us," she said. "Why should we care about them?"

"I'll take it over anyway," the Harris boy said. "Maybe it's good news for them. Maybe they need something happy tonight, too. Like us."

Sadly, holding hands, they wandered off down the dark street, the Harris boy carrying Miss Strangeworth's pink envelope in his hand.

Miss Strangeworth awakened the next morning with a feeling of intense happiness, and for a minute wondered why, and then remembered that this morning three people would open her letters. Harsh, perhaps, at first, but wickedness was never easily banished, and a clean heart was a scoured heart. She washed her soft old face and brushed her teeth, still sound in spite her seventy-one years, and dressed herself carefully in her sweet, soft clothes and buttoned shoes. Then, coming downstairs and reflecting that perhaps a little waffle would be agreeable for breakfast in the sunny dining room, she found the mail on the hall floor and bent to pick it up. A bill, the morning paper, a letter in a green envelope that looked oddly familiar. Miss Strangeworth stood perfectly still for a minute, looking down at the green envelope with the pencilled printing, and thought: It looks like one of my letters. Was one of my letters sent back? No, because no one would know where to send it. How did this get here?

Miss Strangeworth was a Strangeworth of Pleasant Street. Her hand did not shake as she opened the envelope and unfolded the sheet of green paper inside. She began to cry silently for the wickedness of the world when she read the words: LOOK OUT AT WHAT USED TO BE YOUR ROSES.

RESPONDING PERSONALLY

1. With another student, compare your understandings of the story's title. Does Miss Strangeworth get her "just desserts"? Explain.
2. Is Miss Strangeworth's attitude toward her neighbours common in our society today? What does she not understand?

RESPONDING CRITICALLY

3. What is Miss Strangeworth's motivation in sending her poison pen letters. What is she trying to accomplish?
4. This story is about the circularity of evil, that "what goes around, comes around." What mistake does the protagonist make? Why does she get a nasty letter herself at the end? How will her life and standing likely change in the community?
5. What is the purpose of the setting and atmosphere at the beginning of the story? How does the mood change at the end of the story?
6. In a paragraph, explain the symbolism of the roses and characters' names in the story.

RESPONDING CREATIVELY

7. Compose a ballad about Miss Strangeworth of Pleasant Street. Share it with others.
8. Write a letter of apology from Miss Strangeworth to one of the people she insulted or hurt.

PROBLEM-SOLVING/DECISION-MAKING

9. Imagine that concerned citizens in the story get together to decide what they should do about Miss Strangeworth. As a member of the community, write a persuasive speech you would give at the meeting.

Walter Van Tilburg Clark
The Portable Phonograph

The red sunset, with narrow, black cloud strips like threats across it, lay on the curved horizon of the prairie. The air was still and cold, and in it settled the mute darkness and greater cold of night. High in the air there was wind, for through the veil of the dusk the clouds could be seen gliding rapidly south and changing shapes. A queer sensation of torment, of two-sided, unpredictable nature, arose from the stillness of the earth air beneath the violence of the upper air. Out of the sunset, through the dead, matted grass and isolated weed stalks of the prairie, crept the narrow and deeply rutted remains of a road. In the road, in places, there were crusts of shallow, brittle ice. There were little islands of an old oiled pavement in the road, too, but most of it was mud, now frozen rigid. The frozen mud still bore the toothed impress of great tanks, and a wanderer on the neighboring undulations might have stumbled, in this light, into large, partially filled-in and weed-grown cavities, their banks channelled and beginning to spread into badlands. These pits were such as might have been made by falling meteors, but they were not. They were the scars of gigantic bombs, their rawness already made a little natural by rain, seed, and time. Along the road, there were rakish remnants of fence. There was also, just visible, one portion of tangled and multiple barbed wire still erect, behind which was a shelving ditch with small caves, now very quiet and empty, at intervals in its back wall. Otherwise, there was no structure or remnant of a structure visible over the dome of the darkling earth, but only, in sheltered hollows, the darker shadows of young trees trying again.

Under the withering arch of the high wind, a V of wild geese fled south. The rush of their pinions sounded briefly, and the faint, plaintive notes of their expeditionary talk. Then they left a still greater vacancy. There was the smell and the expectation of snow, as there is likely to be when the wild geese fly south. From the remote distance, towards the red sky, came faintly the protracted howl and quick yap-yap of a prairie wolf.

North of the road perhaps a hundred yards, lay the parallel and deeply intrenched course of a small creek, lined with leafless alders and willows. The creek was already silent under ice. In the bank above it was dug a sort of cell, with a single opening, like the mouth of a mine tunnel. Within the cell there was a little red of fire, which showed dully through the opening, like a reflection or a deception of the imagination. The light came from the chary burning of four blocks of poorly aged peat, which gave off a petty warmth and much acrid smoke. But the precious remnants of wood, old fence posts and timbers from the long-deserted dugouts, had to be saved for the real cold, for the time when a man's breath blew white, the moisture in his nostrils stiffened at once when he stepped out, and the expansive blizzards paraded for days over the vast open, swirling and settling and thickening, till the dawn of the cleared day when the sky was thin blue-green and the terrible cold, in which a man could not live for three hours unwarmed, lay over the uniformly drifted swell of the plain.

Around the smoldering peat, four men were seated cross-legged. Behind them, traversed by their shadows, was the earth bench, with two old and dirty army blankets, where the owner of the cell slept. In a niche in the opposite wall were a few tin utensils which caught the glint of the coals. The host was rewrapping in a piece of daubed burlap four fine, leather-bound books. He worked slowly and very carefully, and at last tied the bundle securely with a piece of grass-woven cord. The other three looked intently upon the process, as if a great significance lay in it. As the host tied the cord, he spoke. He was an old man, his long, matted beard and hair grey to nearly white. The shadows made his brows and cheekbones appear gnarled, his eyes and cheeks deeply sunken. His big hands, rough with frost and swollen by rheumatism, were awkward but gentle at their task. He was like a prehistoric priest performing a fateful ceremonial rite. Also his voice had in it a suitable quality of deep, reverent despair, yet perhaps at the moment, a sharpness of selfish satisfaction.

"When I perceived what was happening," he said, "I told myself, 'It is the end. I cannot take much; I will take these.'

"Perhaps I was impractical," he continued. "But for myself, I do not regret, and what do we know of those who will come after us? We are the doddering remnant of a race of mechanical fools. I have saved what I love; the soul of what was good in us is here; perhaps the new ones will make a strong enough beginning not to fall behind when they become clever."

He rose with slow pain and placed the wrapped volumes in the niche with his utensils. The others watched him with the same ritualistic gaze.

"Shakespeare, the Bible, *Moby Dick*, the *Divine Comedy*," one of them said softly. "You might have done worse, much worse."

"You will have a little soul left until you die," said another harshly. "That is more than is true of us. My brain becomes thick, like my hands." He held the big, battered hands, with their black nails, in the glow to be seen.

"I want paper to write on," he said. "And there is none."

The fourth man said nothing. He sat in the shadow farthest from the fire, and sometimes his body jerked in its rags from the cold. Although he was still young, he was sick and coughed often. Writing implied a greater future than he now felt able to consider.

The old man seated himself laboriously, and reached out, groaning at the movement, to put another block of peat on the fire. With bowed heads and averted eyes, his three guests acknowledged his magnanimity.

"We thank you, Dr. Jenkins, for the reading," said the man who had named the books.

They seemed then to be waiting for something. Dr. Jenkins understood, but was loathe to comply. In an ordinary moment he would have said nothing. But the words of *The Tempest* which he had been reading, and the religious attention of the three, made this an unusual occasion.

"You wish to hear the phonograph," he said grudgingly.

The two middle-aged men stared into the fire, unable to formulate and expose the enormity of their desire.

The young man, however, said anxiously, between suppressed coughs, "Oh, please," like an excited child.

The old man rose again in his difficult way, and went to the back of the cell. He returned and placed tenderly upon the packed floor, where the firelight might fall upon it, an old portable phonograph in a black case. He smoothed the top with his hand, and then opened it. The lovely green felt-covered disk became visible.

"I have been using thorns as needles," he said. "But tonight, because we have a musician among us," he bent his head to the young man, almost invisible in the shadow, "I will use a steel needle. There are only three left."

The two middle-aged men stared at him in speechless adoration. The one with the big hands, who wanted to write, moved his lips, but the whisper was not audible.

"Oh, don't!" cried the young man, as if he were hurt. "The thorns will do beautifully."

"No," the old man said. "I have become accustomed to the thorns, but they are not really good. For you, my young friend, we will have good music tonight.

"After all," he added generously, and beginning to wind the phonograph, which creaked, "they can't last forever."

"No, nor we," the man who needed to write said harshly. "The needle, by all means."

"Oh, thanks," said the young man. "Thanks," he said again in a low, excited voice, and then stifled his coughing with a bowed head.

"The records, though," said the old man when he had finished winding, "are a different matter. Already they are very worn. I do not play them more than once a week. One, once a week, that is what I allow myself.

"More than a week I cannot stand it; not to hear them," he apologized.

"No, how could you," cried the young man. "And with them here like this."

"A man can stand anything," said the man who wanted to write, in his harsh, antagonistic voice.

"Please, the music," said the young man.

"Only the one," said the old man. "In the long run, we will remember more that way."

He had a dozen records with luxuriant gold and red seals. Even in that light the others could see that the threads of the records were becoming worn. Slowly he read out the titles, and the tremendous, dead names of the composers and the artists and the orchestras. The three worked upon the names in their minds, carefully. It was difficult to select from such a wealth what they would at once most like to remember. Finally, the man who wanted to write named Gershwin's *New York*.

"Oh, no!" cried the sick young man, and then could say nothing more because he had to cough. The others understood him, and the harsh man withdrew his selection and waited for the musician to choose.

The musician begged Dr. Jenkins to read the titles again, very slowly, so that he could remember the sounds. While they were read, he lay back against the wall, his eyes closed, his thin hard hand pulling at his light beard, and listened to the voices and the orchestras and the single instruments in his mind.

When the reading was done he spoke despairingly. "I have forgotten," he complained; "I cannot hear them clearly.

"There are things missing," he explained.

"I know," said Dr. Jenkins. "I thought that I knew all of Shelley by heart. I should have brought Shelley."

"That's more soul than we can use," said the harsh man. "*Moby Dick* is better."

"By God, we can understand that," he emphasized.

The Doctor nodded.

"Still," said the man who had admired the books, "we need the absolute if we are to keep a grasp on anything.

"Anything but these sticks and peat clods and rabbit snares," he said bitterly.

"Shelley desired an ultimate absolute," said the harsh man. "It's too much," he said. "It's no good; no earthly good."

The musician selected a Debussy nocturne. The others considered and approved. They rose to their knees to watch the Doctor prepare for the playing, so that they appeared to be actually in an attitude of worship. The peat glow showed the thinness of their bearded faces, and the deep lines in them, and revealed the condition of their garments. The other two continued to kneel as the old man carefully lowered the needle onto the spinning disk, but the musician suddenly drew back against the wall again, with his knees up, and buried his face in his hands.

At the first notes of the piano, the listeners were startled. They stared at each other. Even the musician lifted his head in amazement, but then quickly bowed it again, strainingly, as if he were suffering from a pain he might not be able to endure. They were all listening deeply, without movement. The wet, blue-green notes tinkled forth from the old machine, and were individual, delectable presences in the cell. The individual delectable presences swept into a sudden tide of unbearably beautiful dissonance, and then continued fully the swelling and ebbing of that tide, the dissonant inpourings, and the resolutions, and the diminishings, and the little, quiet wavelets of interlude lapping between. Every sound was piercing and singularly sweet. In all the men except the musician, there occurred rapid sequences of tragically heightened recollection. He heard nothing but what was there. At the final, whispering disappearance, but moving quietly so that the others would not hear him and look at him, he let his head fall back in agony, as if it were drawn there by the hair, and clenched the fingers of one hand over his teeth. He sat that way while the others were silent, and until they began to breathe again normally. His drawn-up legs were trembling violently.

Quickly Dr. Jenkins lifted the needle off, to save it and not to spoil the recollection with scraping. When he had stopped the whirling of the sacred disk, he courteously left the phonograph open and by the fire in sight.

The others, however, understood. The musician rose last, but then abruptly, and went quickly out at the door without saying anything. The others stopped at the door and gave their thanks in low voices. The Doctor nodded magnificently.

"Come again," he invited, "in a week. We will have the *New York*."

When the two had gone together, out towards the rimed road, he stood in the entrance, peering and listening. At first, there was only the resonant boom of the wind overhead, and then far over the dome of the dead, dark plain, the wolf cry lamenting. In the rifts of clouds the Doctor saw four stars flying. It impressed the Doctor that one of them had just been obscured by the beginning of a flying cloud at the very moment he heard what he had been listening for, a sound of suppressed coughing. It was not nearby, however. He believed that down against the pale alders he could see the moving shadow.

With nervous hands he lowered the piece of canvas which served as a door, and pegged it at the bottom. Then quickly and quietly, looking at the piece of canvas frequently, he slipped the records into the case, snapped the lid shut, and carried the phonograph to his couch. There, pausing often to stare at the canvas and listen, he dug earth from the wall and disclosed a piece of board. Behind this there was a deep hole in the wall, into which he put the phonograph. After a moment's consideration, he went over and reached down his bundle of books and inserted it also. Then, guardedly, he once more sealed up the hole with the board and the earth. He also changed his blankets, and the grass-stuffed sack which served as a pillow, so that he could lie facing the entrance. After carefully placing two more blocks of peat upon the fire, he stood for a long time watching the stretched canvas, but it seemed to billow naturally with the first gusts of a lowering wind. At last he prayed, and got in under his blankets, and closed his smoke-smarting eyes. On the inside of the bed, next to the wall, he could feel with his hands, the comfortable piece of lead pipe.

RESPONDING PERSONALLY

1. With a partner, decide what is the atmosphere of the story, the mood of the men, and your own mood as the reader. Why do the characters feel as they do?
2. In your response journal, describe the way a piece of music of your choice makes you feel.

RESPONDING CRITICALLY

3. When is the story set? What has happened recently? Support your opinion with details from the story.
4. What is the purpose of the men's meeting? Why does the author compare the unwrapping of the book bundle to a ceremonial rite?
5. What is the significance of the books and music that were saved? What do they symbolize?
6. Why is Dr. Jenkins clutching a lead pipe at the end of the story? What do you think might happen next? Using references from the story, compare ideas in a group.

RESPONDING CREATIVELY

7. Write two contrasting diary entries, one for Dr. Jenkins and another for the musician.
8. On audiotape, dub a favourite song or instrumental piece. In a paragraph, explain its meaning and value to you.

PROBLEM-SOLVING/DECISION-MAKING

9. If you had a choice of three works of art (books, records, or videos) you could preserve for posterity, what would they be? In three paragraphs (one for each work), describe your reasons for preserving these particular works. Be sure to mention the merits and strengths of each work of art.

Coming of Age

Growing up and maturing is a significant part of our lives and, not surprisingly, this stage of life becomes a focal point or theme for many writers. The gaining of maturity, the learning about how the world works, and the maintaining of relationships are all a necessary part of a person's growing up.

The first story, "Boys and Girls," provides a perceptive and moving account of a girl's awakening from childhood to maturity. The girl initially is a free spirit and has dreams about doing significant things with her life. Slowly though, she finds herself pressured by her parents and her circumstances to let go of her dreams, and to become merely the narrowly-defined daughter they want and expect.

The second story, "Fear of the Sea," originates from the West Indies. Ossie, the main character, has never been to the sea. Eventually he will get there, even though tragedy looms in the background. Often memorable defining moments can make young people older, sadder, yet possibly wiser in their understanding of life's experiences.

The third story, "The Metaphor," follows a narrator from junior to senior high school. The girl loves Miss Hancock in grade 7, because of her teacher's attention and caring. But by grade 10, the narrator is caught between the peer pressure of her classmates and her former feelings for her once-beloved teacher. Emotionally torn, the girl wrestles with the callousness of those around her, producing the internal conflict of this story.

The stories in this unit reveal much about the typical rites of passage for young people. Not surprisingly, each of the characters experiences an epiphany that marks their transition from the innocence of youth to the problems of adulthood.

Alice Munro
Boys and Girls

My father was a fox farmer. That is, he raised silver foxes, in pens; and in the fall and early winter, when their fur was prime, he killed them and skinned them and sold their pelts to the Hudson's Bay Company or the Montreal Fur Traders. These companies supplied us with heroic calendars to hang, one on each side of the kitchen door. Against a background of cold blue sky and black pine forests and treacherous northern rivers, plumed adventurers planted the flags of England or of France; magnificent savages bent their backs to the portage.

For several weeks before Christmas, my father worked after supper in the cellar of our house. The cellar was white-washed, and lit by a hundred-watt bulb over the work-table. My brother Laird and I sat on the top step and watched. My father removed the pelt inside-out from the body of the fox, which looked surprisingly small, mean and rat-like, deprived of its arrogant weight of fur. The naked, slippery bodies were collected in a sack and buried at the dump. One time the hired man, Henry Bailey, had taken a swipe at me with this sack, saying, "Christmas present!" My mother thought that was not funny. In fact, she disliked the whole pelting operation—that was what the killing, skinning, and preparation of the furs was called—and wished it did not have to take place in the house. There was the smell. After the pelt had been stretched inside-out on a long board, my father scraped away delicately, removing the little clotted webs of blood vessels, the bubbles of fat; the smell of blood and animal fat, with the strong primitive odor of the fox itself, penetrated all parts of the house. I found it reassuringly seasonal, like the smell of oranges and pine needles.

Henry Bailey suffered from bronchial troubles. He would cough and cough until his narrow face turned scarlet, and his light blue, derisive eyes filled up with tears; then he took the lid off the stove, and, standing well back, shot out a great clot of phlegm—hsss—straight into the heart of the flames. We admired him for this performance and for his ability to make his stomach growl at will, and for his laughter, which was full of high whistlings and gurglings and involved the whole faulty machinery of his chest. It was sometimes hard to tell what he was laughing at, and always possible that it might be us.

After we had been sent to bed, we could still smell fox and still hear Henry's laugh, but these things, reminders of the warm, safe, brightly lit downstairs world, seemed lost and diminished, floating on the stale cold air upstairs. We were afraid at night in the winter. We were not afraid of *outside* though this was the time of year when snowdrifts curled around our house like sleeping whales and the wind harassed us all night, coming up from the buried fields, the frozen swamp, with its old bugbear chorus of threats and misery. We were afraid of *inside*, the room where we slept. At this time, the upstairs of our house was not finished. A brick chimney went up one wall. In the middle of the floor was a square hole, with a wooden railing around it; that was where the stairs came up. On the other side of the stairwell were the things that nobody had any use for any more—a soldiery roll of linoleum, standing on end, a wicker baby carriage, a fern basket, china jugs and basins with cracks in them, a picture of the Battle of Balaclava, very sad to look at. I had told Laird, as soon as he was old enough to understand such things, that bats and skeletons lived over there; whenever a man escaped from the country jail, twenty miles away, I imagined that he had somehow let himself in the window and was hiding behind the linoleum. But we had rules to keep us safe. When the light was on, we were safe as long as we did not step off the square of worn carpet which defined our bedroom space; when the light was off, no place was safe but the beds themselves. I had to turn out the light kneeling on the end of my bed, and stretching as far as I could to reach the cord.

In the dark we lay on our beds, our narrow life rafts, and fixed our eyes on the faint light coming up the stairwell, and sang songs. Laird sang "Jingle Bells," which he would sing any time, whether it was Christmas or not, and I sang "Danny Boy." I loved the sound of my own voice, frail and supplicating, rising in the dark. We could make out the tall frosted shapes of the windows now, gloomy and white. When I came to the part, *When I am dead, as dead I well may be*—a fit of shivering caused not by the cold sheets but by pleasurable emotion almost silenced me. *You'll kneel and say, an Ave there above me*—What was an Ave? Every day I forgot to find out.

Laird went straight from singing to sleep. I could hear his long, satisfied bubbly breaths. Now for the time that remained to me, the most perfectly private and perhaps the best time of the whole day, I arranged myself tightly under the covers and went on with one of the stories I was telling myself from night to night. These stories were about myself, when I had grown a little older; they took place in a world that was recognizably mine, yet one that presented opportunities for courage, boldness and self-sacrifice, as mine never did. I rescued people from a bombed building (it discouraged me that the real war had gone on so far away from Jubilee). I shot two rabid wolves who were menacing the school-yard (the teachers cowered terrified at my back). I rode a fine horse spiritedly down the main street of Jubilee, acknowledging the townspeople's gratitude for some yet-to-be-worked-out piece of heroism (nobody ever rode a horse there, except King Billy in the Orangemen's Day parade). There was always riding and shooting in these stories, though I had only been on a horse twice—bareback because we did not own a saddle—and the second time I had slid right around and dropped under the horse's feet; it had stepped placidly over me. I was really learning to shoot, but I could not hit anything yet, not even tin cans on fence posts.

Alive, the foxes inhabited a world my father made for them. It was surrounded by a high guard fence, like a medieval town, with a gate that was padlocked at night. Along the streets of this town were ranged large, sturdy pens. Each of them had a real door that a man could go through, a wooden ramp along the wire, for the foxes to run up and down on, and a kennel—something like a clothes chest with airholes—where they slept and stayed in winter and had their young. There were feeding and watering dishes attached to the wire in such a way that they could be emptied and cleaned from the outside. The dishes were made of old tin cans, and the ramps and kennels of odds and ends of old lumber. Everything was tidy and ingenious; my father was tirelessly inventive and his favorite book in the world was *Robinson Crusoe*. He had fitted a tin drum on a wheelbarrow, for bringing water down to the pens. This was my job in summer, when the foxes had to have water twice a day. Between nine and ten o'clock in the morning, and again after supper, I filled the drum at the pump and trundled it down through the barnyard to the pens, where I parked it, and filled my watering can and went along the streets. Laird came too, with his little cream and green gardening can, filled too full and knocking against his legs and slopping water on his canvas shoes. I had the real watering can, my father's though I could only carry it three-quarters full.

The foxes all had names, which were printed on a tin plate and hung beside their doors. They were not named when they were born, but when they survived the first year's pelting and were added to the breeding stock. Those my father had named were called names like Prince, Bob, Wally, and Betty. Those I had named were called Star or Turk, or Maureen or Diana. Laird named one Maud after a hired girl we had when he was little, one Harold after a boy at school, and one Mexico, he did not say why.

Naming them did not make pets out of them, or anything like it. Nobody but my father ever went into the pens, and he had twice had blood-poisoning from bites. When I was bringing them their water they prowled up and down on the paths they had made inside their pens, barking seldom—they saved that for nighttime, when they might get up a chorus of community frenzy—but always watching me, their eyes burning, clear gold, in their pointed, malevolent faces. They were beautiful for their delicate legs and heavy, aristocratic tails and the bright fur sprinkled on dark down their backs—which gave them their name—but especially for their faces, drawn exquisitely sharp in pure hostility, and their golden eyes.

Besides carrying water, I helped my father when he cut the long grass, and the lamb's quarter and flowering money-musk, that grew between the pens. He cut with the scythe and I raked into piles. Then he took a pitchfork and threw fresh-cut grass all over the top of the pens, to keep the foxes cooler and shade their coats, which were browned by too much sun. My father did not talk to me unless it was about the job we were doing. In this he was quite different from my mother, who, if she was feeling cheerful, would tell me all sorts of things—the name of a dog she had had when she was a little girl, the names of boys she had gone out with later on when she was grown up, and what certain dresses of hers had looked like—she could not imagine now what had become of them. Whatever thoughts and stories my father had were private, and I was shy of him and would never ask him questions. Nevertheless, I worked willingly under his eyes, and with a feeling of pride. One time a feed salesman came down into the pens to talk to him and my father said, "Like to have you meet my new hired man." I turned away and raked furiously, red in the face with pleasure.

"Could of fooled me," said the salesman. "I thought it was only a girl."

After the grass was cut, it seemed suddenly much later in the year. I walked on stubble in the earlier evening, aware of the reddening skies, the entering silences, of fall. When I wheeled the tank out of the gate and put the padlock on, it was almost dark. One night at this time, I saw my mother and father standing talking on the little rise of ground we called the gangway, in front of the barn. My father had just come from the meathouse; he had his stiff bloody apron on, and a pail of cut-up meat in his hand.

It was an odd thing to see my mother down at the barn. She did not often come out of the house unless it was to do something—hang out the wash or dig potatoes in the garden. She looked out of place, with her bare lumpy legs, not touched by the sun, her apron still on and damp across the stomach from the supper dishes. Her hair was tied up in a kerchief, wisps of it falling out. She would tie her hair up like this in the morning, saying she did not have time to do it properly, and it would stay tied up all day. It was true, too; she really did not have time. These days our back porch was piled with baskets of peaches and grapes and pears, bought in town, and onions and tomatoes and cucumbers grown at home, all waiting to be made into jelly and jam and preserves, pickles and chili sauce. In the kitchen, there was a fire in the stove all day, jars clinked in boiling water, sometimes a cheesecloth bag was strung on a pole between two chairs, straining blue-black grape pulp for jelly. I was given jobs to do and I would sit at the table peeling peaches that had been soaked in the hot water, or cutting up onions, my eyes smarting and streaming. As soon as I was done, I ran out of the house, trying to get out of earshot before my mother thought of what she wanted me to do next. I hated the hot dark kitchen in summer, the green blinds and the flypapers, the same old oilcloth table and wavy mirror and bumpy linoleum. My mother was too tired and preoccupied to talk to me; she had no heart to tell about the Normal School Graduation Dance; sweat trickled over her face and she was always counting under her breath, pointing at jars, dumping cups of sugar. It seemed to me that work in the house was endless, dreary, and peculiarly depressing; work done out of doors, and in my father's service, was ritualistically important.

I wheeled the tank up to the barn, where it was kept, and I heard my mother saying, "Wait till Laird gets a little bigger, then you'll have a real help."

What my father said I did not hear. I was pleased by the way he stood listening, politely as he would to a salesman or a stranger, but with an air of wanting to get on with his real work. I felt my mother had no business down here and I wanted him to feel the same way. What did she mean about Laird? He was no help to anybody. Where was he now? Swinging himself sick on the swing, going around in circles, or trying to catch caterpillars. He never once stayed with me till I was finished.

"And then I can use her more in the house," I heard my mother say. She had a dead-quiet, regretful way of talking about me that always made me uneasy. "I just get my back turned and she runs off. It's not like I had a girl in the family at all."

I went and sat on a feed bag in the corner of the barn, not wanting to appear when this conversation was going on. My mother, I felt, was not to be trusted. She was kinder than my father and more easily fooled, but you could not depend on her, and the real reasons for the things she said and did were not to be known. She loved me, and she sat up late at night making a dress of the difficult style I wanted, for me to wear when school started, but she was also my enemy. She was always plotting. She was plotting now to get me to stay in the house more, although she knew I hated it (*because* she knew I hated it) and keep me from working for my father. It seemed to me she would do this simply out of perversity, and to try her power. It did not occur to me that she could be lonely, or jealous. No grown-up could be; they were too fortunate. I sat and kicked my heels monotonously against a feedbag, raising dust, and did not come out till she had gone.

At any rate, I did not expect my father to pay any attention to what she said. Who could imagine Laird doing my work—Laird remembering the padlock and cleaning out the watering-dishes with a leaf on the end of a stick, or even wheeling the tank without it tumbling over? It showed how little my mother knew about the way things really were.

I have forgotten to say what the foxes were fed. My father's bloody apron reminded me. They were fed horsemeat. At this time, most farmers still kept horses, and when a horse got too old to work, or broke a leg or got down and would not get up, as they sometimes did, the owner would call my father, and he and Henry went out to the farm in the truck. Usually they shot and butchered the horse there, paying the farmer from five to twelve dollars. If they had already too much meat on hand, they would bring the horse back alive, and keep it for a few days or weeks in our stable, until the meat was needed. After the war, the farmers were buying tractors and gradually getting rid of horses altogether, so it sometimes happened that we got a good healthy horse, that there was just no use for any more. If this happened in the winter, we might keep the horse in our stable till spring, for we had plenty of hay and if there was a lot of snow—and the plow did not always get our road cleared—it was convenient to be able to go to town with a horse and cutter.

The winter I was eleven years old we had two horses in the stable. We did not know what names they had had before, so we called them Mack and Flora. Mack was an old black workhorse, sooty and indifferent. Flora was a sorrel mare, a driver. We took them both out in the cutter. Mack was slow and easy to handle. Flora was given to fits of violent alarm, veering at cars and even at other horses, but we loved her speed and high-stepping, her general air of gallantry and abandon. On Saturdays, we went down to the stable and as soon as we opened the door on its cosy, animal-smelling darkness Flora threw up her head, rolled her eyes, whinnied despairingly and pulled herself through a crisis of nerves on the spot. It was not safe to go into her stall, she would kick.

This winter also I began to hear a great deal more on the theme my mother had sounded when she had been talking in front of the barn. I no longer felt safe. It seemed that in the minds of the people around me there was a steady undercurrent of thought, not to be deflected, on this one subject. The word *girl* had formerly seemed to me innocent and unburdened, like the word *child*: now it appeared that it was no such thing. A girl was not, as I had supposed, simply what I was; it was what I had become. It was a definition, always touched with emphasis, with reproach and disappointment. Also it was a joke on me. Once Laird and I were fighting, and for the first time ever I had to use all my strength against him; even so, he caught and pinned my arm for a moment, really hurting me. Henry saw this, and laughed, saying,

"Oh, that there Laird's gonna show you, one of these days!" Laird was getting a lot bigger. But I was getting bigger too.

My grandmother came to stay with us for a few weeks and I heard other things. "Girls don't slam doors like that." "Girls keep their knees together when they sit down." And worse still, when I asked some questions, "That's none of girls' business." I continued to slam the doors and sit as awkwardly as possible, thinking that by such measures I kept myself free.

When spring came, the horses were let out in the barnyard. Mack stood against the barn wall trying to scratch his neck and haunches, but Flora trotted up and down and reared at the fences, clattering her hooves against the rails. Snow drifts dwindled quickly, revealing the hard grey and brown earth, the familiar rise and fall of the ground, plain and bare after the fantastic landscape of winter. There was a great feeling of opening-out, of release. We just wore rubbers now, over our shoes; our feet felt ridiculously light. One Saturday we went out to the stable and found all the doors open, letting in the unaccustomed sunlight and fresh air. Henry was there, just idling around looking at his collection of calendars which were tacked up behind the stalls in a part of the stable my mother had probably never seen.

"Come to say goodbye to your old friend Mack?" Henry said. "Here, you give him a taste of oats." He poured some oats into Laird's cupped hand and Laird went to feed Mack. Mack's teeth were in bad shape. He ate very slowly, patiently shifting the oats around in his mouth, trying to find a stump of a molar to grind it on. "Poor old Mack," said Henry, mournfully. "When a horse's teeth's gone, he's gone. That's about the way."

"Are you going to shoot him today?" I said. Mack and Flora had been in the stable so long I had almost forgotten they were going to be shot.

Henry didn't answer me. Instead, he started to sing in a high, trembly, mocking-sorrowful voice, *Oh, there's no more work, for poor Uncle Ned, he's gone where the good darkies go.* Mack's thick, blackish tongue worked diligently at Laird's hand. I went out before the song ended and sat down on the gangway.

I had never seen them shoot a horse, but I knew where it was done. Last summer Laird and I had come upon a horse's entrails before they were buried. We had thought it was a big black snake, coiled up in the sun. That was around in the field that ran up beside the barn. I thought that if we went inside the barn, and found a wide crack or a knothole to look through, we would be able to see them do it. It was not something I wanted to see; just the same, if a thing really happened, it was better to see it, and know.

My father came down from the house, carrying the gun.

"What are you doing here?" he said.

"Nothing."

"Go on up and play around the house."

He sent Laird out of the stable. I said to Laird, "Do you want to see them shoot Mack?" and without waiting for an answer led him around to the front door of the barn, opened it carefully, and went in. "Be quiet or they'll hear us," I said. We could hear Henry and my father talking in the stable, then the heavy, shuffling steps of Mack being backed out of his stall.

In the loft it was cold and dark. Thin, crisscrossed beams of sunlight fell through the cracks. The hay was low. It was a rolling country, hills and hollows, slipping under our feet. About four feet up was a beam going around the walls. We piled hay up in one corner and I boosted Laird up and hoisted myself. The beam was not very wide; we crept along it with our hands flat on the barn walls. There were plenty of knotholes, and I found one that gave me the view I wanted—a corner of the barnyard, the gate, part of the field. Laird did not have a knothole and began to complain.

I showed him a widened crack between two boards. "Be quiet and wait. If they hear you, you'll get us in trouble."

My father came in sight carrying the gun. Henry was leading Mack by the halter. He dropped it and took out his cigarette papers and tobacco; he rolled cigarettes for my father and himself. While this was going on, Mack nosed around in the old, dead grass along the fence. Then my father opened the gate and they took Mack through. Henry led Mack away from the path to a patch of ground and they talked together, not loud enough for us to hear. Mack again began searching for a mouthful of fresh grass, which was not to be found. My father walked away in a straight line, and stopped short at a distance which seemed to suit him. Henry was walking away from Mack too, but sideways, still negligently holding on to the halter. My father raised the gun and Mack looked up as if he had noticed something and my father shot him.

Mack did not collapse at once, but swayed, lurched sideways and fell, first on his side, then he rolled over on his back and, amazingly kicked his legs for a few seconds in the air. At this Henry laughed, as if Mack had done a trick for him. Laird, who had drawn a long, groaning breath of surprise when the shot was fired, said out loud, "He's not dead." And it seemed to me it might be true. But his legs stopped, he rolled on his side again, his muscles quivered and sank. The two men walked over and looked at him in a businesslike way; they bent down and examined his forehead where the bullet had gone in, and now I saw his blood on the brown grass.

"Now they just skin him and cut him up," I said. "Let's go." My legs were a little shaky and I jumped gratefully down into the hay. "Now you've seen how they shoot a horse," I said in a congratulatory way, as if I had seen it many times before. "Let's see if any barn cat's had kittens in the hay." Laird jumped. He seemed young and obedient again. Suddenly I remembered how, when he was little, I had brought him into the barn and told him to climb the ladder to the top beam. That was in the spring, too, when the hay was low. I had done it out of a need for excitement, a desire for something to happen so that I could tell about it. He was wearing a little bulky brown-and-white checked coat, made down from one of mine. He went all the way up, just as I had told him, and sat down on the top beam with the hay far below him on one side, and barn floor and some old machinery on the other. Then I ran screaming to my father, "Laird's up on the top beam!" My father came, my mother came, my father went up the ladder talking

very quietly and brought Laird down under his arm, at which my
mother leaned against the ladder and began to cry. They said to
me, "Why weren't you watching him?" but nobody ever knew the
truth. Laird did not know enough to tell. But whenever I saw the
brown-and-white checked coat hanging in the closet, or at the
bottom of the rag bag, which was where it ended up, I felt a
weight in my stomach, the sadness of unexorcised guilt.

I looked at Laird who did not even remember this, and I did
not like the look on his thin, winter-pale face. His expression was
not frightened or upset, but remote, concentrating. "Listen," I
said, in an unusually bright and friendly voice, "you aren't going
to tell, are you?"

"No," he said absently.

"Promise."

"Promise," he said. I grabbed the hand behind his back to
make sure he was not crossing his fingers. Even so, he might have
a nightmare; it might come out that way. I decided I had better
work hard to get all thoughts of what he had seen out of his
mind—which, it seemed to me, could not hold very many things
at a time. I got some money I had saved and that afternoon we
went into Jubilee and saw a show, with Judy Canova, at which we
both laughed a great deal. After that I thought it would be all
right.

Two weeks later I knew they were going to shoot Flora. I knew
from the night before, when I heard my mother ask if the hay was
holding out all right, and my father said, "Well, after tomorrow
there'll just be the cow, and we should be able to put her out to
grass in another week." So I knew it was Flora's turn in the morning.

This time I didn't think of watching it. That was something to
see just one time. I had not thought about it very often since, but
sometimes when I was busy, working at school, or standing in
front of the mirror combing my hair and wondering if I would be
pretty when I grew up, the whole scene would flash into my
mind: I would see the easy, practised way my father raised the
gun, and heard Henry laughing when Mack kicked his legs in the

air. I did not have any great feeling of horror and opposition, such as a city child might have had; I was too used to seeing the death of animals as a necessity by which we lived. Yet I felt a little ashamed and there was a new wariness, a sense of holding-off, in my attitude to my father and his work.

It was a fine day, and we were going around the yard picking up tree branches that had been torn off in winter storms. This was something we had been told to do, and also we wanted to use them to make a teepee. We heard Flora whinny, and then my father's voice and Henry's shouting, and we ran down to the barnyard to see what was going on.

The stable door was open. Henry had just brought Flora out, and she had broken away from him. She was running free in the barnyard, from one end to the other. We climbed up on the fence. It was exciting to see her running, whinnying, going up on her hind legs, prancing and threatening like a horse in a Western move, an unbroken ranch horse, though she was just an old driver, an old sorrel mare. My father and Henry ran after her and tried to grab the dangling halter. They tried to work her into a corner, and they had almost succeeded when she made a run between them, wild-eyed, and disappeared around the corner of the barn. We heard the rails clatter down as she got over the fence, and Henry called, "She's into the field now!"

That meant she was in the long L-shaped field that ran up by the house. If she got around the centre, heading toward the lane, the gate was open; the truck had been driven into the field this morning. My father shouted to me, because I was on the other side of the fence, nearest the lane, "Go shut the gate!"

I could run very fast. I ran across the garden, past the tree where our swing was hung, and jumped across a ditch into the lane. There was the open gate. She had not got out, I could not see her up on the road; she must have run to the other end of the field. The gate was heavy. I lifted it out of the gravel and carried it across the roadway. I had it half-way across when she came in sight, galloping straight towards me. There was just time to get the chain on. Laird came scrambling through the ditch to help me.

Instead of shutting the gate, I opened it as wide as I could. I did not make any decision to do this, it was just what I did. Flora never slowed down; she galloped straight past me, and Laird jumped up and down, yelling, "Shut it, shut it!" even after it was too late. My father and Henry appeared in the field a moment too late to see what I had done. They only saw Flora heading for the township road. They would think I had not got there in time.

They did not waste any time asking about it. They went back to the barn and got the gun and the knives they used, and put these in the truck; then they turned the truck around and came bouncing up the field toward us. Laird called to them, "Let me go too, let me go too!" and Henry stopped the truck and they took him in. I shut the gate after they were all gone.

I supposed Laird would tell. I wondered what would happen to me. I had never disobeyed my father before, and I could not understand why I had done it. Flora would not really get away. They would catch up with her in the truck. Or if they did not catch her this morning somebody would see her and telephone us this afternoon or tomorrow. There was no wild country here for her to run to, only farms. What was more, my father had paid for her, we needed the meat to feed the foxes, we needed the foxes to make our living. All I had done was make more work for my father who worked hard enough already. And when my father found out about it he was not going to trust me any more; he would know that I was not entirely on his side. I was on Flora's side, and that made me no use to anybody, not even to her. Just the same, I did not regret it; when she came running at me and I held the gate open, that was the only thing I could do.

I went back to the house, and my mother said, "What's all the commotion?" I told her that Flora had kicked down the fence and got away. "Your poor father," she said, "now he'll have to go chasing over the countryside. Well, there isn't any use planning dinner before one." She put up the ironing board. I wanted to tell her, but thought better of it and went upstairs and sat on my bed.

Lately, I had been trying to make my part of the room fancy, spreading the bed with old lace curtains, and fixing myself a dressing table with some leftovers of cretonne for a skirt. I planned to put up some kind of barricade between my bed and Laird's, to keep my section separate from his. In the sunlight, the lace curtains were just dusty rags. We did not sing at night any more. One night when I was singing Laird said, "You sound silly," and I went right on but the next night I did not start. There was not so much need to anyway, we were no longer afraid. We knew it was just old furniture over there, old jumble and confusion. We did not keep to the rules. I still stayed awake after Laird was asleep and told myself stories, but even in these stories something different was happening; mysterious alterations took place. A story might start off in the old way, with a spectacular danger, a fire or wild animals, and for a while I might rescue people; then things would change around, and instead, somebody would be rescuing me. It might be a boy from our class at school, or even Mr. Campbell, our teacher, who tickled girls under the arms. And at this point the story concerned itself at great length with what I looked like—how long my hair was, and what kind of dress I had on; by the time I had these details worked out, the real excitement of the story was lost.

It was later than one o'clock when the truck came back. That tarpaulin was over the back, which meant there was meat in it. My mother had to heat dinner up all over again. Henry and my father had changed from their bloody overalls into ordinary working overalls in the barn, and they washed their arms and necks and faces at the sink, and splashed water on their hair and combed it. Laird lifted his arm to show of a streak of blood. "We shot old Flora," he said, "and cut her up in fifty pieces."

"Well, I don't want to hear about it," my mother said. "And don't come to my table like that."

My father made him go and wash the blood off.

We sat down and my father said grace and Henry pasted his chewing gum on the end of his fork, the way he always did, when he took it off, he would have us admire the pattern. We began to pass the bowls of steaming, overcooked vegetables. Laird looked across the table at me and said proudly, distinctly, "Anyway it was her fault Flora got away."

"What?" my father said.

"She could of shut the gate and she didn't. She just open' it up and Flora ran out."

"Is that right?" my father said.

Everybody at the table was looking at me. I nodded, swallowing food with great difficulty. To my shame, tears flooded my eyes.

My father made a curt sound of disgust. "What did you do that for?"

I did not answer. I put down my fork and waited to be sent from the table, still not looking up.

But this did not happen. For some time nobody said anything, then Laird said matter-of-factly, "She's crying."

"Never mind," my father said. He spoke with resignation, even good humour, the words which absolved and dismissed me for good. "She's only a girl," he said.

I didn't protest that, even in my heart. Maybe it was true.

RESPONDING PERSONALLY

1. Write your thoughts and feelings as you read this selection. OR Write about some of your childhood memories that this story evokes.

2. With another student, decide what is the value of this story in relation to the topics of gender identity and differences.

RESPONDING CRITICALLY

3. For paragraph writing: What is the initial relationship between the protagonist and Laird? How does it change by the end of the story? Why?

4. Which parent and which roles does the protagonist identify with at various times in the story? What foreshadows her sympathy for Flora and her own act of rebellion?

5. What are the reactions of the family members to the narrator letting the horse escape? What do you think she feels at the conclusion of the story?

6. With a partner, decide what is the symbolism of the opened gate and the various animals in the story.

RESPONDING CREATIVELY

7. Write a sequel to the ending, revealing what the girl says as she talks with her mother.
8. Watch the Atlantis video adaptation of this story. How has the ending been altered? Write a review, giving your response to the adaptation.

PROBLEM-SOLVING/DECISION-MAKING

9. In a paragraph, describe a decision you or someone you know made that consciously defied authority or the status quo.

He seemed to be staring
vacantly, without focusing on
anything or anyone in particular.

Earl McKenzie
Fear of the Sea

Before that outing Ossie had never seen the sea. He had heard grownups talk about it, and they had described it as a big deep thing made of water, which was sometimes very rough, and in which people caught fish. Those descriptions, however, did not tell him very much. Perhaps the best description he got was from an old man who said it was like the biggest field of cabbage one could imagine.

One year, a few weeks before Easter, a man named Mass Aston went around the district selling tickets for an outing to the beach. Ossie's father bought tickets for the three members of his family. Ossie had never been on an outing and began to itch all over with excitement. During the days that followed, his parents had only to threaten not to take him along and he would rush to do anything they requested.

The day before the outing he got up early and completed all his chores. Then he bathed in the river which ran near their house. He regarded this river as an enormous quantity of water, and he found it hard to believe when people told him that compared with the sea it was almost nothing. They said it was just one of the hundreds of little rivers which flowed into the big rivers which in turn flowed into the sea. Ossie wondered about this strange thing which they said was like the sky but made of water, which had the colour of the mountains but was flat and rolling, and which was so irresistible people paid to visit it time and time again.

Near sunset he went to the square to see what was happening there. The truck in which they would be travelling had already returned from its daily trip to Kingston, and it was now parked at its usual spot beside the wooden two-storey building at the northern end of the square. One of the sidemen was washing the cab, and two others were bent over the spare tyre and pumping air into it. Some of the people in the square stood around the sidemen and watched; others were moving in and out of the shops in haste, going home to prepare food for the trip.

Ossie left the square at dusk and began running home. His feet were light with anticipation as he ran. He swung around a kerb and crashed into Adassa

"Boy, why you don't look where you going?" she shouted angrily as she shoved him away.

In the half-light he noticed that her normally pretty face was contorted with anger, an anger too deep to be entirely the result of his bumping into her.

"Sorry, ma'am," said Ossie.

"Cho!" she said as she brushed past him.

"I didn't see you," he called after her.

She didn't answer and the grey form of her dress and headtie quickly disappeared around the bent.

A little further down the road he saw Caswell, her boyfriend, sitting on a bank with his head and hands bent over his knees. Ossie said "Good evening" as he passed, but Caswell did not answer.

At home his mother and one of his aunts were in the kitchen preparing food for the outing. Ossie went into the house and sat by the window where he could smell the fried chicken and rice and peas, and where he could listen to the women's voices while he watched the flickering of the fire behind the rows of bamboo wattling.

He slept lightly that night; he woke up at the slightest sound, and he interpreted every crowing of a cock as a sign of daylight. When it was finally daybreak he was sleeping soundly and had to be awakened. It was still dark outside, but his parents had surer ears and noses for the sounds and smells of morning than he had.

They got up, dressed, and had breakfast. Then they set off for the square. They had the food in a bamboo basket with a lid, and they took turns carrying it up the hill.

The square was full of colourfully dressed people who were greeting each other, chatting and laughing. The truck was now out on the main road between two of the shops; the back-board was lowered and people were climbing in. People were also climbing in through the side-door to the left. Ossie's mother and father climbed in through the side-door, and he left them to join in the scramble for a seat on the back row. These seats were in great demand since you got a better view from them. Ossie managed to squeeze in between two of his friends. There was a space in the middle to let people through, and one of the sidemen asked that it be saved for him. Ossie settled down comfortably and waited for the trip to begin.

Neville, the driver of the truck, lived in a rented room on the top storey of the wooden building. A few minutes later, he and Adassa appeared at the top of the outside stairway. Adassa was wearing a tight-fitting red dress, and her thick hair was combed back with only a few plaits and pins to keep it in place. Her face was fixed in a defiant smile, and she kept close to Neville as they walked down the stairway.

The image of Caswell sitting alone on the bank came back to Ossie, and he tried to remember if he had seen him since arriving at the square. Ossie stood up and looked around the square, then inside the truck. Caswell was sitting in the right corner four rows away, and he was watching the square through the space between the wooden bars at his eye level. He seemed to be staring vacantly, without focusing on anything or anyone in particular. Ossie turned and noticed that Neville and Adassa were about to walk along the right side of the truck. He remained standing to see if Caswell would react to them. They came into his view and his body shook. Then he turned away from them and pretended to be watching the sidemen who were collecting baskets over the wings of the truck. He turned away from the sidemen, and, with bowed head and drooping shoulders, he stared at the floor of the truck. Most of the passengers were chatting and laughing. But Caswell was the loneliest person Ossie had ever seen.

Then everyone could hear Neville and Mass Aston having an argument outside.

"I want mi wife and myself to drive in the cab," said Mass Aston. "Is me in charge of this trip."

"Is only Adassa I want inside there with me," said Neville. "If I don't drive unu can't go."

When they saw Mass Aston and his wife coming through the side-door they knew that Neville had had his way.

Mass Aston stood in front and counted the passengers. He ordered the sidemen to pull up the back-board. Then he reached over the wings and pulled the cord attached to the bicycle bell close to the driver's seat. The truck started and people began waving to those who were staying behind. Some were watching with obvious envy. Others showered them with so many blessings and good wishes it was as if they were leaving for a foreign country.

The truck stopped a few times to pick up additional passengers. Soon they were out on the open road. Conversation slackened and they began singing. They sang "Roll Jordan Roll" and "Chi-Chi Bud O." When they began driving on asphalted road they broke into the gear-box song:

Mass Aston	Mr. Driver!
Passengers	Drop in a gear for me.
Mass Aston	Mr. Driver!
Passengers	Drop in a gear for me.
	For when you are driving
	Remember your gear-box
	Drop in a gear for me.

Neville was famous for being a "sweet-foot" driver, and at the end of each round of the song he changed gears with so much music and rhythm the people shouted with pleasure. He also tapped out the rhythm of the song on his horn.

Later they drove past enormous cane fields, and large pastures in which herds of cattle grazed. They drove beside a large river which began to open Ossie's eyes to what the grownups had said about rivers and the sea. Then they began climbing into hilly territory. Ossie noticed the many small and thickly forested hills which were so different from the large mountains he was accustomed to seeing.

Ossie will never forget his first sight of the sea. Suddenly an enormous stretch of deep indigo hit his eyes; it seemed as if it had risen up suddenly out of the earth, then it fell again. People rushed to the wings. "The sea, the sea!" they shouted. "Look at the sea!" The truck turned away and the wide expanse of blue quickly shrank to a long strip before it was swallowed up into the vegetation. Ossie found that his heart was pounding, that he was breathing heavily, and that his palms were moist.

For several minutes the sea seemed to be playing hide-and-seek with them. Sometimes they were so close to it they could see the white spots people in the truck said were waves. The next time they saw it, it was a mere strip in the distance. It took some time for Ossie to realise that they were seeing the same sea from different directions as they followed the winding road along the coast.

Suddenly they were right up beside the sea, separated from it only by a concrete wall. Ossie looked out at the vast expanse of blue-green water, and he felt nostalgia for the friendly intimacy of his little village stream. Now he could see the waves crashing against the wall, and he could hear the sea breathing and panting as if it were alive. They drove in silence as if it were somehow irreverent to laugh and sing in the presence of the awesome being beside them.

After a few minutes they turned into a side entrance, and they drove through a colonnade of coconut trees until they came to an open area where a number of vehicles, including a bus and a truck, were parked. At the far end of the open area Ossie could see a strip of white sand; beside it the sea lay quietly as if it had suddenly fallen asleep.

There were three buildings beside the beach: two thatched huts which were used as dressing rooms, and a large club-house, also thatched, which contained a restaurant, a bar and a place for dancing. The beach was already crowded with people from the other vehicles. There were also a few tourists with cameras. Some of the tourists had a motor boat and they were taking turns going out into the sea and coming back.

Most of the members of Mass Aston's party assembled in families and began eating. Later, a few changed into swimsuits and went into the sea. Very few of them could swim, so they splashed around at the edge of the water, or sat on the sand. As soon as they were through eating, most of the men headed for the bar.

Ossie did not go into the water; he had no swimsuit and he could not swim. He also felt a growing fear of the sea. So he walked along the shore with his friends and collected shells and driftwood.

Later in the afternoon a wind started blowing, and Ossie noticed the increased intensity of the waves. He heard a man telling his listeners that the waves had the power to pull you in, and if they did, they would bring you back to the shore twice, but after the third pull you would be gone for ever.

When they were tired of the beach, Ossie and his friends went into the club-house. There was a jukebox and people were dancing. Neville and Adassa were by themselves in a corner and they were close-dancing. Neville had a bottle of beer in his left hand and he hugged Adassa with his right. Their cheeks were pressed together as they danced.

After watching the dancers for a few minutes, Ossie and his friends turned their attention to the jukebox. They were admiring the way the jukebox changed records when they heard the sound of someone screaming outside. The screams got closer and a woman rushed into the club-house.

"Caswell drownin'!" she cried. "Caswell drownin'!"

People stopped dancing and rushed out of the club-house. Ossie and his friends followed. The beach was lined with people who were all looking out into the sea.

When Ossie and his friends got to the front they saw a tall black man coming towards the shore with Caswell's body slung sideways across his shoulders. The man lay Caswell's body face down on the sand. Caswell was wearing only his striped underpants.

One of the tourists, a middle-aged woman with red hair, went forward and knelt beside the body. She rested her palms on his back and began moving forward and backward as she tried to squeeze the water from his body. Each time she pressed forward the water spouted from his nose and mouth.

The woman who had taken the news to the club-house began describing what she had seen:

"I noticed that he wasn't lookin' too happy since mornin'. But is not my business what goin' on. Everybody can see what goin' on between Adassa and Neville. This is their business. But when I saw Caswell goin' into the sea I thought he was just going in to bathe. It didn't occur to me at the time that he might have something else on his mind. Then a little later I looked out and didn't see him any more. Then I spread the alarm."

A few minutes later the tourist got to her feet with a dejected look on her face. "I'm sorry," she said. "I've done everything I can. I'm very sorry. But he's dead."

The woman began wailing. "Look at the news we goin' 'ave to carry back! Look at the news we goin' 'ave to carry back to his parents!"

The tourists hitched their boat to their car and prepared to leave. The man who had taken Caswell's body from the sea asked them to report the death to the nearest police station. Most of the people began heading toward their vehicles. A number of vehicles left the beach. The people who came in the bus had to wait; the man who had taken Caswell from the sea was a member of their party and he would be required to give a statement to the police.

As Ossie walked back to the truck he noticed that Neville and Adassa were sitting in the cab. Neville's eyes were red and he was pulling hard at a cigarette and inhaling deeply. Adassa was leaning back in her seat and her face was cold and expressionless.

It was almost dusk when the police finally arrived. Ossie did not want to see what they were doing so he remained in his seat at the back of the truck. It was getting uncomfortably cold. Finally he heard the bus and the police van leaving the beach. The members of their party who had watched the examination and removal of the body began climbing into the truck. Soon afterwards the truck began retracing its path through the colonnade of coconut trees.

As they drove along the coast Ossie had his final glimpse of the sea, the sea that had taken Caswell. He glimpsed sections of its sad and immense loneliness. Each time he saw it he shivered at the thought of its unimaginable depths. He heard its panting as it intimidated the shore. Again, they kept moving closer and away from it; gradually it merged into the encapsulating darkness.

They drove in silence for many miles. Then they began to sing. The truck became a wake on wheels. For Ossie the songs were as sad as his memory of the sea. And every time he thought of the sea, he felt a cold fear approaching his heart.

RESPONDING PERSONALLY

1. In your personal response journal, write about your own feelings for the sea.
2. Do you think Caswell intended to die? In a group, compare your opinions.

RESPONDING CRITICALLY

3. Explain what Ossie's opinion of the sea is before and after he saw it. Why do his feelings change?
4. Write a character sketch of Ossie. What is he like? How do you know? Compare your sketch with those written by others.

5. What, if any, foreshadowing of Caswell's death is there? Could anyone have prevented it? How does his death affect the other travellers?

6. What epiphany does Ossie have at the end of the story? How does the experience change him?

RESPONDING CREATIVELY

7. Write Ossie's sympathy letter to Caswell's parents.

8. Write a poem dedicated to the sea in which you reveal your own feelings about the sea.

PROBLEM-SOLVING/DECISION-MAKING

9. With a partner, describe a time in which you or someone you know dealt with the death of a friend, family member, or relative.

"My mother is a flawless, modern
building, created of glass and the
smoothest of pale concrete."

Budge Wilson
The Metaphor

Miss Hancock was plump and unmarried and overenthusiastic.
She was fond of peasant blouses encrusted with embroidery, from
which loose threads invariably dangled. Like a heavy bird, she
fluttered and flitted from desk to desk, inspecting notebooks,
making suggestions, dispensing eager praise. Miss Hancock was
our teacher of literature and creative writing.

If one tired of inspecting Miss Hancock's clothes, which were
nearly always as flamboyant as her nature, one could still contemplate her face with considerable satisfaction. It was clear that
this was a face that had once been pretty, although cloakroom dis-
cussions of her age never resulted in any firm conclusions. In any
case, by now it was too late for simple unadorned prettiness.
What time had taken away from her, Miss Hancock tried to replace by mechanical means, and she applied her makeup with an
excess of zeal and a minimum of control. Her face was truly
amazing. She was fond of luminous frosted lipsticks—in hot pink
or something closer to purple or magenta. Her eyelashes curled
up and out singly, like a row of tiny bent sticks. Surrounding her
eyes, the modulations of color, toners, shadows, could keep a student interested for half an hour if he or she were bored with a
grammar assignment. Her head was covered with a profusion of
small busy curls, which were brightly, aggressively, golden—"in
bad taste," my mother said, "like the rest of her."

However, do not misunderstand me. We were fond of Miss
Hancock. In fact, almost to a person, we loved her. Our class, like
most groups that are together for long periods of time have developed a definite personality. By some fluke of geography or biology or school administration, ours was a cohesive group

composed of remarkably backward grade 7 pupils—backward in
that we had not yet embraced sophistication, boredom, cruelty,
drugs, alcohol, or sex. Those who did not fit into our mold were
in the minority and made little mark upon us. We were free to respond positively to Miss Hancock's literary excesses without fear
of the mockery of our peers, and with an open and uninhibited
delight that is often hard to find in any classroom above the level
of grade 5. So Miss Hancock was able to survive, even to flourish,
in our unique, sheltered environment.

Miss Hancock was equally at home in her two fields of creative
writing and literature. It was the first time I had been excited,
genuinely moved, by poems, plays, stories. She could analyse
without destroying a piece of literature, and we argued about
meanings and methods and creative intentions with passionate
caring. She had a beautiful deeply modulated voice, and when
she read poetry aloud, we sat bewitched, transformed. We could
not have said which we loved best, Miss Hancock or her subject.
They were all of a piece.

But it was in the area of composition, in her creative writing
class, that Miss Hancock made the deepest mark upon me. She
had that gift of making most of us want to write, to communicate,
to make a blank sheet of paper into a beautiful or at least an interesting thing. We were as drugged by words as some children
are by electronic games.

One October day, just after Thanksgiving, Miss Hancock came
into the classroom and faced us, eyes aglitter, hands clasped in
front of her embroidered breasts.

"Today," she announced, clapping her dimpled hands together, her charm bracelets jingling, "we are going to do a lovely exercise. Such *fun!*" She raised her astonishing eyes to the classroom
ceiling. "A whole new world of composition is about to open for
you in one glorious *woosh.*" She stood there, arms now raised, elbows bent, palms facing up, enjoying her dramatic pause. "After
today," she announced in a loud, confidential whisper, "you will
have a brand-new weapon in your arsenal of writing skills. You
will possess" (pause again) "The Metaphor!" Her arms fell, and

she clicked to the blackboard in her patent leather pumps to start the lesson. Her dazzling curls shone in the afternoon sunlight and jiggled as she wrote. Then, with a board full of examples and suggestions, she began her impassioned discourse on The Metaphor. I listened, entranced. Miss Hancock may have been in poor taste, but at that time in my life she was my entry to something I did not yet fully understand but which I knew I wanted.

"And now," Miss Hancock announced, after the lucid and fervent presentation of her subject, "The Metaphor is yours—to *use*, to *enjoy*, to *enrich*." She stood poised, savoring one of her breathless pauses. "I now want you to take out your notebooks," she continued, "and make a list. Write down the members of your family, your home, your pets, anything about which you feel *deeply*. Then," she went on, "I want you to describe everyone and everything on your list with a pungent and a telling metaphor." She gave a little clap. "Now *start!*" she cried. She sat down at her desk, clasping her hands together so tightly that the knuckles looked polished. Smiling tensely, frilled eyes shining, she waited.

All but the dullest of us were excited. This was an unfamiliar way of looking at things. Better still, it was a newfangled method of talking about them.

Miss Hancock interrupted us just one more time. "Write quickly," she urged from her glowing expectant position at the desk. "Don't think too hard. Let your writing, your words, emerge from you like a mysterious and elegant blossom. Let it all *out*," she closed her lacy eyes, "without restraint, without inhibition, with *verve*."

Well, we did. The results, when we read them out to her were, as one might expect, hackneyed, undistinguished, ordinary. But we were delighted with ourselves. And she with us. She wrote our metaphors on the blackboard and expressed her pleasure with small delighted gasping sounds.

"My dog is a clown in a spotted suit."

"My little brother George is a whirling top."

"The spruce tree was a tall lady in a stiff dress."

"My dad is a warm wood stove."

And so it went. Finally it was my turn. I offered metaphors for my father, my grandmother, my best friend, the waves at Peggy's Cove. Then I looked at the metaphor for my mother. I had not realized I had written so much.

"Miss Hancock," I hesitated, "the one for my mother is awfully long. You probably don't want to write all this stuff down."

"Oh *heavens*, Charlotte," breathed Miss Hancock, "of *course* I want it! Read it all to us. Do, Charlotte. Oh, *do!*"

I began: "My mother is a flawless, modern building, created of glass and the smoothest of pale concrete. Inside are business offices furnished with beige carpets and gleaming chromium. In every room there are machines—computers, typewriters, intricate copiers. They are buzzing and clicking way, absorbing and spitting out information with the speed of sound. Downstairs, at ground level, people walk in and out, tracking mud and dirt over the steel-grey tiles, marring the cool perfection of the building. There are no comfortable chairs in the lobby."

I sat down, eyes on my desk. There was a pause so long that I finally felt forced to look up. Miss Hancock was standing there at the front of the room, chalk poised, perfectly still. Then she turned around quickly and wrote the whole metaphor verbatim (verbatim!) on the board. When she faced us again, she looked normal once more. Smiling brightly, she said, "Very *very* good, class! I had planned to discuss with you what you all *meant* by your metaphors; I had hoped to probe their *significance*. But I have to leave early today because of a dental appointment." Then, with five vigorous sweeps of her blackboard eraser, the whole enticing parade of metaphors disappeared from the board, leaving us feeling vaguely deprived. It also left me feeling more than vaguely relief. "Class dismissed!" said Miss Hancock cheerfully, and then, "Charlotte. May I see you for a moment before you go."

When everyone had gathered up their books and their leftover lunches, they disappeared into the corridor. I went up to the front of the room to Miss Hancock's desk. She was sitting there soberly, hands still, eyes quiet.

"Yes, Miss Hancock?" I inquired, mystified.

"Charlotte," she began, "your metaphors were unusually good, unusually interesting. For someone your age, you have quite a complex vocabulary, a truly promising way of expressing yourself."

Ah. So this was why she wanted to see me. But apparently it was not.

"I wonder," she continued slowly, carefully, "do you have anything you would like to discuss about your mother's metaphor?"

I thought about that.

"No," I replied. "I don't think so. I don't really know what it means. It just sort of came out. I feel kind of funny about it."

"Lots of things just sort of come out when you're writing," said Miss Hancock quietly, oh so quietly, as though she were afraid something fragile might break if she spoke too quickly, too loudly. "And there's no need to feel funny about it. I don't want to push you even a little bit, but are you really sure you don't want to discuss it?" I could tell that she was feeling concerned and kind, not nosy.

"Lookit," I said, using an expression that my mother particularly disliked, "that's really nice of you, but I can't think of anything at all to say. Besides, even though you say there's no need to feel funny, I really do feel sort of creepy about it. And I'm not all that crazy about the feeling." I paused, not sure of what else to say.

Miss Hancock was suddenly her old self again. "*Well!*" she said cheerfully, as she rose. "That's perfectly fine. I just wanted you to know that your writing was very intriguing today, and that it showed a certain maturity that surprised and delighted me." She gathered up her books, her purse, her pink angora cardigan, and started off toward the corridor. At the door, she stopped and turned around, solemn and quiet once more. "Charlotte," she said, "if you ever need any help—with your writing or, well, with any other kind of problem, just let me know." Then she turned abruptly and clicked off in the direction of the staff room, waving her hand in a fluttery farewell. "My dental appointment," she called merrily.

I walked home slowly, hugging my books to my chest. The mid-October sun shone down upon the colored leaves that littered the sidewalk, and I kicked and shuffled as I walked, enjoying the swish and scrunch, savoring the sad-sweet feeling of doom that October always gives me. I thought for a while about my metaphor—the one Miss Hancock had asked about—and then I decided to push it out of my head.

When I arrived home, I opened the door with my key, entered the front porch, took off my shoes and read the note on the hall table. It was written in flawless script on a small piece of bond paper. It said; "At a Children's Aid Board Meeting. Home by 5. Please tidy your room."

The hall table was polished, antique, perfect. It contained one silver salver for messages and a small ebony lamp with a white shade. The floor of the entrance was tiled. The black and white tiles shone in the sunlight, unmarked by any sign of human contact. I walked over them carefully, slowly, having slipped and fallen once too often.

Hunger I went into the kitchen and surveyed it thoughtfully. More black and white tiles dazzled the eye, and the cupboards and walls were a blinding spotless white. The counters shone, empty of jars, leftovers, canisters, appliances. The whole room looked as though it were waiting for the movers to arrive with the furniture and dishes. I made myself a peanut-butter sandwich, washed the knife and plate, and put everything away. Then I went upstairs to my room, walking on the grey stair carpet beside the off-white walls, glancing absently at the single lithograph in its black fame. "My home," I said aloud, "is a box. It is cool and quiet and empty and uninteresting. Nobody lives in the box." Entering my room, I looked around. A few magazines were piled on the floor beside my bed. On my dresser, a T-shirt lay on top of my ivory brush and comb set. Two or three books were scattered over the top of my desk. I picked up the magazines, removed the T-shirt and put the books back in the bookcase. There. Done.

Then I called Julia Parsons, who was my best friend, and went over to her house to talk about boys. When I returned at 6 o'clock, my mother, who had been home only one hour, had prepared a complicated three-course meal—expert, delicious, nutritious. "There's food in the box," I mused.

Since no one else had much to say at dinner, I talked about school. I told them about Miss Hancock's lesson on The Metaphor. I said what a marvellous teacher she was, how even the dumbest of us had learned to enjoy writing compositions, how she could make the poetry in our textbook so exciting to read and to hear.

My father listened attentively, enjoying my enthusiasm. He was not a lively or an original man, but he was an intelligent person who liked to watch eagerness in others. "You're very fortunate, Charlotte," he said, "to find a teacher who can wake you up and make you love literature."

"Is she that brassy Miss Hancock whom I met at the Home and School meeting?" asked my mother.

"What do you mean, brassy?"

"Oh. You know. Overdone, too much enthusiasm. Flamboyant. Orange hair. Is she the one?"

"Yes," I said.

"Oh," said my mother without emphasis of any kind. "Her. Charlotte, would you please remove the dishes and bring in the dessert. Snow pudding. In the fridge, top left-hand side. Thank you."

That night I lay in the bath among the Estée Lauder bubbles (gift of my father on my last birthday) and created metaphors. I loved baths. The only thing nicer than one bath a day was two. Julia said that if I kept taking so many baths, my skin would get dry and crisp, and that I would be wrinkled before I was 30. That was too far away to worry about. She also said that taking baths was disgusting and that showers were more hygienic. She pointed out that I was soaking in my own dirt, like Indians in the fetid Ganges. I thought this a bit excessive and said so. "For Pete's sake," I exclaimed, "if I have two baths a day, I can't be sitting in very much dirt. Besides, it's *therapeutic*."

"It's *what*?"

"Therapeutic. Water play. I read about it in *Reader's Digest* at the doctor's office. They let kids play with water when they're wild and upset. And now they're using warm baths to soothe the patients in mental hospitals."

"So?"

"So it could be useful if I happen to end up crazy." I laughed. I figured that would stop her. It did.

In the bath I always did a lot of things besides wash. I lifted up mounds of the tiny bubbles and held them against the fluorescent light over the sink. The patterns and shapes were delicate, like minute filaments of finest lace. I poked my toes through the bubbles and waved their hot pinkness to and fro among the static white waves. I hopefully examined my breasts for signs of sudden growth. If I lay down in the tub and brought the bubbles up over my body and squeezed my chest together by pressing my arms inward, I could convince myself that I was full-breasted and seductive. I did exercise to lengthen my hamstrings, in order to improve my splits for the gymnastics team. I thought about Charles Swinimer. I quoted poetry, out loud with excessive feeling and dramatic emphasis, waving my soapy arms around and pressing my eloquent hand upon my flat chest. And from now on, I also lay there and made up metaphors, most of them about my mother.

"My mother is a white picket fence—straight, level. The fence stands in a field full of weeds. The field is bounded on its other sides by thorny bushes and barbed wire."

"My mother is a lofty mountain capped by virgin snow. The air around the mountain is clear and clean and very cold." I turned on more hot water. "At the base of the mountain grow gnarled and crooked trees, surrounded by scrub brush and poison ivy."

Upon leaving the bath, I would feel no wiser. Then I would clean the tub very carefully indeed. It was necessary.

Not, mind you, that my mother ranted and raved about her cleanliness. Ranting and raving were not part of her style. "I know you will agree," she would say, very oh ever so sweetly, implying in some oblique way that I certainly did not agree, "that it is an inconsiderate and really ugly thing to leave a dirty tub." Then she would lead me with a subtle soft-firm pressure into the bathroom, so that we might inspect together a bathtub ringed with sludge, sprinkled with hair and dried suds. "Not," she would say quietly, "a very pretty sight."

And what, I would ask myself, is so terrible about that? Other mothers, I know, I had heard them, nagged, yelled, scolded, did terrible and noisy things. But what was it about my mother's methods that left me feeling so depraved, so unsalvageable?

But of course I was 13 by now, and knew all about cleaning tubs and wiping off countertops and sweeping up crumbs. A very small child must have been a terrible test to that cool and orderly spirit. I remember those days. A toy ceased to be a toy and began to be a mess, the moment it left the toy cupboard. "I'm sure," she would say, evenly, "that you don't want to have those blocks all over the carpet. Why not keep them all in one spot, over here behind Daddy's chair?" From time to time, I attempted argument.

"But Mother. I'm making a garden."

"Then make a *little* garden. They're every bit as satisfying as large, sprawling unmanageable farms."

And since no one who was a truly nice person would want a large, sprawling unmanageable farm, I would move my blocks behind the chair and make my small garden there. Outside, our backyard was composed of grass and flowers, plus one evergreen tree that dropped neither fuzzy buds in the spring nor ragged leaves in the fall. No swing set made brown spots on that perfect lawn, nor was there a sandbox. Cat were known to use sandboxes as community toilets. Or so my mother told me. I assume she used the term "toilet" (a word not normally part of her vocabulary) instead of "washroom," lest there be any confusion as to her meaning.

But in grade 7, you no longer needed a sandbox. My friends marvelled when they came to visit, which was not often. How serene my mother seemed, how lovely to look at, with her dark-blond hair, her flawless figure, her smooth hands. She never acted frazzled or rushed or angry, and her forehead was unmarked by age lines or worry marks. Her hair always looked as though a hairdresser had arrived at 6 A.M. to ready her for the day. "Such a peaceful house," my friends would say, clearly impressed, "and no one arguing or fighting." Then they would leave and go somewhere else for their snacks, their music, their hanging around.

No indeed, I thought. No fights in this house. It would be like trying to down an angel with a BB gun—both sacrilegious and futile, all at the same time. My father was thin and nervous, and was careful about hanging up his clothes and keeping his sweaters in neat piles. He certainly did not fight with my mother. In fact, he said very little to her at all. He had probably learned early that to complain is weak, to rejoice is childish, to laugh is noisy. And moving around raises dust.

This civilized, this clean, this disciplined woman who was and is my mother, was also, if one were to believe her admirers, the mainstay of the community, the rock upon which the town was built. She chaired committees, ran bazaars, sat on boards. When I first heard about this, I thought it a very exciting thing that she sat on boards. If my mother, who sat so correctly on the needlepoint chair with her nylon knees pressed so firmly together, could actually sit on *boards*, there might be a rugged and reckless side to her that I had not yet met. The telephone rang constantly, and her softly controlled voice could be heard, hour after hour, arranging and steering and manipulating the affairs of the town.

Perhaps because she juggled her community jobs, her housework, her cooking, and her grooming with such quiet calm efficiency, she felt scorn for those less able to cope. "Mrs. Langstreth says she is too *tired* to take on a table at the bazaar," she might say. It was not hard to imagine. Mrs. Langstreth lounging on a sofa, probably in a turquoise chenille dressing gown, surrounded by full ashtrays and neglected children. Or my mother might comment quietly, but with unmistakable emphasis, "Gillian Monroe is having trouble with her children. And in my opinion, she has only herself to blame." The implication seemed to be that if Gillian Monroe's children were left in my mother's care for a few weeks, she could make them all into a perfectly behaved family. Which was probably true.

Certainly in those days I was well-behaved. I spoke quietly, never complained, ate what was put before me, and obeyed all rules without question or argument. I was probably not even very unhappy, although I enjoyed weekdays much more than weekends. Weekends did not yet include parties or boys. It is true that Julia and I spent a lot of our time together talking about boys. I also remember stationing myself on the fence of the vacant lot on Seymour Street at 5 o'clock, the hour when Charles Swinimer could be expected to return from high school. As he passed, I would be too absorbed in my own activity to look at him directly. I would be chipping the bark off the fence, or reading, or pulling petals from a daisy—he loves me, he loves me not. Out of the corner of my eye, I feasted upon his jawline, his confident walk, his shoulders. On the rare days when he would toss me a careless "Hi" (crumbs to a pigeon), I would have to dig my nails into the wood to keep from falling off, from fainting dead away. But that was the extent of my thrills. No boys had yet materialized in the flesh to offer themselves to me. Whatever else they were looking for, it was not acne, straight, brown stringy hair, or measurements of 32-32-32.

So weekdays were still best. Weekdays meant school and particularly English class, where Miss Hancock delivered up trays of succulent literature for our daily consumption. *Hamlet* was the thing that spring, the spring before we moved into junior high. So were a number of poems that left me weak and changed. And our composition class gathered force, filling up with a creative confidence that was heady stuff. We wrote short stories, played with similes, created poems that did and did not rhyme, felt we were capable of anything and everything; if Shakespeare, if Wordsworth could do it, why couldn't we? Over it all, Miss Hancock presided, hands fluttering, voice atremble with raw emotion.

But best of all was *Hamlet*. Like all serious students, we agonized and argued over its meaning, Hamlet's true intent, his sanity, his goal. Armed with rulers, we fought the final duel and its bloody sequence, and a four-foot Fortinbras stepped among the dead bodies between the desks to proclaim the ultimate significance of it all. At the end, Miss Hancock stood, hands clasped, knuckles white, tears standing in her eyes. And I cannot pretend that all of ours were dry.

At the close of the year, our class bought an enormous, tasteless card of thanks and affixed it to a huge trophy. The trophy was composed of two brass-colored Ionic pillars that were topped by a near-naked athlete carrying a spiky wreath. On the plate below was inscribed: "For you and Hamlet with love. The grade 7 class. 1965."

When my mother saw it, she came close to losing her cool control.

"Who *chose* it?" she asked, tight-lipped.

"Horace Hennigar," I answered. Oh don't spoil it, don't spoil it.

"That explains it," she said, and mercifully that was all.

Junior high school passed, and so did innocence and acne. Hair curled, makeup intact, I entered high school the year that Charles Swinimer left for university. But there would be other fish to fry. Outwardly blasé, single-minded and 16, I came into my first grade 10 class with a mixture of intense apprehension and a burning unequivocal belief that high school could and would deliver up to me all life's most precious gifts—the admiration of my peers, local fame, boys, social triumphs. During August of that year, my family had moved to another school district. I entered high school with a clean slate. It was terrifying to be so alone. I also knew that it was a rare and precious opportunity; I could approach life without being branded with my old failures, my old drawbacks. I was pretty; I was shapely; I was anonymous; I melted into the crowd. No one here would guess that I had once been such a skinny, pimply wretch.

Our first class was Geography, and I knew enough of the material to be able to let my eyes and other senses wander. Before the end of the period, I knew that the boy to pursue was Howard Oliver, that the most prominent and therefore the most potentially useful or dangerous girl was Gladys Simpson, that Geography was uninteresting, that the teacher was strict. To this day I can smell the classroom during that first period—the dry and acrid smell of chalk, the cool, sweet fragrance of the freshly waxed floors, the perspiration that travelled back to me from Joey Elliott's desk.

The next period was English. My new self-centred and self-conscious sophistication had not blunted my love of literature, my desire to write, to play with words, to express my discoveries and confusions. I awaited the arrival of the teacher with masked but real enthusiasm. I was not prepared for the entrance of Miss Hancock.

Hiss Hancock's marked success with 15 years of grade 7 students had finally transported her to high places. She entered the classroom, wings spread, ready to fly. She was used to success, and she was eager to sample the gift of a group of older and more perceptive minds. Clad in royal blue velour, festooned with gold chains, hair glittering in the sun pouring in from the east window, fringed eyes darting, she faced the class, arms raised. She paused.

"Let us pray!" said a deep male voice from the back row. It was Howard Oliver. Laughter exploded in the room. Behind my Duo Tang folder, I snickered fiercely.

Miss Hancock's hands fluttered wildly. It was as though she were waving off an invasion of poisonous flies.

"Now, now, class!" she exclaimed, with a mixture of tense jollity and clear panic. "We'll have none of *that*! Please turn to page 7 in your textbook. I'll read the selection aloud to you first, and then we'll discuss it." She held the book high in the palm of one hand; the other was raised like an admonition, an artistic beckoning.

The reading was from Tennyson's *Ulysses*. I had never heard it before. As I listened to her beautiful voice, the old magic took hold, and no amount of peer pressure could keep me from thrilling to the first four lines she read:

"I am a part of all that I have met;
Yet all experience is an arch where-thro'

Gleams that untravell'd world whose margin fades
For ever and for ever when I move."
But after that, it was difficult even to hear her. Guffaws sprang
up here and there throughout the room. Gladys Simpson whispered something behind her hand to the girl beside her, and then
broke into fits of giggles. Paper airplanes flew. The wits of grade
10 offered comments: "Behold the Bard!" "Bliss! Oh poetic bliss!"
"Hancock! Whocock? Hancock! Hurray!" "Don't faint, class! *Don't
faint!*"

I was caught in a stranglehold somewhere between shocked
embarrassment and a terrible desire for concealment. No other
members of the class shared my knowledge of Miss Hancock or
my misery. But I knew I could not hide behind that Duo Tang
folder forever.

It was in fact 10 days later that Miss Hancock recognized me.
It could not have been easy to connect the eager, skinny fan of
grade 7 with the cool and careful person I had become. And she
would not have expected to find a friend in that particular classroom By then, stripped of 15 years of overblown confidence, she
offered her material shyly, hesitantly, certain of rejection, of humiliation. When our eyes met in class, she did not rush up to me
to claim alliance or allegiance. Her eyes merely held mine for a
moment, slid off and then periodically slid back. There was a desperate hope in them that I could hardly bear to witness. At the
end of the period, I waited until everyone had gone before I
walked toward her desk on the way to the corridor. Whatever was
going to happen, I wanted to be sure that it would not be wit-
nessed.

When I reached her, she was sitting quietly, hands folded on
top of her lesson book. I was reminded of another day, another
meeting, but the details were blurred. But I knew I had seen this
Miss Hancock before. She looked at me evenly and said quietly,
simply, "Hello, Charlotte. How nice to see you."

I looked at her hands, the floor, the blackboard, anywhere but
at those searching eyes. "Hello, Miss Hancock," I said.

"Still writing metaphors?" she asked, with a tentative smile.

"Oh, I dunno," I replied. But I was. Nightly, in the bathtub. And I kept a notebook in which I wrote them all own.

"Your writing showed promise, Charlotte." Her eyes were quiet, pleading. "I hope you won't forget that."

Or anything else, I thought. Oh Miss Hancock, let me go. Aloud I said, "French is next, and I'm late."

She looked directly into my eyes and held them for a moment. Then she spoke. "Go ahead, Charlotte. Don't let me keep you."

She did not try to reach me again. She taught, or tried to teach her classes, as though I were not there. Week after week, she entered that room white with tension and left it defeated. I did not tell a living soul that I had ever seen her before.

One late afternoon in March of that year, Miss Hancock stepped off the curb in front of the school and was killed instantly by a school bus.

The next day, I was offered this piece of news with that mixture of horror and delight that so often attends the delivery of terrible tidings. When I heard it, I felt as though my chest and throat were constricted by a band of dry ice. During Assembly, the Principal came forward and delivered a short announcement of the tragedy, peppered with little complimentary phrases: "... a teacher of distinction ..." "... a generous colleague ..." "... a tragic end to a promising career ..." Howard Oliver was sitting beside me; he had been showing me flattering attention of late. As we got up to disperse for classes, he said, "Poor old Whocock Hancock. Quoting poetry to the angels by now." He was no more surprised than I was when I slapped him full across his handsome face, before I ran down the aisle of the Assembly Room, up to the long corridor of the first floor, down the steps and out into the parking lot. Shaking with dry and unsatisfying sobs, I hurried home through the back streets of the town and let myself in by the back door.

"What on earth is wrong, Charlotte?" asked my mother when she saw my stricken look, my heaving shoulders. There was real concern in her face.

"Miss Hancock is dead," I whispered.

"Miss *who*? Charlotte, speak up please."

"Miss Hancock. She teaches—*taught*—us grade 10 English."

"You mean that same brassy creature from grade 7?"

I didn't answer. I was crying out loud, with the abandon of a preschooler or of someone who is under the influence of drugs.

"Charlotte, do please blow your nose and try to get hold of yourself. I can't for the life of me see why you're so upset. You never even told us she was your teacher this year."

I was rocking back and forth on the kitchen chair, arms crossed over my chest. My mother stood there erect, invulnerable. It crossed my mind that no grade 10 class would throw paper airplanes in any group that *she* chose to teach.

"Well then," she said, "why or how did she die?"

I heard myself shriek, "I killed her! I killed her!"

Halting, gasping, I told her all of it. I described her discipline problems, the cruelty of the students, my own blatant betrayal.

"For goodness's sake, Charlotte," said my mother, quiet but clearly irritated, "don't lose perspective. She couldn't keep order and she had only herself to blame." That phrase sounded familiar to me. "A woman like that can't survive for five minutes in the high schools of today. There was nothing you could have done."

I was silent. I could have *said something*. Like thank you for grade 7. Or yes, I still have fun with The Metaphor. Or once, just once in this entire year, I could have *smiled* at her.

My mother was speaking again. "There's a great deal of ice. It would be very easy to slip under a school bus. And she didn't strike me as the sort of person who would exercise any kind of sensible caution."

"Oh dear God," I was whispering, "I wish she hadn't chosen a *school bus*."

I cried some more that day and excused myself from supper. I heard my father say, "I think I'll just go up and see if I can help." But my mother said, "Leave her alone, Arthur. She's 16 years old. It's time she learned how to cope. She's acting like a hysterical child." My father did not appear. Betrayal, I thought, runs in the family.

The next day I stayed home from school. I kept having periods of uncontrollable weeping, and even my mother could not send me off in that condition. Once again I repeated to her, to my father, "I killed her. We all killed her. But especially me."

"Charlotte."

Oh I knew that voice, that tone. So calm, so quiet, so able to silence me with one word. I stopped crying and curled up in a tight ball on the sofa.

"Charlotte. I know you will agree with what I'm going to say to you. There is no need to speak so extravagantly. A sure and perfect control is what separates the civilized from the uncivilized." She inspected her fingernails, pushing down the quick of her middle finger with her thumb. "If you would examine this whole, perfectly natural situation with a modicum of rationality, you would see that she got exactly what she deserved."

I stared at her.

"Charlotte," she continued, "I'll have to ask you to stop this nonsense. You're disturbing the even tenor of our home."

I said nothing. With a sure and perfect control, I uncoiled myself from my fetal position on the sofa. I stood up and left the living room.

Upstairs in my bedroom I sat down before my desk. I took my pen out of the drawer and opened my notebook. Speaking extravagantly, without a modicum of rationality, I began to write.

"Miss Hancock was a birthday cake," I wrote. "The cake was frosted by someone unschooled in the art of cake decoration. It was adorned with a profusion of white roses and lime-green leaves, which dropped and dribbled at the edges where the pastry tube had slipped. The frosting was of an intense peppermint flavor, too sweet, too strong. Inside, the cake had two layers—chocolate and vanilla. The chocolate was rich and soft and very delicious. No one who stopped to taste it could have failed to enjoy it. The vanilla was subtle and delicate; only those thoroughly familiar with cakes, only those with great sensitivity of taste, could have perceived its true fine flavor. Because it was a birthday cake, it was filled with party favors. If you stayed long enough at the party, you could amass quite a large collection of these treasures. If you kept them for many years, they would amaze you by turning into pure gold. Most children would have been delighted by this cake. Most grown-ups would have thrown it away after one brief glance at the frosting.

"I wish that the party wasn't over."

Responding Personally

1. In your response journal, describe a teacher or school situation this story reminded you of.
2. What is *peer pressure*? What role does it play in the outcome of this story?

Responding Critically

3. Who are the protagonist and antagonist in this story? Defend your choices using examples from the story.
4. What is the purpose of the subplot between Charlotte and her mother?
5. What is the mother's attitude toward Miss Hancock? Why does she feel this way? Is she callous or honest? Explain.
6. For paragraph writing: With another student, brainstorm ideas and then write an analysis of the symbolism in the last paragraph. Compare what you have written with another partner.

Responding Creatively

7. This story uses the convention of an adult narrator looking back at her past. Write your own short story, reflecting on a memorable character from your childhood.
8. Compose the poem Charlotte writes dedicated to her late teacher.

Problem-Solving/Decision-Making

9. For small group discussion: Describe a difficult decision you or someone you know had to make while under the influence of peer pressure. What did you finally decide? Why?

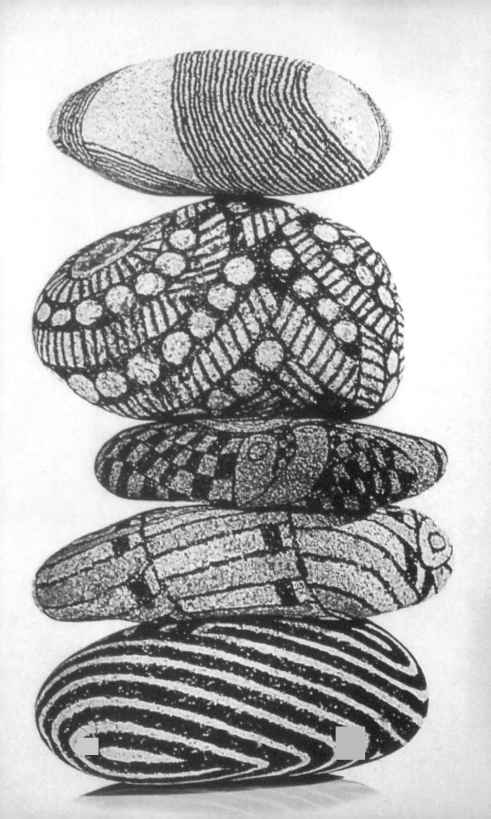

More Themes to Explore

Although this book explores certain common literary themes in the first eight units, much of the joy and satisfaction of being a reader comes from discovering themes and exploring stories on one's own. The stories of this unit take us through diverse and ranging themes not explored in previous units.

Carol Shields' "Fragility" is a serious story about a young couple's search for a new home and for peace from a tragedy. One of Canada's best fiction writers reveals her understanding of psychology and human relationships to render the very fragility of life itself.

"The Organized Woman Story" is another ironic story, this time about connections and the search for meaning in daily relationships. The author, Birk Sproxton, enjoys playing with words, rhythms, and formula sentences to present the overlapping nuances of a memorable character and the strange uncanny patterns we sometimes discover in our busy, changing world.

"Another Evening at the Club," presents a relationship in which the cultural concept of "maintaining face," even at the expense of others, is explored. The story reveals the terrible price paid so that comfortable illusions and superficial social appearances may be maintained.

From the genre of science fiction comes Isaac Asimov's entertaining story "All the Troubles of the World." This story's main premise is that computers will one day be able to detect and prevent crime before it happens. What the humans don't reckon on, however, are human flaws inherent in the moods and character of the computer, Multivac.

Wallace Stegner is best-known for his prairie fiction, so "Volcano" will come as a surprise for many of his fans. This is a tale of an American tourist in Mexico who travels to see a treacherous volcano, itself a vision of hell with the awesome forces of nature. What he finds, as well, is that the journey itself can be as intriguing as his destination.

"The Merman of Olsen's Island" is a romantic dreamy fantasy about a woman mourning her lost lover. The depth of the young woman's passion transcends her immediate suffering and engages us with its hypnotic spell. By the end of the story, we have learned what the protagonist has learned and vicariously experienced, a resolution of her emotional, psychological, and spiritual anguish.

The final story, "Edward's Rocks," originating from Newfoundland, is a quaint, quirky yarn about some seal hunters who run into a baffling obstacle on one of their runs. "Edward's Rocks" affirms the dignity of hard-working people and offers us a positive focus on their adventures and unique culture.

A few gulps of oxygen are all
that stand between us and
death.

Carol Shields
Fragility

We are flying over the Rockies on our way to Vancouver, and there sits Ivy with her paperback. I ask myself: should I interrupt and draw her attention to the grandeur beneath us?

In a purely selfish sense, watching Ivy read is as interesting as peering down at those snowy mountains. She turns the pages of a book in the same way she handles every object, with a peculiar, respectful gentleness, as though the air around it were more tender than ordinary air. I've watched her lift a cup of tea with this same abstracted grace, cradling a thick mug in a way that transforms it into something precious and fragile. It's a gift some people have.

I decide not to disturb her; utterly absorbed in what she's reading, she's seen the Rockies before.

In the seat ahead of us is a young man wearing a bright blue jacket— I remember that once I had a similar jacket in a similar hue. Unlike us, he's clearly flying over the Rockies for the first time. He's in a half-standing position at the window, snapping away with his camera, pausing only to change the film. From where I'm sitting I can see his intense, eager trigger hand, his steadying elbow, his dropped lower lip. In a week he'll be passing his slides around the office, holding them delicately at their edges up to the light. He might set up a projector and screen them one evening in his living room; he might invite a few friends over, and his wife—who will resemble the Ivy of fifteen years ago—will serve coffee and wedges of cheesecake; these are the Rockies, he'll say—magnificent, stirring, one of the wonders of the continent.

I tell myself that I would give a great deal to be in that young man's shoes, but this is only a half-truth, the kind of lie Ivy and I sometimes spin for our own amusement. We really don't want to go back in time. What we envy in the young is that fine nervous edge of perception, the ability to take in reality afresh. I suppose, as we grow older, that's what we forfeit, acquiring in its place a measure of healthy resignation.

Ivy puts down her book suddenly and reaches for my hand. A cool, light, lazy touch. She's smiling.

"Good book?"

"Hmmm," she says, and stretches.

Now, as a kind of duty, I point out the Rockies.

"Beautiful," she exclaims, leaning toward the window.

And it is beautiful. But unfortunately the plane is flying at a height that extracts all sense of dimension from the view. Instead of snow-capped splendor, we see a kind of Jackson-Pollock dribbling of white on green. It's a vast, abstract design, a linking of incised patterns, quite interesting in its way, but without any real suggestion of height or majesty.

"It looks a little like a Jackson Pollock," Ivy says in that rhythmic voice of hers.

"Did you really say that?"

"I think so." Her eyebrows go up, her mouth crimps at the edges. "At least, if I didn't, someone did."

I lift her hand—I can't help myself—and kiss her fingertips.

"And what's that for?" she asks, still smiling.

"An attack of poignancy."

"A serious new dietary disease, I suppose," Ivy says, and at that moment the steward arrives with our lunch trays.

Ivy and I have been to Vancouver fairly often on business trips or for holidays. This time it's different; in three months we'll be moving permanently to Vancouver, and now the two of us are engaged in that common-enough errand, a house-hunting expedition.

Common, I say, but not for us.

We know the statistics: that about half of all North Americans move every five years, that we're a rootless, restless, portable society. But for some reason, some failing on our part or perhaps simple good fortune, Ivy and I seem to have evaded the statistical pattern. The small, stone-fronted, bow-windowed house we bought when Christopher was born is the house in which we continue to live after twenty years.

If there had been another baby, we would have considered a move, but we stayed in the same house in the middle of Toronto. It was close to both our offices and close too to the clinic Christopher needed. Curiously enough, most of our neighbors also stayed there year after year. In our neighborhood we know everyone. When the news of my transfer came, the first thing Ivy said was, "What about the Mattisons and the Levensons? What about Robin and Sara?"

"We can't very well take everyone on the street along with us."

"Oh Lordy," Ivy said and bit her lip. "Of course not. It's only—"

"I know," I said.

"Maybe we can talk Robin and Sara into taking their holidays on the coast next year. Sara always said—"

"And we'll be back fairly often. At least twice a year."

"If only—"

"If only what?"

"Those stupid bulbs." (I love the way Ivy pronounces the word stupid: *stewpid*, giving it a patrician lift.)

"Bulbs?"

"Remember last fall, all those bulbs I put in?"

"Oh," I said, remembering.

She looked at me squarely: "You don't mind as much as I do, do you?"

"Of course I do. You know I do."

"Tell me the truth."

What could I say? I've always been impressed by the accuracy of Ivy's observations. "The truth is—"

"The truth is—?" she helped me along.

"I guess I'm ready."

"Ready for what?" Her eyes filled with tears. This was a diffi-cult time for us. Christopher had died in January. He was a tough kid and lived a good five years longer than any of us ever thought he would. His death was not unexpected, but still, Ivy and I were feeling exceptionally fragile.

"Ready for what?" she asked again.

"For something," I admitted. "For anything, I guess."

The first house we look at seems perfect. The settled neighbor-hood is dense with trees and shrubbery and reminds us both of our part of Toronto. There are small repairs that need doing, but nothing major. Best of all, from the dining room there can be seen a startling lip of blue water meeting blue sky.

I point this out to Ivy; a view was one of the things we had put on our list. There is also a fireplace, another must, and a capa-cious kitchen with greenhouse windows overlooking a garden.

"And look at the bulbs," I point out. "Tulips halfway up. Daffodils."

"Lilies," Ivy says.

"I think we've struck it lucky," I tell the real-estate woman who's showing us around, a Mrs. Marjorie Little. ("Call me Marge," she'd said to us with West coast breeziness.)

Afterwards, in the car, Ivy is so quiet I have to prompt her. "Well?"

Marge Little, sitting at the wheel, peers at me, then at Ivy.

"It's just," Ivy begins, "it's just so depressing."

Depressing? I can't believe she's saying this. A view, central lo-cation, a fireplace. Plus bulbs.

"Well," Ivy says slowly, "it's a divorce house. You must have no-ticed?"

I hadn't. "A divorce house? How do you know?"

"I looked in the closets. Her clothes were there but *his* weren't."
"Oh."
"And half the pictures had been taken off the wall. Surely you noticed that."

I shake my head.

"I know it sounds silly, but wouldn't you rather move into a house with some good"—she pauses—"some good vibrations?"

"Vibrations?"

"Did you notice the broken light in the bathroom? I'll bet someone threw something at it. In a rage."

"We could always fix the light. And the other things. And with our own furniture—"

Ivy is an accountant. Once I heard a young man in her firm describe her as a *crack* accountant. For a number of years now she's been a senior partner. When this same young man heard she was leaving because of my transfer, he couldn't help ragging her a little, saying he thought women didn't move around at the whim of their husbands anymore, and that, out of principle, she ought to refuse to go to Vancouver or else arrange some kind of compromise life—separate apartments, for instance, with weekend rendezvous in Winnipeg.

Ivy had howled at this. She's a positive, good-natured woman and, as it turned out, she had no trouble finding an opening in a good Vancouver firm at senior level. As I say, she's positive. Which is why her apprehension over good or bad vibrations is puzzling. Can it be she sees bad times ahead for the two of us? Or is it only that she wants solid footing after these long years with Christopher? Neither of us is quite glued back together again. Not that we ever will be.

"I can't help it," Ivy is saying. "It just doesn't feel like a lucky house. There's something about—"

Marge Little interrupts with a broad smile. "I've got all kinds of interesting houses to show you. Maybe you'll like the next one better."

"Does it have good vibes?" Ivy asks, laughing a little to show she's only half-serious.

"I don't know," Marge Little says. "They don't put that kind of info on the fact sheet."

The next house is perched on the side of the canyon. No, that's not quite true. It is, in fact, falling into the canyon. I notice, but don't mention, the fact that the outside foundation walls are cracked and patched. Inside, the house is alarmingly empty; the cool settled air seems proof that it's been vacant for some time.

Marge consults her fact sheet. Yes, the house has been on the market about six months. The price has been reduced twice. But—she glances at us—perhaps we noticed the foundation....

"Yes," I say. "Hopeless."

"Damn," Ivy says.

We look at two more houses; both have spectacular views and architectural distinction. But one is a bankruptcy sale and the other is a divorce house. By now I'm starting to pick up the scent: it's a compound of petty carelessness and strenuous neglect, as though the owners had decamped in a hurry, angry at the rooms themselves.

To cheer ourselves up, the three of us have lunch in a sunny Broadway restaurant. It seems extraordinary that we can sit here and see mountains that are miles away; the thought that we will soon be able to live within sight of these mountains fills us with optimism. We order a little wine and linger in the sunlight. Vancouver is going to be an adventure. We're going to be happy here. Marge Little, feeling expansive, tells us about her three children and about the problem she has keeping her weight down. "Marge Large they'll be calling me soon," she says. It's an old joke, we sense, and the telling of it makes us feel we're old friends. She got into the business, she says, because she loves houses. And she has an instinct for matching houses with people. "So don't be discouraged," she tells us. "We'll find the perfect place this afternoon."

We drive through narrow city streets to a house where a famous movie idol grew up. His mother still lives in the house, a spry, slightly senile lady in her eighties. The tiny house—we quickly see it is far too small for us—is crowded with photographs of the famous son. He beams at us from the hallway, from the dining room, from the bedroom bureau.

"Oh, he's a good boy. Comes home every two or three years," his mother tells us, her large teeth shining in a diminished face. "And once I went down there, all the way down to Hollywood, on an airplane. He paid my way, sent me a ticket. I saw his swimming pool. They all have swimming pools. He has a cook, a man who does all the meals, so I didn't have to lift a finger for a whole week. What an experience, like a queen. I have some pictures someplace I could show you—"

"That would be wonderful," Marge Little says, "but"—she glances at her watch—"I'm afraid we have another appointment."

"—I saw those pictures just the other day. Now where—? I think they're in this drawer somewhere. Here, I knew it. Take a look at this. Isn't that something? That's his swimming pool. Kidney-shaped. He's got another one now, even bigger."

"Beautiful," Ivy says.

"And here he is when he was little. See this? He's be about nine there. We took a trip east. That's him and his dad standing by Niagara Falls. Here's another—"

"We really have to—"

"A good boy. I'll say that for him. Didn't give any trouble. Sometimes I see his movies on the TV and I can't believe the things he does, with women and so on. I have to pinch myself and say it's only pretend—"

"I think—"

"I'm going into this senior citizen place. They've got a nice TV lounge, big screen, bigger than this little bitty one, color too. I always—"

"Sad," Ivy says, when we escape at last and get into the car.

"The house or the mother?" I ask her.

"Both."

"At least it's not a D.H." (This has become our shorthand expression for divorce house.)

"Wait'll you see the next place," Marge Little says, swinging into traffic. "The next place is fabulous."

Fabulous, yes. But far too big. After that, in a fit of desperation, we look at a condo. "I'm not quite ready for this," I have to admit.

"No garden," Ivy says in a numb voice. She looks weary, and we decide to call it a day.

The ad in the newspaper reads: *Well-Loved Family Home.* And Ivy and Marge Little and I are there, knocking on the door at 9:30 A.M.

"Come in, come in," calls a young woman in faded jeans. She has a young child on one hip and another—they must be twins—by the hand. Sunlight pours in the front window and there is freshly baked bread cooling on the kitchen counter.

But the house is a disaster, a rabbit warren of narrow hallways and dark corners. The kitchen window is only feet away from a low, brick building where bodywork is being done on imported sportscars. The stairs are uneven. The bedroom floors slope and the paint is peeling off the bathroom ceiling.

"It just kills us to leave this place," the young woman says. She's following us through the rooms, pointing with unmistakable sorrow at the wall where they were planning to put up shelving, at the hardwood floors they were thinking of sanding. Out of the blue, they got news of a transfer.

Ironically, they're going to Toronto, and in a week's time they'll be there doing what we're doing, looking for a house they can love. "But we just know we'll never find a place like this," she tells us with sad shake of her head. "Not in a million zillion years."

After that we lose track of the number of houses. The day bends and blurs; square footage, zoning regulations, mortgage schedules, double-car garages, cedar-siding only two years old—was that the place near that little park? No, that was the one on that little crescent off Arbutus. Remember? The one without the basement.

Darkness is falling as Marge Little drives us back to our hotel. We are passing hundreds—it seems like thousands—of houses, and we see lamps being turned on, curtains being closed. Friendly smoke rises from substantial chimneys. Here and there, where the curtains are left open, we can see people sitting down to dinner. Passing one house I see a woman in a window, leaning over with a match in her hand, lighting a pair of candles. Ivy sees it too, and I'm sure she's feeling as I am, a little resentful that everyone but us seems to have a roof overhead.

"Tomorrow for sure," Marge calls cheerily. (Tomorrow is our last day. Both of us have to be home on Monday.)

"I suppose we could always rent for a year." Ivy says this with low enthusiasm.

"Or," I say, "we could make another trip in a month or so. Maybe there'll be more on the market."

"Isn't it funny? The first house we saw, remember? In a way, it was the most promising place we've seen."

"The one with the view from the dining room? With the broken light in the bathroom?"

"It might not look bad with a new fixture. Or even a skylight."

"Wasn't that a divorce house?" I ask Ivy.

"Yes," she shrugs, "but maybe that's just what we'll just have to settle for."

"It *was* listed at a good price."

"I live in a divorce house," Marge Little says, pulling up in front of our hotel. "It's been a divorce house for a whole year now."

"Oh, Marge," Ivy says. "I didn't mean—" she stops. "Forgive me."

"And it's not so bad. Sometimes it's darned cheerful."

"I just—" Ivy takes a breath, "I just wanted a lucky house. Maybe there's no such thing—"

"Are you interested in taking another look at that first house? I might be able to get you an appointment this evening. That is, if you think you can stand one more appointment today."

"Absolutely," we say together.

This time we inspect the house inch by inch. Ivy makes a list of the necessary repairs and I measure the windows for curtains. We hadn't realized that there was a cedar closet off one of the bedrooms. The lights of the city are glowing through the dining-room window. A spotlight at the back of the house picks out the flowers just coming into bloom. There'll be room for our hi-fi across from the fireplace. The basement is dry and very clean. The wallpaper in the downstairs den is fairly attractive and in good condition. The stairway is well-proportioned and the banister is a beauty. (I'm a sucker for banisters.) There's an alcove where the pine buffet will fit nicely. Trees on both sides of the house should give us greenery and privacy. The lawn, as far as we can tell, seems to be in good shape. There's a lazy susan in the kitchen, also a built-in dishwasher, a later model than ours. Plenty of room for a small table and a couple of chairs. The woodwork in the living room has been left natural, a wonder since so many people, a few years back, were painting over their oak trim.

Ivy says something that makes us laugh. "Over here," she says, "over here is where we'll put the Christmas tree." She touches the edge of one of the casement windows, brushes it with the side of her hand, and says, "It's hard to believe that people could live in such a beautiful house and be unhappy."

For a moment there's silence, and then Marge says, "We could put in an offer tonight. I don't think it's too late. What do you think?"

And now, suddenly, it's the next evening, and Ivy and I are flying back to Toronto. Here we are over the Rockies again, crossing them this time in darkness. Ivy sits with her head back, eyes closed, her shoulders so sharply her own; she's not quite asleep, but not quite awake either.

Our plane seems a fragile vessel, a piece of jewelry up here between the stars and the mountains. Flying through dark air like this makes me think that life itself is fragile. The miniature accidents of chromosomes can spread unstoppable circles of grief. A dozen words carelessly uttered can dismantle a marriage. A few gulps of oxygen are all that stand between us and death.

I wonder if Ivy is thinking, as I am, of the three months ahead, of how tumultuous they'll be. There are many things to think of when you move. For one, we'll have to put our own house up for sale. The thought startles me, though I've no idea why.

I try to imagine prospective buyers arriving for appointments, stepping through our front doors with polite murmurs and a sharp eye for imperfections.

They'll work their way through the downstairs, the kitchen (renewed only four years ago), the living room (yes, a real fireplace, a good draft), the dining room (small, but you can seat ten in a pinch). Then they'll make their way upstairs (carpet a little worn, but with lots of wear left). The main bedroom is a fair size (with good reading lamps built in, also bookshelves).

And then there's Christopher's bedroom.

Will the vibrations announce that here lived a child with little muscular control, almost no sight or hearing, and no real consciousness as that word is normally perceived? He had, though— and perhaps the vibrations will acknowledge the fact—his own kind of valor and perhaps his own way of seeing the world. At least Ivy and I always rewallpapered his room every three years or so out of a conviction that he took some pleasure in the sight of ducks swimming on a yellow sea. Later, it was sailboats; then tigers and monkeys dodging jungle growth; then a wild op-art checkerboard; and then, the final incarnation, a marvellous green cave of leafiness with amazing flowers and impossible birds sitting in branches.

I can't help wondering if these prospective buyers, these people looking for God only knows what, if they'll enter this room and feel something of his fragile presence alive in a fragile world.

Well, we shall see. We shall soon see.

RESPONDING PERSONALLY

1. In your journal or notebook, discuss what the story reveals about the stress and hardships of ordinary people living today.

2. Who is Christopher? What is his story?

RESPONDING CRITICALLY

3. What is the significant antecedent action of the story? Why are the couple looking for a house in Vancouver?
4. What are the various problems encountered in the house search? Are they ever resolved? What is the couple's final decision? How does Marge influence them?
5. How does the airplane trip reflect the meaning of the story's title and theme?
6. Assess the strength of Ivy, her husband, and the two as a couple. Is their relationship successful? Comment.

RESPONDING CREATIVELY

7. Write the stream of consciousness thoughts of a prospective buyer visiting the couple's old home in Toronto.
8. Make a collage about today's world based on your associations with the word *fragility*.

PROBLEM-SOLVING/DECISION-MAKING

9. Assume the role of a family counsellor who has been meeting with Ivy and her husband. Write a report indicating how they are coping with their grief.

"Wayne, it's time to lasso those kids and tuck them in the back seat."

Birk Sproxton
The Organized Woman Story

Carol is an organized woman. You will understand what I mean by an organized woman when I tell you about her love life, or what I know of her love life, for she has never never been in love with me. Not like that, anyways. I have the wrong name.

By organized, I don't mean that she can always find her car keys, though it is true, or that she can remember to phone her third cousin Sally on the third Sunday of every third month, though she does that, too. She phones me on the same day, the third Sunday of every third month, and she tells me that Sally has taken to lassoing the children at supper time, or whatever it is that Sally is up to, and she tells me the latest news about Michael. Michael and I correspond every few days on electronic mail, but no matter. She calls me regularly. On the third Sunday.

I first realized she was an organized woman when she fell in love with my friend. He is her second husband named Michael. The second Michael, my friend, is a different man from the first, but they have the same first name. Then I realized that she always falls in love with men named Michael. Not every Michael, of course, for she can be a very fussy woman, but every man she falls in love with turns out to be named Michael.

You may think that because her brother is named Michael and her father is named Michael that she is simply picking variants of her father, each man a copy of her father with his quiet laugh and confident walk, the way you fall in love with, say, a special kind of doughnut and each time you hanker for a doughnut you go to the same shop, the warm yeasty smells as you open the door always remind you of what you want, and you order the same kind

of doughnut you did the last time you were struck by the doughnut urge. Something like that.

Now you may argue husbands are not like doughnuts, but I
must tell you I once said that to her, I said, men are not like
doughnuts, you don't have to choose the same kind every time,
and she pointed out, in a rather peckish way I thought, that I certainly had not divorced myself from my last round of doughnuts,
but in fact I seemed to embrace and nurture and hold on to
doughnuts and let them root and ripen and grow into huge bal-
loon tires around my waist. I, she said—meaning me, your story
teller—seem to have clutched those chocolate doughnuts to my
very loins for life. She has this way of zeroing in on your weak
spots. So I dropped the subject.

But she was not looking for variants of her father.

I know this because she was once courted by Wayne, a pharmacist in my neighbourhood. In fact, she was infatuated with
Wayne, quite wrapped up in him, you might say, after she
chucked out her first husband named Michael, even to the point
of trying to persuade her brother to go by the name Wayne.

"After all," she said to her brother, "Wayne is your second name,
and this Wayne is very nice. I'd like you to be Wayne, too." She did
not approach her father, of course, whose second name is also
Wayne, because she knew that he would give in to anything his
darling-poo wanted and so it would not be a proper test. Therefore
she approached her brother first. But her brother remained adamant.
Michael was the name he preferred. Wayne wouldn't do, even if it
was his second name and one she was currently infatuated with. So
she dropped him. The pharmacist, I mean. If she could not get all her
men to go by the name Wayne, if she was stuck with Michael, then
Michael it would be. She'd have to find another Michael.

Wayne the pharmacist had to go. She thanked him very much
for giving her the cardboard boxes she had used to pack up her
first husband's things, and for allowing her a small discount on
the several tons of packing paper she had used to wrap every single item that Michael owned, each sock in its own wrapper, before she chucked him out.

That was the Saturday she broke tradition. She phoned me, even though it was Saturday, to say that Michael had departed, his possessions all neatly wrapped in tissue paper and tucked in solid cardboard cartons the nice pharmacist had given her. I thought I would say something to cheer her up, though she gave no sign of being upset, so I said, No, Michael hadn't gone, in fact he was sitting in my living room.

She said, "Oh, you silly man, what's he doing at your place?" And I, thinking she deserved a diversion though I knew she would find my place a deplorable mess, said, "Well, why don't you come over and find out?"

So she came over and that's how she met Michael, my friend, and that's why Michael and I now use electronic mail to talk. She phoned me the next day, Sunday, the third Sunday of the month, to say that Sally was building a huge jungle gym for the kids to climb on, she was bolting planks onto the third storey. Sally was, and then she, Carol, apologized for hauling Michael off like that last night, and wasn't he a nice man?

I said, of course you think he's a nice man because his name is Michael.

It was the wrong thing to say. I won't tell you exactly what she replied because it might make her look bad, but it had something to do with my feeling sorry for myself about all the poems I can't get anybody to buy, or read, and why didn't I get off my blossoming derrière and lift the telephone receiver and give Sally a call, she of the lasso and the jungle gym and the herd of howling kids.

So I did. I lifted the phone and did that very thing. That very day. The third Sunday of the month. Right after I fortified myself with a little nibble of chocolate doughnut and a somewhat larger nip on a heel of Johnny Walker Red Label and a thorough re-read of the more kindly rejection letters I have in my files.

"Sally," I said, in my most charming poet-voice, "Sally, I'm coming over."

"But," she said, "I don't even know you."

"So what," said I, "I don't know you either. That makes us even. Besides that, you have a lasso."

She said, "What will we do when you get here?"

I said, "I will read you my poems."

She said, with only a small hesitation, "What kind of poems?"

"Apple poems," I said, "Peach and orange and banana poems. Pomegranate and eggplant and rhubarb poems. I have apricots, I have blueberries, I have kiwi and squash, I have scarlet runners and carrots and beets, I have peas and pumpkins and pears and kohlrabi. I have delicate grapes and crunchy celery, I have potato poems, flowering reds and bristling whites, I have turnips and cabbage and broccoli and Brussels sprouts ..."

She interrupted me. It's a small failing of hers, not to be a telephone person; long telephone calls don't agree with her.

Then she said, in a quiet voice, she said, "I want a salad, I want you to read me a salad."

A minute ago the phone rang. You can hear it plainly from up here on the third floor of the jungle gym, despite the cries of the children and despite the tiny wet bottom planted on my knee. That will be Carol calling. She will be talking now to Sally. It is the third Sunday of the month. Carol will be asking us to drop over after supper for a visit. Bring the kids, she will say. And Wayne, bring him too, tell him I have some chocolate doughnuts.

She's an organized woman, Carol is. They won't talk long. We will drive over, and sit and visit, and Michael will ask about my latest crop of poems. Have I thought of maybe doing some weeding, he will ask in his gentle way. Then I will say, no, no weeding, I'm a fertilizer man, let them grow.

And Carol will agree with me, "Fertilizer, I'll say," and then give the little laugh that makes Michael's eyes shine.

And Sally, well, Sally will say in her sing-song voice how she likes the fruit and vegetables we grow together and how the kids grow like bad weeds and maybe we should gather them up now if we can disentangle them from the jungle of Michael's computer cords and get on our way, for we have to stop at the pharmacy to buy some radish seeds.

And then Sally will turn to me and say, "Wayne, it's time to lasso those kids and tuck them in the back seat."

And I will lasso those kids and tuck them and strap them tight with belts and hugs and kisses, and Sally will drive us home to make poems and salads together until the next time the phone rings on the third Sunday of the month. Then I will dust the fertilizer from my latest poems. The kids will howl as only kids can do. Sally will twirl her lasso as she picks up the receiver. It will be Carol. She's an organized woman.

RESPONDING PERSONALLY

1. With a partner, list the main characters in the story and their connections to one another. Note any other people mentioned by name only.

2. In your journal, write notes describing people you know whom this story reminded you of.

RESPONDING CRITICALLY

3. How is Carol an "organized woman"? Is that expression intended to be a compliment by the narrator? How can you tell?

4. What is the significance of the various names and connections between characters in the story? What is the author saying about names and their influence on people? Are the lives of people mainly determined by character, accident, coincidence, or fate? Explain.

5. For small group discussion—Decide what is the significance of:
   a) the references to doughnuts
   b) the narrator's fruit and vegetable poems
   c) the references to gardening
   d) the references to lassos.

6. Find and quote three examples of humour involving the characters.

RESPONDING CREATIVELY

7. Write a profile about the most intriguing person you have ever met.

8. Design a set of trading cards for the characters in this story. Post them for others to see.

PROBLEM-SOLVING/DECISION-MAKING

9. Create a brochure inspired by this story about strategies for becoming a positive person who has fulfilling relationships.

"We'd be the laughing-stock of
the town."

Alifa Rifaat
Another Evening at the Club

In a state of tension, she awaited the return of her husband. At a
loss to predict what would happen between them, she moved
herself back and forth in the rocking chair on the wide wooden
verandah that ran along the bank and occupied part of the river
itself. Its supports being fixed in the river bed, while around it
grew grasses and reeds. As though to banish her apprehension,
she passed her fingers across her hair. The spectres of the euca-
lyptus trees ranged along the garden fence rocked before her gaze,
with white egrets slumbering on the high branches like huge
white flowers among the thin leaves.

The crescent moon rose from behind the eastern mountains and
the peaks of the gently stirring waves glistening in its feeble rays,
intermingled with threads of light leaking from the houses of
Manfalout scattered along the opposite bank. The coloured bulbs
fixed to the trees in the garden of the club at the far end of the town
stood out against the surrounding darkness. Somewhere over there
her husband now sat, most likely engrossed in a game of chess.

It was only a few years ago that she had first laid eyes on him
at her father's house, meeting his gaze that weighed up her

beauty and priced it before offering the dowry. She had noted his eyes ranging over her as she presented him with the coffee in the Japanese cups that were kept safely locked away in the cupboard for important guests. Her mother had herself laid them out on the silver-plated tray with its elaborately embroidered spread. When the two men had taken their coffee, her father had looked up at her with a smile and had told her to sit down, and she had seated herself on the sofa facing them, drawing the end of her dress over her knees and looking through lowered lids at the man who might choose her as his wife. She had been glad to see that he was tall, well-built and clean-shaven except for a thin greying moustache. In particular she noticed the well-cut coat of English tweed and the silk shirt with gold links. She had felt herself blushing as she saw him returning her gaze. Then the man turned to her father and took out a gold case and offered him a cigarette.

"You really shouldn't, my dear sir," said her father, patting his chest with his left hand and extracting a cigarette with trembling fingers. Before he could bring out his box of matches Abboud Bey had produced his lighter.

"No, after you, my dear sir," said her father in embarrassment. Mingled with her sense of excitement at this man who gave out such an air of worldly self-confidence was a guilty shame at her father's inadequacy.

After lighting her father's cigarette Abboud Bey sat back, crossing his legs, and took out a cigarette for himself. He tapped it against the case before putting it in the corner of his mouth and lighting it, then blew out circles of smoke that followed each other across the room.

"It's a great honour for us, my son," said her father, smiling first at Abboud Bey, then at his daughter, at which Abboud Bey looked across at her and asked:

"And the beautiful little girl's still at second school?"

She lowered her head modestly and her father had answered:

"As from today she'll be staying at home in readiness for your happy life together, Allah permitting," and at a glance from her father she had hurried off to join her mother in the kitchen.

"You're a lucky girl," her mother had told her. "He's a real find. Any girl would be happy to have him. He's an Inspector of Irrigation though he's not yet forty. He earns a big salary and gets a fully furnished government house wherever he's posted, which will save us the expense of setting up a house—and I don't have to tell you what our situation is—and that's besides the house he owns in Alexandria where you'll be spending your holidays."

Samia had wondered to herself how such a splendid suitor had found his way to her door. Who had told him that Mr. Mahmoud Barakat, a mere clerk at the Court of Appeal, had a beautiful daughter of good reputation?

The days were then taken up with going the rounds of Cairo's shops and choosing clothes for the new grand life she would be living. This was made possible by her father borrowing on the security of his government pension. Abboud Bey, on his part, never visited her without bringing a present. For her birthday, just before they were married, he bought her an emerald ring that came in a plush box bearing the name of a well-known jeweller in Kasr el-Nil Street. On her wedding night, as he put a diamond bracelet round her wrist, he had reminded her that she was marrying someone with a brilliant career in front of him and that one of the most important things in life was the opinion of others, particularly one's equals and seniors. Though she was still only a young girl she must try to act with suitable dignity.

"Tell people you're from the well-known Barakat family and that your father was a judge," and he went up to her and gently patted her cheeks in a fatherly, reassuring gesture that he was often to repeat during their times together.

Then, yesterday evening, she had returned from the club somewhat light-headed from the bottle of beer she had been required to drink on the occasion of someone's birthday. Her husband, noting the state she was in, hurriedly took her back home. She had undressed and put on her nightgown, leaving her jewellery on the dressing-table, and was fast asleep seconds after getting into bed. The following morning, fully recovered, she slept late, then rang the bell as usual and had breakfast brought to her. It was only as she was putting her jewellery away in the wooden and mother-of-pearl box that she realized her emerald ring was missing.

Could it have dropped from her finger at the club? In the car on the way back? No, she distinctly remembered it last thing at night, remembered the usual difficulty she had in getting it off her finger. She stripped the bed of its sheets, turned over the mattress, looked inside the pillow cases, crawled on hands and knees, under the bed. The tray of breakfast lying on the small bedside table caught her eye and she remembered the young servant coming in that morning with it, remembered the noise of the tray being put down, the curtains being drawn, the tray then being lifted up again and placed on the beside table. No one but the servant had entered the room. Should she call her and question her?

Eventually, having taken two aspirins, she decided to do nothing and await the return of her husband from work.

Directly he arrived she told him what had happened and he took her by the arm and seated her down beside him:

"Let's just calm down and go over what happened."

She repeated, this time with further details, the whole story.

"And you've looked for it?"

"Everywhere. Every possible and impossible place in the bedroom and the bathroom. You see, I remember distinctly taking it off last night."

He grimaced at the thought of last night, then said:

"Anybody been in the room since Gazia when she brought in the breakfast?"

"Not a soul. I've even told Gazia not to do the room today."

"And you've not mentioned anything to her?"

"I thought I'd better leave it to you."

"Fine, go and tell her I want to speak to her. There's no point in your saying anything but I think it would be as well if you were present when I talk to her."

Five minutes later Gazia, the young servant girl they had recently employed, entered behind her mistress. Samia took herself to a far corner of the room while Gazia stood in front of Abboud Bey, her hands folded across her chest, her eyes lowered.

"Yes, sir?"

"Where's the ring?"

"What ring are you talking about, sir?"

"Now don't make out you don't know. The one with the green stone. It would be better for you if you hand it over and then nothing more need be said."

"May Allah blind me if I've set eyes on it."

He stood up and gave her a sudden slap on the face. The girl reeled back, put one hand to her cheek, then lowered it again to her chest and made no answer to any of Abboud's questions. Finally he said to her:

"You've got just fifteen seconds to say whether you've hidden the ring or else, I swear to you, you're not going to have a good time of it."

As he lifted up his arms to look at his watch the girl flinched slightly but continued in her silence. When he went to the telephone Samia raised her head and saw that the girl's cheeks were wet with tears. Abboud Bey got through to the Superintendent of Police and told him briefly what had occurred.

"Of course I haven't got any actual proof but seeing that no one else entered the room, it's obvious she's pinched it. Anyway I'll leave the matter in your capable hands—I know your people have their ways and means."

He gave a short laugh, then listened for a while and said: "I'm really most grateful to you."

He put down the receiver and turned round to Samia:

"That's it, my dear. There's nothing more to worry about. The Superintendent has promised me we'll get it back. The patrol car's on the way."

The following day, in the late afternoon, she'd been sitting in front of her dressing-table rearranging her jewellery in its box when an earring slipped from her grasp and fell to the floor. As she bent to pick it up she saw the emerald ring stuck between the leg of the table and the wall. Since that moment she had sat in a state of panic awaiting her husband's return from the club. She even felt tempted to walk down to the water's edge and throw it into the river so as to be rid of the unpleasantness that lay ahead.

At the sound of the screech of tyres rounding the house to the garage, she slipped the ring on to her finger. As he entered she stood up and raised her hand to show him the ring. Quickly, trying to choose her words but knowing that she was expressing herself clumsily, she explained what an extraordinary thing it was that it should have lodged itself between the dressing-table and the wall, what an extraordinary coincidence she should have dropped the earring and so seen it, how she'd thought of ringing him at the club to tell him the good news but ...

She stopped in mid-sentence when she saw his frown and added weakly: "I'm sorry. I can't think how it could have happened. What do we do now?"

He shrugged his shoulders as though in surprise.

"Are you asking me, my dear lady? Nothing of course."

"But they've been beating up the girl—you yourself said they'd not let her be till she confessed."

Unhurriedly, he sat himself down as though to consider this new aspect of the matter. Taking out his case, he tapped a cigarette against it in his accustomed manner, then moistened his lips, put the cigarette in place and lit it. The smoke rings hovered in the still air as he looked at his watch and said:

"In any case she's not got all that long before they let her go. They can't keep her for more than forty-eight hours without getting any evidence or a confession. It won't kill her to put up with things for a while longer. By now the whole town knows the servant stole the ring—or would you like me to tell everyone: 'Look, folks, the fact is that the wife got a bit tiddly on a couple of sips of beer and the ring took off on its own and hid itself behind the dressing-table.' What do you think?"

"I know the situation's a bit awkward ..."

"Awkward? It's downright ludicrous. Listen, there's nothing to be done but to give it to me and the next time I go down to Cairo I'll sell it and get something else in its place. We'd be the laughing-stock of the town."

He stretched out his hand and she found herself taking off the ring and placing it in the outstretched palm. She was careful that their eyes should not meet. For a moment she was on the point of protesting and in fact uttered a few words:

"I'd just like to say we could ..."

Putting the ring away in his pocket, he bent over her and with both hands gently patted her on the cheeks. It was a gesture she had long become used to, a gesture that promised her continued security, that told her that this man who was her husband and the father of her child had also taken the place of her father who, as though assured that he had found her a suitable substitute, had followed up her marriage with his own funeral. The gesture told her more eloquently than any words that he was the man, she the woman, he the one who carried the responsibilities, made the decisions, she the one whose role it was to be beautiful, happy, carefree. Now, though, for the first time in their life together the gesture came like a slap in the face.

Directly he removed his hands her whole body was seized with an uncontrollable trembling. Frightened he would notice, she rose to her feet and walked with deliberate steps towards the large window. She leaned her forehead against the comforting cold surface and closed her eyes tightly for several seconds. When she opened them she noticed that the café lights strung between the trees on the opposite shore had been turned on and that there were men seated under them and a waiter moving among the tables. The dark shape of a boat momentarily blocked out the café scene; in the light from the hurricane lamp hanging from its bow she saw it cutting through several of those floating islands of Nile waterlilies that, rootless, are swept along with the current.

Suddenly she became aware of his presence alongside her.

"Why don't you go and change quickly while I take the car out? It's hot and it would be nice to have supper at the club."

"As you like. Why not?"

By the time she had turned round from the window she was smiling.

RESPONDING PERSONALLY

1. Describe how you felt when you lost something valuable and explain what happened afterwards.
2. What does it mean to "save face"? Why are people too often unwilling to admit error or take responsibility for their own mistakes and misjudgements?

RESPONDING CRITICALLY

3. How does the protagonist first meet her husband? How does he win her hand in marriage? Why does he tell her about his background?
4. The incident of dealing with the lost ring is foreshadowed by characterization earlier in the story. Explain.
5. How does the wife feel when she finds the ring? How does her husband react to her discovery? Why?
6. What does the ending reveal about the couple individually and their relationship?

RESPONDING CREATIVELY

7. Write a letter the wife might submit to a newspaper advice columnist. Then write the columnist's response.
8. With two other students, adapt this story for a reader's theatre presentation. Perform the finished script for the class.

PROBLEM-SOLVING/DECISION-MAKING

9. For small group discussion: Offer your views on what the couple did. Were they right or wrong in their choices? Give reasons for your position.

"Multivac will have a complete
analysis of all of you in its
files."

Isaac Asimov
All the Troubles of the World

The greatest industry on Earth centred around Multivac—
Multivac, the giant computer that had grown in fifty years until
its various ramifications had filled Washington, D.C., to the sub-
urbs and had reached out tendrils into every city and town on
Earth.

An army of civil servants fed it data constantly and another
army correlated and interpreted the answers it gave. A corps of
engineers patrolled its interior while mines and factories consumed themselves in keeping its reserve stocks of replacement
parts ever complete, ever accurate, ever satisfactory in every way.

Multivac directed Earth's economy and helped Earth's science.
Most important of all, it was the central clearing house of all
known facts about each individual Earthman.

And each day it was part of Multivac's duties to take the four
billion sets of facts about individual human beings that filled its
vials and extrapolate them for an additional day of time. Every
Corrections Department on Earth received the data appropriate to
its own area of jurisdiction, and the overall data was presented in
one large piece to the Central Board of Corrections in
Washington, D.C.

Bernard Gulliman was in the fourth week of his year term as
Chairman of the Central Board of Corrections and had grown casual enough to accept the morning report without being frightened by it. As usual, it was a sheaf of paper some six inches thick.
He knew by now he was not expected to read it. (No human
could.) Still, it was amusing to glance through it.

There was the usual list of predictable crimes: frauds of all
sorts, larcenies, riots, manslaughters, arsons.

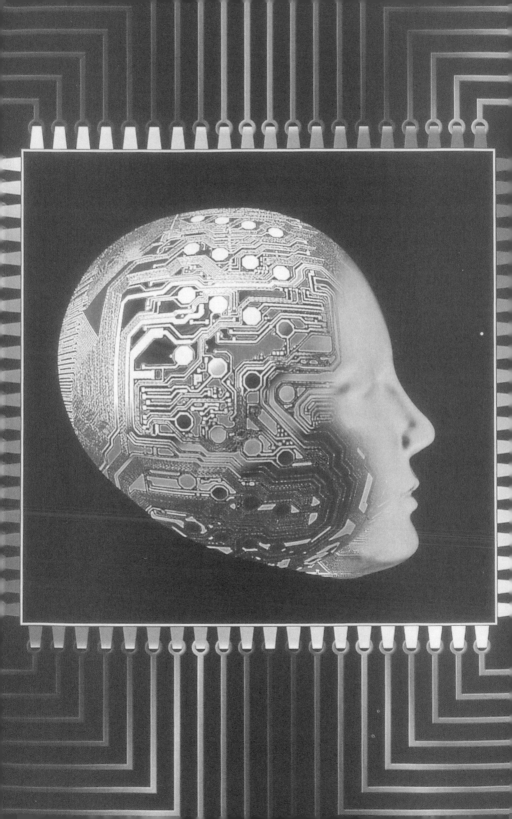

He looked for one particular heading and felt a slight shock at finding it there at all, then another one at seeing two entries. Not one, but two. *Two* first-degree murders. He had not seen two in one day in all his term as Chairman so far.

He punched the knob of the two-way intercom and waited for the smooth face of his co-ordinator to appear on the screen.

"Ali," said Gulliman. "There are two first-degrees this day. Is there any unusual problem?"

"No, sir." The dark-complexioned face with its sharp, black eyes seemed restless, "Both cases are quite low probability."

"I know that," said Gulliman. "I observed that neither probability is higher than 15 percent. Just the same, Multivac has a reputation to maintain. It has virtually wiped out crime, and the public judges that by its record on first-degree murder which is, of course, the most spectacular crime."

Ali Othman nodded. "Yes, sir. I quite realize that."

"You also realize, I hope," Gulliman said, "that I don't want a single consummated case of it during my term. If any other crime slips through, I may allow excuses. If a first-degree murder slips through, I'll have your hide. Understand?"

"Yes, sir. The complete analyses of the two potential murders are already at the district offices involved. The potential criminals and victims are under observation. I have rechecked the probabilities of consummation and they are already dropping."

"Very good," said Gulliman, and broke connection.

He went back to the list with an uneasy feeling that perhaps he had been overpompous. —But then, one had to be firm with these permanent civil-service personnel and make sure they didn't imagine they were running everything, including the Chairman. Particularly this Othman, who had been working with Multivac since both were considerably younger, and had a proprietary air that could be infuriating.

To Gulliman, this matter of crime was the political chance of a lifetime. So far, no Chairman had passed through his term without a murder taking place somewhere on Earth, some time. The previous Chairman had ended with a record of eight, three more (*more*, in fact) than his predecessor.

Now Gulliman intended to have *none*. He was going to be, he had decided, the first Chairman without any murder at all anywhere on Earth during his term. After that, and the favorable publicity that would result—

He barely skimmed the rest of the report. He estimated that there were at least two thousand cases of prospective wife-beatings listed. Undoubtedly, not all would be stopped in time. Perhaps thirty percent would be consummated. But the incidence was dropping and consummations were dropping even more quickly.

Multivac had added wife-beating to its list of predictable crimes only some five years earlier and the average man was not yet accustomed to the thought that if he planned to wallop his wife, it would be known in advance. As the conviction percolated through society, women would first suffer fewer bruises and then, eventually, none.

Some husband-beatings were on the list too, Gulliman noticed.

Ali Othman closed connections and stared at the screen from which Gulliman's jowled and balding head had departed. Then he looked across at his assistant, Rafe Leemy, and said, "What do we do?"

"Don't ask me. *He's* worried about just a lousy murder or two."

"It's an awful chance trying to handle this thing on our own. Still if we tell him, he'll have a first-class fit. These elective politicians have their skins to think of, so he's bound to get in our way and make things worse."

Leemy nodded his head and put a thick lower lip between his teeth. "Trouble is, though, what if we miss out? It would just about be the end of the world, you know."

"If we miss out, who cares what happens to us? We'll just be part of the general catastrophe." Then he said in a more lively manner, "But hell, the probability is only 12.3 percent. On anything else, except maybe murder, we'd let the probabilities rise a bit before taking any action at all. There could still be spontaneous correction."

"I wouldn't count on it," said Leemy dryly.

"I don't intend to. I was just pointing the fact out. Still, at this probability, I suggest we confine ourselves to simple observation for the moment. No one could plan a crime like this alone; there must be accomplices."

"Multivac didn't name any."

"I know. Still—" His voice trailed off

So they stared at the details of the one crime not included on the list handed out to Gulliman; the one crime much worse than first-degree murder; the one crime never before attempted in the history of Multivac; and wondered what to do.

Ben Manners considered himself the happiest sixteen-year-old in Baltimore. This was, perhaps, doubtful. But he was certainly one of the happiest, and one of the most excited.

At least, he was one of the handful admitted to the galleries of the stadium during the swearing in of the eighteen-year-olds. His older brother was going to be sworn in so his parents had applied for spectators' tickets and they had allowed Ben to do so, too. But when Multivac chose among all the applicants, it was Ben who got the ticket.

Two years later, Ben would be sworn in himself, but watching big brother Michael now was the next best thing.

His parents had dressed him (or supervised the dressing, at any rate) with all care, as representative of the family and sent him off with numerous messages for Michael, who had left days earlier for preliminary physical and neurological examinations.

The stadium was on the outskirts of town and Ben, just bursting with self-importance, was shown to his seat. Below him, now, were rows upon rows of hundreds upon hundreds of eighteen-year-olds (boys to the right, girls to the left), all from the second district of Baltimore. At various times in the years, similar meetings were going on all over the world, but this was Baltimore, this was the important one. Down there (somewhere) was Mike, Ben's own brother.

Ben scanned the tops of heads, thinking somehow he might recognize his brother. He didn't, of course, but then a man came out of the raised platform in front of all the crowd and Ben stopped looking to listen.

The man said, "Good afternoon, swearers and guests. I am Randolph T. Hoch, in charge of the Baltimore ceremonies this year. The swearers have met me several times now during the progress of the physical and neurological portions of this examination. Most of the task is done, but the most important matter is left. The swearer himself, his personality, must go into Multivac's records.

"Each year, this requires some explanation to the young people reaching adulthood. Until now" (he turned to the young people before him and his eyes went no more to the gallery) "you have not been adult; you have not been individuals in the eyes of Multivac, except where you were especially singled out as such by your parents or your government.

"Until now, when the time for the yearly up-dating of information came, it was your parents who filled in the necessary data on you. Now the time has come for you to take over that duty yourself. It is a great honor, a great responsibility. Your parents have told us what schooling you've had, what diseases, what habits; a great many things. But now you must tell us a great deal more; your innermost thoughts; your most secret deeds.

"This is hard to do the first time, embarrassing even, but it *must* be done. Once it is done, Multivac will have a complete analysis of all of you in its files. It will understand your actions and reactions. It will even be able to guess with fair accuracy at your future actions and reactions.

"In this way, Multivac will protect you. If you are in danger of accident, it will know. If someone plans harm to you, it will know. If you plan harm, it will know and you will be stopped in time so that it will not be necessary to punish you.

"With its knowledge of all of you, Multivac will be able to help Earth adjust its economy and its laws for the good of all. If you have a personal problem, you may come to Multivac with it and with its knowledge of all of you, Multivac will be able to help you.

"Now you will have many forms to fill out. Think carefully and answer all questions as accurately as you can. Do not hold back through shame or caution. No one will ever know your answers except Multivac unless it becomes necessary to learn the answers in order to protect you. And then only authorized officials of the government will know.

"It may occur to you to stretch the truth a bit here or there. Don't do this. We will find out if you do. All your answers put together form a pattern. If some answers are false, they will not fit the pattern and Multivac will discover them. If all your answers are false, there will be a distorted pattern of a type that Multivac will recognize. So you must tell the truth."

Eventually, it was all over, however; the form-filling, the ceremonies and speeches that followed. In the evening, Ben, standing tiptoe, finally spotted Michael, who was still carrying the robes he had worn in the "parade of the adults." They greeted one another with jubilation.

They shared a light supper and took the expressway home, alive and alight with the greatness of the day.

They were not prepared, then, for the sudden transition of the homecoming. It was a numbing shock to both of them to be stopped by a cold-faced young man in uniform outside their own front door; to have their papers inspected before they could enter their own house; to find their own parents sitting forlornly in the living room, the mark of tragedy on their faces.

Joseph Manners, looking much older than he had that morning, looked out of his puzzled, deep-sunken eyes at his sons (one with the robes of new adulthood still over his arm) and said, "I seem to be under house arrest."

Bernard Gulliman could not and did not read the entire report. He read only the summary and that was most gratifying indeed.

A whole generation, it seemed, had grown up accustomed to the fact that Multivac could predict the commission of major crimes. They learned that Corrections agents would be on the scene before the crime could be committed. They found out that consummation of the crime led to inevitable punishment. Gradually, they were convinced that there was no way anyone could outsmart Multivac.

The result was, naturally, that even the intention of crime fell off. And as such intentions fell off and as Multivac's capacity was enlarged, minor crimes could be added to the list it would predict each morning, and these crimes, too, were now shrinking in incidence.

So Gulliman had ordered an analysis made (by Multivac naturally) of Multivac's capacity to turn its attention to the problem of predicting probabilities of disease incidence. Doctors might soon be alerted to individual patients who might grow diabetic in the course of the next year, or suffer an attack of tuberculosis or grow a cancer.

An ounce of prevention—

And the report was a favorable one!

After that, the roster of the day's possible crimes arrived and there was not a first-degree murder on the list.

Gulliman put in an intercom call to Ali Othman in high good humor. "Othman, how do the numbers of crimes in the daily lists of the past week average compare with those in my first week as chairman?"

It had gone down, it turned out, by 8 percent and Gulliman was happy indeed. No fault of his own, of course, but the electorate would not know that. He blessed his luck that he had come in at the right time, at the very climax of Multivac, when disease, too, could be placed under its all-embracing and protecting knowledge.

Gulliman would prosper by this.

Othman shrugged his shoulders. "Well, he's happy."

"When do we break the bubble?" said Leemy. "Putting Manners under observation just raised the probabilities and house arrest gave it another boost."

"Don't I know it?" said Othman peevishly. "What I don't know is why."

"Accomplices, maybe, like you said. With Manners in trouble, the rest have to strike at once or be lost."

"Just the other way around. With our hand on one, the rest would scatter for safety and disappear. Besides, why aren't the accomplices named by Multivac?"

"Well, then do we tell Gulliman?"

"No, not yet. The probability is still only 17.3 percent. Let's get a bit more drastic first."

Elizabeth Manners said to her younger son, "You go to your room, Ben."

"But what's it all about, Mom?" asked Ben, his voice breaking at this strange ending to what had been a glorious day.

"Please!"

He left reluctantly, passing through the door to the stairway, walking up it nosily and down again quietly.

And Mike Manners, the older son, the new-minted adult and the hope of the family, said in a voice and tone that mirrored his brother's, "What's it all about?"

Joe Manners said, "As heaven is my witness, son, I don't know. I haven't done anything."

"Well, sure you haven't done anything." Mike looked at his small-boned, mild-mannered father in wonder. "They must be here because you're *thinking* of doing something."

"I'm not."

Mrs. Manners broke in angrily, "How can he be thinking of doing something worth all—all this." She cast her arm about, in a gesture toward the enclosing shell of government men about the house. "When I was a little girl, I remember the father of a friend of mine was working in a bank, and they once called him up and said to leave the money alone and he did. It was fifty thousand dollars. He hadn't really taken it. He was just thinking about taking it. They didn't keep those things as quiet in those days as they do now; the story got out. That's how I know about it.

"But I mean," she went on, rubbing her plump hands slowly together, "that was fifty thousand dollars; fifty—thousand—dollars.

Yet all they did was call him; one phone call. What could your father be planning that would make it worth having a dozen men
come down and close off the house?"

Joe Manners said, eyes filled with pain, "I am planning no
crime, not even the smallest. I swear it."

Mike, filled with the conscious wisdom of a new adult, said,
"Maybe it's something subconscious, Pop. Some resentment
against your supervisor."

"So that I would want to kill him? No!"

"Won't they tell you what it is, Pop?"

His mother interrupted again, "No, they won't. We've asked. I
said they were ruining our standing in the community just being
here. The least they could do is tell us what it's all about so we
could fight it, so we could explain."

"And they wouldn't?"

"They wouldn't."

Mike stood with his legs spread apart and his hands deep in
his pockets. He said, troubled, "Gee, Mom, Multivac doesn't
make mistakes."

His father pounded his fist helplessly on the arm of the sofa. "I
tell you I'm not planning any crime."

The door opened without a knock and a man in uniform
walked in with a sharp, self-possessed stride. His face had a
glazed, official appearance. He said, "Are you Joseph Manners?"

Joe Manners rose to his feet. "Yes. Now what is it you want of
me?"

"Joseph Manners, I place you under arrest by order of the government," and curtly he showed his identification as a
Corrections officer. "I must ask you to come with me."

"For what reason? What have I done?"

"I am not at liberty to discuss that."

"But I can't be arrested just for planning a crime even if I were
doing that. To be arrested I must actually have *done* something.
You can't arrest me otherwise. It's against the law."

The officer was impervious to the logic. "You will have to come
with me."

Mrs. Manners shrieked and fell on the coach, weeping hyster-
ically. Joseph Manners could not bring himself to violate the code
drilled into him all his life by actually resisting an officer, but he
hung back at least, forcing the Corrections officer to use muscular power to drag him forward.

And Manners called out as he went, "But tell me what it is. Just
tell me. If I *knew*—Is it murder? Am I supposed to be planning
murder?"

The door closed behind him and Mike Manners, white-faced
and suddenly feeling not the least bit adult, stared first at the
door, then at his weeping mother.

Ben Manners, behind the door and suddenly feeling quite
adult, pressed his lips tightly together and thought he knew exactly what to do.

If Multivac took away, Multivac could also give. Ben had been
at the ceremonies that very day. He had heard this man, Randolph
Hoch, speak of Multivac and all that Multivac could do. It could
direct the government and it could also unbend and help out
some plain person who came to it for help.

Anyone could ask help of Multivac and anyone meant Ben.
Neither his mother nor Mike were in any condition to stop him
now, and he had some money left of the amount they had given
him for his great outing that day. If afterward they found him
gone and worried about it, that couldn't be helped. Right now, his
first loyalty was to his father.

He ran out the back way and the officer at the door cast a
glance at his papers and let him go.

Harold Quimby handled the complaints department of the
Baltimore substation of Multivac. He considered himself to be a
member of that branch of the civil service that was most important of all. In some ways, he may have been right, and those who
heard him discuss the matter would have had to be made of iron
not to feel impressed.

For one thing, Quimby would say, Multivac was essentially an
invader of privacy. In the past fifty years, mankind had had to

acknowledge that its thoughts and impulses were no longer secret, that it owned no inner recess where anything could be hidden. And mankind had to have something in return.

Of course, it got prosperity, peace, and safety, but that was abstract. Each man and woman needed something personal as his or her own reward for surrendering privacy, and each one got it. Within reach of every human being was a Multivac station with circuits into which he could freely enter his own problems and questions without control or hindrance, and from which, in a matter of minutes, he could receive answers.

At any given moment, five million individual circuits among the quadrillion or more within Multivac might be involved in this question-and-answer program. The answers might not always be certain, but they were the best available, and every questioner *knew* the answer to be the best available and had faith in it. That was what counted.

And now an anxious sixteen-year-old had moved slowly up the waiting line of men and women (each face in that line illuminated by a different mixture of hope with fear or anxiety or even anguish—always with hope predominating as the person stepped nearer and nearer to Multivac).

Without looking up, Quimby took the filled-out form being handed him and said, "Booth 5-B."

Ben said, "How do I ask the question, sir?"

Quimby looked up then, with a bit of surprise. Pre-adults did not generally make use of the service. He said kindly, "Have you ever done this before, son?"

"No, sir."

Quimby pointed to the model on his desk. "You use this. You see how it works? Just like a typewriter. Don't you try to write or print anything by hand. Just use the machine. Now you take Booth 5-B, and if you need help, just press the red button and someone will come. Down that aisle, son, on the right."

He watched the youngster go down the aisle and out of view and smiled. No one was ever turned away from Multivac. Of course, there was always a certain percentage of trivia: people who asked personal questions about their neighbors or obscene questions about prominent personalities; college youths trying to outguess their professors or thinking it clever to stump Multivac by asking it Russell's class-of-all-classes paradox and so on.

Multivac could take care of all that. It needed no help.

Besides, each question and answer was filed and formed but another item in the fact assembly for each individual. Even the most trivial question and the most impertinent, insofar as it reflected the personality of the questioner, helped humanity by helping Multivac know about humanity.

Quimby turned his attention to the next person in line, a middle-aged woman, gaunt and angular, with the look of trouble in her eye.

Ali Othman strode the length of his office, his heels thumping desperately on the carpet. "The probability still goes up. It's 22.4 percent now. Damnation! We have Joseph Manners under actual arrest and it still goes up." He was perspiring freely.

Leemy turned away from the telephone. "No confession yet. He's under Psychic Probing and there is no sign of crime. He may be telling the truth."

Othman said, "Is Multivac crazy then?"

Another phone sprang to life. Othman closed connections quickly, glad of the interruption. A Corrections officer's face came to life in the screen. The officer said, "Sir, are there any new directions as to Manners' family? Are they to be allowed to come and go as they have been?"

"What do you mean, as they have been?"

"The original instructions were for the house arrest of Joseph Manners. Nothing was said of the rest of the family, sir."

"Well, extend it to the rest of the family until you are informed otherwise."

"Sir, that is the point. The mother and older son are demanding information about the younger son. The younger son is gone and they claim he is in custody and wish to go to headquarters to inquire about it."

Othman frowned and said in almost a whisper, "Younger son? How young?"

"Sixteen, sir," said the officer.

"Sixteen and he's gone. Don't you know where?"

"He was allowed to leave, sir. There were no orders to hold him."

"Hold the line. Don't move." Othman put the line into suspension, then clutched at his coal-black hair with both hands and shrieked, "Fool! Fool! Fool!'

Leemy was startled, "What the hell?"

"The man has a sixteen-year-old son," choked out Othman. "A sixteen-year-old is not an adult and he is not filed independently in Multivac, but only as part of his father's file." He glared at Leemy. "Doesn't everyone know that until eighteen a youngster does not file his own reports with Multivac but that his father does it for him? Don't I know it? Don't you?"

"You mean Multivac didn't mean Joe Manners?" said Leemy.

"Multivac meant his minor son, and the youngster is gone, now. With officers three deep around the house, he calmly walks out and goes on you know what errand."

He whirled to the telephone circuit to which the Corrections officer still clung, the minute break having given Othman just time enough to collect himself and to assume a cool and self-possessed mien. (It would never have done to throw a fit before the eyes of the officer, however much good it did in purging his spleen.)

He said, "Officer, locate the younger son who has disappeared. Take every man you have, if necessary. Take every man available in the district, if necessary. I shall give the appropriate orders. You must find that boy at all costs."

"Yes, sir."

Connection was broken. Othman said, "Have another rundown on the probabilities, Leemy."

Five minutes later, Leemy said, "It's down to 19.6 percent. It's *down*."

Othman drew a long breath. "We're on the right track at last."

Ben Manners sat in Booth 5-B and punched out slowly, "My name is Benjamin Manners, number MB-71833412. My father, Joseph Manners, has been arrested but we don't know what crime he is planning. Is there any way we can help him?"

He sat and waited. He might be only sixteen but he was old enough to know that somewhere those words were being whirled into the most complex structure ever conceived by man; that a trillion facts would blend and co-ordinate into a whole, and that from that whole, Multivac would abstract the best help.

The machine clicked and a card emerged. It had an answer on it, a long answer. It began, "Take the expressway to Washington, D.C., at once. Get off at the Connecticut Avenue stop. You will find a special exit, labelled 'Multivac' with a guard. Inform the guard you are a special courier for Dr. Trumbull and he will let you enter.

"You will be in a corridor. Proceed along it till you reach a small door labelled 'Interior.' Enter and say to the men inside, 'Message for Dr. Trumbull!' You will be allowed to pass. Proceed on—"

It went on in this fashion. Ben could not see the application to his question, but he had complete faith in Multivac. He left at a run, heading for the expressway to Washington.

The Corrections officers traced Ben Manners to the Baltimore station an hour after he had left. A shocked Harold Quimby found himself flabbergasted at the number and importance of the men who had focussed on him in the search for a sixteen-year-old.

"Yes, a boy," he said, "but I don't know where he went to after he was through here. I had no way of knowing that anyone was looking for him. We accept all comers here. Yes, I can get the record of the question and answer."

They looked at the record and televised it to Central Headquarters at once.

Othman read it through, turned up his eyes, and collapsed. They brought him to almost at once. He said to Leemy weakly, "Have them catch that boy. And have a copy of Multivac's answer made out for me. There's no way anymore, no way out. I must see Gulliman now."

Bernard Gulliman had never seen Ali Othman as much perturbed before, and watching the co-ordinator's wild eyes now sent a trickle of ice water down his spine.

He stammered, "What do you mean, Othman? What do you mean worse than murder?"

"Much worse than just murder."

Gulliman was quite pale. "Do you mean assassination of a high government official?" (It did cross his mind that he himself—)

Othman nodded. "Not just a government official. *The* government official."

"The *Secretary-General*?" said Gulliman in an appalled whisper.

"More than that, even. Much more. We deal with a plan to assassinate Multivac!"

"WHAT!"

"For the first time in the history of Multivac, the computer came up with the report that it itself was in danger."

"Why was I not at once informed?"

Othman half-truthed out of it. "The matter was so unprecedented, sir, that we explored the situation first before daring to put it on official record."

"But Multivac has been saved, of course? It's been saved?"

"The probabilities of harm have declined to under 4 percent. I am waiting for the report now."

"Message for Dr. Trumbull," said Ben Manners to the man on the high stool, working carefully on what looked like the controls of a stratojet cruiser, enormously magnified.

"Sure, Jim," said the man. "Go ahead."

Ben looked at his instructions and hurried on. Eventually, he would find a tiny control lever which he was to shift to a DOWN position at a moment when a certain indicator spot would light up red.

He heard an agitated voice behind him, then another, and suddenly, two men had him by his elbows. His feet were lifted off the floor.

One man said, "Come with us, boy."

Ali Othman's face did not noticeably lighten at the news, even though Gulliman said with great relief, "If we have the boy, then Multivac is safe."

"For the moment."

Gulliman put a trembling hand to his forehead. "What a half hour I've had. Can you imagine what the destruction of Multivac for even a short time would mean? The government would have collapsed; the economy broken down. It would have meant devastation worse—" His head snapped up, "What do you mean *for the moment?*"

"The boy, this Ben Manners, had no intention of doing harm. He and his family must be released and compensation for false imprisonment given them. He was only following Multivac's instructions in order to help his father and it's done that. His father is free now."

"Do you mean Multivac ordered the boy to pull a lever under circumstances that would burn out enough circuits to require a month's repair work? You mean Multivac would suggest its own destruction for the comfort of one man?"

"It's worse than that, sir. Multivac not only gave those instructions but selected the Manners family in the first place because Ben Manners looked exactly like one of Dr. Trumbull's pages so that he could get into Multivac without being stopped."

"What do you mean the family was selected?"

"Well, the boy would have never have gone to ask the question if his father had not been arrested. His father would never have been arrested if Multivac had not blamed him for planning the destruction of Multivac. Multivac's own action started the chain of events that almost led to Multivac's destruction."

"But there's no sense to that," Gulliman said in a pleading voice. He felt small and helpless and he was virtually on his knees, begging this Othman, this man who had spent nearly a lifetime with Multivac, to reassure him.

Othman did not do so. He said, "This is Multivac's first attempt along this line as far as I know. In some ways, it planned well.

It chose the right family. It carefully did not distinguish between father and son to send us off the track. It was still an amateur at the game, though. It could not overcome its own instructions that led it to report the probability of its own destruction as increasing with every step we took down the wrong road. It could not avoid recording the answer it gave the youngster. With further practice, it will probably learn deceit. It will learn to hide certain facts, fail to record others. From now on, every instruction it gives may have the seeds in it of its own destruction. We will never know. And however careful we are, eventually Multivac will succeed. I think, Mr. Gulliman, you will be the last Chairman of this organization."

Gulliman pounded his desk in fury. "But why, why, why? Damn you, why? What is wrong with it? Can't it be fixed?"

"I don't think so," said Othman, in soft despair. "I've never thought about this before. I've never had the occasion to until this happened, but now that I think of it, it seems to me we have reached the end of the road because Multivac is too good. Multivac has grown so complicated, its reactions are no longer those of a machine, but those of a living thing."

"You're mad, but even so?"

"For fifty years and more we have been loading humanity's troubles on Multivac, on this living thing. We've asked it to care for us, all together and each individually. We've asked it to take all our secrets into itself; we've asked it to absorb our evil and guard us against it. Each of us brings his troubles to it, adding his bit to the burden. Now we are planning to load the burden of human disease on Multivac, too."

Othman paused a moment, then burst out, "Mr. Gulliman, Multivac bears all the troubles of the world on its shoulders and it is tired."

"Madness. Midsummer madness," muttered Gulliman.

"Then let me show you something. Let me put it to the test. May I have permission to use the Multivac circuit line here in your office?"

"Why?"

"To ask it a question no one has ever asked Multivac before."

"Will you do it harm?" asked Gulliman in quick alarm.

"No. But it will tell us what we want to know."

The Chairman hesitated a trifle. Then he said, "Go ahead."

Othman used the instrument on Gulliman's desk. His fingers punched out the question with deft strokes: "Multivac, what do you yourself want more than anything else?"

The moment between question and answer lengthened unbearably, but neither Othman nor Gulliman breathed.

And there was a clicking and a card popped out. It was a small card. On it, in precise letters, was the answer:

"I want to die."

RESPONDING PERSONALLY

1. In your response journal, list the many troubles of the world likely experienced by Multivac. Compare your list with that of another student.

2. For paragraph writing: Is the story's premise plausible? Can computers be as autonomous, secretive, powerful, and self-conscious as Multivac?

RESPONDING CRITICALLY

3. What evidence from the story suggests that Ben and other characters see Multivac as a god? What effect does their view have on the plot and resolution?

4. How is this future world nearly perfect? What role does Multivac play in this new world order?

5. What is the essential flaw of Multivac? Why does it malfunction? Why don't the humans suspect Multivac? What throws them off from finding the truth?

6. How is suspense created in the story? What are the most suspenseful moments in the story?

RESPONDING CREATIVELY

7. Write a computer doctor's analysis of Multivac's problem.

8. Write an essay describing life in the year 2020. What are the lifestyles and values of the day? What will be the role and place of technology in this era?

PROBLEM-SOLVING/DECISION-MAKING

9. Debate the following resolution: "Be it resolved that technology be reduced in order to improve the quality of life."

Wallace Stegner
Volcano

Once they had turned off the asphalt onto the rough graded road
the driver nursed the car along carefully, creeping across bridges
and through arroyos and along rocky stretches. While lighting a
cigarette he explained to his American passenger.

"It is a car which cost seven thousand pesos," he said. "One
does not treat it as if it were a burro."

"Truly," the American said.

"Partly it is the tires," the driver said. "Tires one cannot buy
without paying too much to those who sell them illegally. But
partly it is the engine. In the dust an engine suffers."

"I believe it," the American said politely. He was watching out
the closed window, seeing how the ash had deepened in the last
mile or two, how the bridge rails now were mounded with it, and
how the pines, growing thickly on the sides of the countless little
volcanic hills, rose listless and gray out of a gray blanket as
smooth as new snow and as light under the wind as feathers.
Across the west the cloud of smoke was blacker and angrier, fun-
neling down so that its compact lower plume was hidden behind
the hills. The sun, at the upper edge of the cloud, was an immense golden orange.

A horn blatted behind them, and the driver pulled half off the
road. A car went by them fast, pouring back a choking, impenetrable fog of dust. The driver stopped philosophically to let it
blow away before he started again. "Loco," he said. "That one has
no respect either for his passengers or his engine."

The American did not answer. He was leaning back in the seat
watching the blasted country outside. Occasionally they crept
past adobe huts half buried in the ash, their corrals drifted deep,

their roofs weighted down, the fields which had once grown corn and beans stretching away on both sides without a track to break their even, slaty gray. He thought of the little animals that had lived in these woods, and whether they had got out before the ash became deep, or had quietly smothered in their holes. A wildcat might make headway through it, perhaps, but not the smaller things, the mice and rabbits and lizards, and it was the small things that one thought of.

"What has become of the people from here?" he asked.

The driver half turned. Some, he said, had gone, many to the United States, being taken away in buses and trains to work as *braceros* in the fields of Arizona and California.

"Where they may be cheated and abused," the American said. "What of those who stay?"

"I will show you one," the driver said. A little further on he pointed to a gray hut under the ash-laden shelter of the pines, a few yards off the road. Peering, the American saw a woman standing in the door, her *rebozo* wrapped across her face, and back of her the cavelike interior and the gleam of a charcoal fire.

"Some, like that one, will not leave," the driver said. "The governor's men have been here and urged them, but they are foolish. It is where they were born; they do not want to leave.'

"But what do they live on? They can't grow anything here."

"There are those who cut wood," the driver said. "Though the trees are dying, they are a thing that can be saved. Others, in San Juan, rent horses and burros for the trip to the *boca*. That one, she has nothing. She will die."

The road turned, and the American lost sight of the hut and the still woman in the doorway. Somehow, though the windows were tight shut and the motor and the punished springs filled the car with sound, he had an impression of great silence.

They curved left along a ridge and dropped into a valley, and the volcano was directly ahead of them, not more than two miles away. From its vent monstrous puffs of black smoke mushroomed upward, were whipped ragged by the wind, belched up again. The side of the cone, looking as straight at that distance as if drawn with a ruler, ran down into a curving lava stream that stopped in a broken wall two hundred yards short of the road. The west side of the cone was lost in smoke.

The driver stopped and pointed. Under the lava, he said, was the village of Paricutín. It was not possible to walk across the lava yet, because it had not cooled completely and there were poisonous fumes, but this was a good place to watch from, with the wind the way it was.

"In San Juan it will be dirty," he said. "One will not be able to see much for the smoke."

"The horses leave from San Juan?"

"At about this time every afternoon."

"And there are people in San Juan still?"

"*Sí.*"

"*Vamanos,*" the American said. "If we wish we can come back here later."

He sat forward in the seat, watching the volcano throw up its gobbets of smoke. Through and behind the smoke, like distant flying specks, he could see the rocks and boulders that were thrown up and fell swiftly again.

"This trip by horse," he said. "What is it like?"

"It is something to be remembered," the driver said. "One goes up in daylight, but on the return it is very dark, so dark that one cannot see the horse's ears. And behind, as one comes down this black trail that one knew a year ago as a cornfield, are always this noise and this glare on the sky as if hell were open." He took his hand off the wheel and raised it over his head. "There is always this feeling of something behind," he said. "It is like fleeing the end of the world."

"You could wait for me if I went up?"

"Why not?" the driver said. "It is an experience."

They passed a corral, a hut, a clutter of sheds, another corral, its gates hanging open under a gray drift. Then the houses closed in suddenly and they were in a street. In the perpetual twilight of this town of San Juan men and women, wrapped to the eyes in *rebozos* and *serapes*, their bare feet gray and silent in the ashes, walked along under the overhang of thatch, and children leaned against the walls, only their eyes showing under the sombrero rims, and watched the car pass.

In the plaza three buses and a half-dozen cars were parked. Only when the motor was cut did the American realize that the silence he had been constantly aware of outside had given place to a thin, gritty patter on the roof. The driver gestured upward. "Here it rains cinders," he said. "It is necessary to keep the head well covered, and something over the mouth and nose." He tied a bandanna across his face and climbed out. "I shall see about these horses," he said.

The American waited. On the far side of the plaza a group of Americans, men and women, were already mounting. In odd mis-matched clothes, suit trousers and leather jackets and sombreros and bandannas, the women in riding breeches or Levi's, all of them with their faces muffled, they looked like members of a comic-opera outlaw gang. The driver was having a conference with two Mexicans who were adjusting stirrups for the women. After five minutes he came back.

"It is a pity," he said. "This crowd which is to go immediately has taken all the horses available."

"It is not important," the American said. "Actually I am not so interested in the insides of this volcano."

He tied his handkerchief across his nose, pulled down his hat, and stepped out into the feathery ash. The air was thick with smoke, and cinders pattered on his hat and shoulders. He slitted his eyes against the gritty rain.

"If you would like me to show you around—" the driver said.

"It is not necessary," the American said. He went poking off up a street that opened on the plaza, his nose filled with the odor that he realized he had been smelling for some time, a sour, acrid, vinegarish odor like fresh-sawn oak. He saw many people, shrouded and silent, but they did not break the stillness in which the falling cinders whispered dryly. Even the handkerchief-muffled calls of the Americans riding off toward the crater, and the tooting of the bus horns in farewell, came through the air as through a thick pillow, and he did not hear his own footsteps in the dust.

Once, as he walked past a doorway into which a trail led through the deep ash, the accumulated ashes on a roof let go and avalanched behind him. He turned to see the last runnels trickling from the thatch, and two little Indian girls, each with a small baby hung over her back in the looped *rebozo*, came out of the doorway and waded experimentally in the knee-deep powder.

The end of the street trailed off into ashen fields, and for a moment the American stood in the unnatural gray dusk looking across toward the cone of Paricutín under its lowering cloud of smoke. At intervals of about a minute there was a grumble like far-off blasting, but because of the smoke which blew directly over the town he could not see the rocks flying up. The cinders were an insistent, sibilant rain on his head and shoulders, and his mouth was bitter with the vinegarish taste.

It was not a place he liked. The village of Paricutín, on the other side, had been buried completely under the lava. That was death both definite and sudden. But this slow death that fell like light rain, this gradual smothering that drooped the pines and covered the holes of the little animals and mounded the roofs and choked the streets, this dying village through which ghosts went in silence, was something else. It was a thing Mexicans had always known, in one form or another, else there would not be in so many of their paintings the figure of the robed skeleton, the walking Death. They were patient under it, they accepted it—but the American did not like to remember how alive the eyes of the Indian girls had been as they waded through the ashes with their little sisters on their backs.

On the way back to the plaza he met a pig that wandered in from a side street. The pig looked at him, wrinkling its snout. Its bristly back was floured with gray ash, and its eyes were red. It grunted softly, querulously, and put its snout to the ground, rooted without hope in the foot-deep powder, walked a few steps with its nose plowing the dry and unprofitable dust.

The American left it and went back to the car. In a moment the driver came from the bus where he had been gossiping. "Let's go," the American said. "Perhaps where we stopped first it is clearer."

They went back through the choked streets, leaving the silent Indians who moved softly as shadows through the dead town and the hog which rooted without hope in the ashes, and pulled off the road in deep ash at the end of the valley. For a few minutes they sat, talking desultorily in polite Spanish and watching the irregular spouting of the cone, opening the windows so that they could hear the ominous low grumble and the faint clatter of falling rocks. The cone was blue-black now, and the lava bed across the foreground was a somber, smoking cliff. It was a landscape without shadows, submerged in gray twilight.

"I have conceived a great hatred for this thing," the American said finally. "It is a thing I have always known and always hated. It is something which kills."

"Truly," the driver said. "I have felt it, as those who are in the war must feel the war."

"Yes," the American said.

"You have friends in the war?"

"Sons," the American said. "One is now a prisoner in Germany."

"Ai," the driver said, with sympathy. He hesitated a minute, as if hunting for the correct thing to say to one whose sons were captives of the enemy. "You hear from him?" he said. "How does he endure his captivity?"

"How does one endure anything?" the American said. "I suppose he hates it and endures it, that is all." He looked out the window, raised his shoulders. "I have heard once only," he said for politeness' sake.

They looked across the gray waste that had once been a *milpa*, toward the smoking front of the lava bed. The light had changed. It was darker, more threatening, like the last ominous moments before a thunderstorm. The west was almost as black as night, but across the field spread a steely dusk that rendered every object sharp-edged and distinct. The American raised his head and looked at the ceiling of the car. The stealthy, light fingering had begun there.

"You see," he said. "That is what I mean. It is something which follows. It is like a doom."

The driver made a deprecating gesture. "The wind has shifted," he said.

"It always shifts," the American said.

He stepped out of the car and stood shin-deep in the gray death, listening to the stealthy whisper and the silence that lay over and under and around. The crater rumbled far off, and boulders fell back with a distant clatter, but the silence still hung like something tangible over the valley.

As he watched, the heavy dusk lightened, and he looked up. By a freak of wind the smoke had been blown high, and though no sign of the setting sun came through the obscured west, a pale, pinkish wash of light came through under the cloud and let an unearthly illumination over the field of ash and the smoking cliff of lava.

Into that lurid dusk an Indian in white pajamas, with a bundle of wood on his back and an axe across his shoulder, came out of the pines at the upper edge of the lava and walked along the clifflike front. Little puffs of dust rose from under his feet. After him, fifteen yards behind, came another, and after him another.

The three strung out across the field, walking as silently in the rosy, metallic light as dream figures. The ones behind did not try to close the gap and walk companionably with the one ahead; the one ahead did not wait for them. They walked in single file, fifteen yards apart, each with his burden of wood on his back, and the little puffs of dust rose under their feet and the punched-hole tracks lengthened behind them across the field.

The American watched them, feeling the silence that weighed on these little figures more heavily than the loads upon their backs, and as he watched he heard the man ahead whistle a brief snatch of tune, drop it, start something else. He went whistling, a ghost in a dead land, toward some hut half buried in ash where a charcoal fire would be burning, and his wife would have ready for him tortillas and beans, with cinders in them, perhaps, like everything else, but still tortillas and beans that would fill a man's belly against the work that must be done tomorrow.

The American watched the three until they were out of sight around the shoulder of the hill. When he climbed into the car and motioned for the driver to start back he was not thinking of the steady smothering fall of the cinders or the death that lay over the streets and cornfields of San Juan. He was thinking of the eyes of the little Indian girls, which were so very alive above the muffling *rebozos.*

"It is a strange thing," he said. "This whistling."

The driver, reaching to turn the ignition key, shrugged, and smiled. "Why not?" he said. "The mouth is not made merely to spit with or curse with. At times it may be used for whistling, or even for kissing, *verdad?*"

RESPONDING PERSONALLY

1. Would you be interested in travelling to see the volcano in the story? Why or why not?
2. In your response journal, write about a famous natural landmark this story reminded you of. What is special and intriguing about it?

RESPONDING CRITICALLY

3. Why does the American want to see the volcano? What is his reaction when he finally views it? How do the references to war connect to the volcano?
4. Through characterization, we slowly get a picture of the protagonist and what he is like. What do his actions and comments reveal about his character and values?
5. The story offers a vision of poverty, evil, and death. Quote three sentences which summarize views of evil and death, and explain in your own words what each means.

6. What is the purpose of the last six paragraphs and the references to whistling?

RESPONDING CREATIVELY

7. Create a postcard from the man, which he sends back to a friend in America.
8. Make a brochure designed to boost tourism to the village.

PROBLEM-SOLVING/DECISION-MAKING

9. At one point, the driver suggests: "It is something to be remembered" and "It is an experience." Write about an unusual or special place that you (or someone you know) have visited which had a similar profound effect on you.

All I know is that my heart is
broken and I miss The Man I
Love.

Anita H. Olsen
The Merman of Olsen's Island

I decide to go to my parents' cabin on the island because my heart is broken. The day is late as I sit by the open window and listen to the sound of the waves lapping against the dock my father had built. *Slap, slap, slap.* The sound has not changed since I was a child, and I close my eyes and remember those happy days of long ago. Now, though, laughter is very foreign to me.

I light a fire in the old stove and start up some soup made from caribou bones that my brother had given me. I throw a birch log into the fire, and soon the soup begins to simmer. It starts to get dark, so I light the kerosene lamp; it casts lurking shadows as I move around the cabin. The season is late, and the fall winds rustle around the windows and shake the verandah screens. The waves are now spewing long frothy arms between the planks of the dock, which begin to creak. I move the curtain aside to have a look. I see a sliver of pale reds and oranges and deep blues blending together to form the black night sky.

The wind whistles into the cabin through the cracks by the window, and I tear strips off the bottom of my long peasant skirt to fill them in. I am sad and lonely and think that maybe my grief has cost me my sanity. Doubt and confusion, too, fill my mind, but I don't really care. All I know is that my heart is broken and I miss The Man I Love.

I sip at some wine I've brought along and try to read but it's impossible to concentrate, so I give up. The fire in the stove dies out and, in front of the window, so does the lamp. Under my goosedown quilt, I listen to the grief in the voice of the wind.

I am breathing still. So is the wind—softer now—its rage has faded out. Time passes and seagulls cry and so do I. The waves keep lapping, but more gently now.

I realize that I have slept, slept without The Man I Love, and when my heart was broken. My dreams were so full—of harvesttimes, large round moons, big feasts and whole casks of ale. I put on my skirt, torn from the ravages of the night, and acutely feel that now, I am truly empty. The dichotomy overwhelms me and I go outside to think on this.

I think about being at the airport, clutching the single rose given to me by The Man I Love. I'd placed it, small, bright and red, upon the counter, and that had made me cry. "It's a man, isn't it?" the ticket agent had asked. Shattered at the blame this implied, I'd responded, *No, no. The Man I Love is special. He's different from everyone else. He would never hurt me, never. Can't you see that?* Then I'd grabbed at my small red rose for comfort, and as proof that what I'd said was true. She looked at me, surprised at the strength and passion in my voice, but I was surprised too, because really I was so weak and depleted. I left then, my heart growing heavier with each step, because I was going further and further away from The Man I Love.

The waves are small and brisk, the late ravens make their sounds among the pine trees over the muskeg and a flock of geese flies southward for the winter.

I go to a rocky point and think that maybe the water is friendly and beckoning me forward, but I really can't make up my mind about this. So I look upwards and see the sun high in the sky and the distant gulls as they hover over the barren stretches of water. The islands around me are like they've always been and nothing seems to have changed, except that I am so very lonely. The wind is rising again and the seagulls start to scream. I need to talk to somebody, just anybody—but especially I need someone to deliver me to The Man I Love.

But none of this seems to be happening, so, miserably, I gaze out at the islands. Then, from among them, I see something very different—a ship rapidly approaching. It is several storeys high with a skull and crossbones flag waving from its highest point. Men are on the deck, and they come so close that we start to talk. I am relieved for the company and greatly excited—can they possibly take me to The Man I Love? One man gives me some roe on seaweed, which is what they have been harvesting. In the west, they say, this is called *gow*, and I put it in my mouth to taste it. It is bitter and salty, and I have a hard time swallowing it. Why are you sitting here on the rocks, one man, the captain, asks. So, unable to hide anything and desperately wanting company, I tell him. I'm here because my heart is broken and The Man I Love is far, far away. He look directly at me like he is remembering something.

Then he speaks loudly to his crew in a foreign language. He's told them to go off and find more *gow*, he says. I pause and look at them gather in several small rowboats, and then watch as they dive into the waters and swim away. The rowboats are left anchored, and the waves slapping against the sides make pleasant hypnotic sounds.

Then I go back to the rocks to sit and think and be alone. The rocks have soaked up the warmth of the afternoon sun, and that makes it easy for me to sit among them with my thoughts. I look at the flagship moored at the dock my father had built and at the *gow*, now on a china plate I was also given. I nibble on it, thinking that perhaps I can acquire a taste for it. Beside the next island, I notice men tugging at the seaweed until it floats to the surface of the water. I watch idly as they heave their harvest into floating bundles. Some of them talk and yell to each other, and laugh. They are telling bad jokes, I think, but it does not bother me.

The gulls cry, as I do, and my tears flow; the raucous voices of the distant crewmen float through the screen window. The wind begins to rise. (Or does it? Or, am I just starting to become aware of it? I can't really tell.)

I go to open another bottle of wine because I suddenly remember the sea captain and think that maybe I can share a glass with him. *If only I can stop crying, and stop missing The Man I Love, then I will be proper company.* But it seems to be a vain hope, and as dusk falls, I ponder on my weaknesses and wish there were something I could do. But instead, I have some thin caribou soup in an exotic flat dish and some bread to go along with it.

There are sounds in this night, but very few of them. Do I hear the hoot of an ancient owl who visits the Chosen for special evil purposes? I'm sure that I do, and begin to wonder if maybe, this time, I am the Chosen one …

Then I feel compelled to leave the cabin and go to the rocks where I'd spent the afternoon. I glance at the outline of the flagship, black and huge, moored at the dock my father had built. Now I hear the cool autumn waters calling, and I wade in as far as I dare. One hand clutches a green wine bottle and the other holds up the torn skirt still hanging from my waist. I am in a state of indecision, and as my skirts falls from my hand, its swirling tatters whisper in the waters around me. The gazing stars are overhead and twinkle as they wait; a waning moon is watching as it plods on a steady and soundless path across the dark night sky.

In the distance, again I hear the ancient owl and no longer wonder about this heavy and foreign night—I know now that sleep will not come to me at all.

Then I hear the murmur of parting waters, and there, in the moonlit darkness, a rowboat appears. I am not afraid, and recognize the sea captain sitting alone in the boat. I understand, without any words, that he has come to get me; his hands are cold as he helps me aboard. I do not ask where we are going for I know that it does not really matter, because I will not see The Man I Love anymore.

The night sounds—what are they? The drops of water as they fall from the oars into the lake; the swishing of the waters as the oars plough through, reaching distant and foreign and watery places.

The sea captain starts to talk, calmly and slowly, but nothing he says seems to fit into my own scattered sense of reality. I do not argue or interrupt, and instead look around and notice that the surroundings have changed. The island is far behind, a black glob on the horizon, and I can only barely see the lights of the flagship moored at the dock my father had built. The sky is huge, wide, black and gaping; the moon and stars are still waiting expectantly for something to happen to me. I look down and noticed that there is no longer a bottom on the rowboat, and that the sea captain is heaving a large forked fin back and forth in the open water. His arms, large and hairy, are still rowing steadily in strong even strokes. My own feet are dragging behind in cold, cold water and my hands clutch at the sides of the rowboat.

The oarlocks are creaking, back and forth, back and forth. The water moves in creases up my legs; in the sky I hear the ancient owl. Once, I am sure I see the brazen and fiery lights in his legendary eyes, and know that I have no chance, no hope at all …

From the light of the moon, I see a rocky shoreline as it looms closer and closer. There is no beach, no warmth at all, and I instinctively know that beyond the never-ending shore, the memories of The Man I Love will no longer exist. So I hastily grab the scenes of the love we shared and bury them into secret recesses. I'm still not sure of what is happening to me, but I know that these are my final farewells to The Man I Love.

I open my eyes, for my arms are aching; I realize that I've been swimming in cold, cold waters. Over towards the big dark shapes on the rocky shoreline, I notice the sea captain tying his long long hair into a single plait behind his back. I am not afraid when I see his arms and the rest of his body below his neck covered in big blue-grey scales. There is something of home in him, something I do not fully understand.

He sees me looking at him, and talks to me about his journeys to the bottom of the sea. There are hundreds of villages down there, he says, filled with many thousands of people from everywhere who have drowned in all the shipwrecks since The Beginning and who now await the Resurrection Day. He describes the ancient rotten ships with giant seaweed growing out of portholes and around all the roped rigging. He mentions the vague dead eyes of the villagers, and the way their hair floats around them in massive waves as they tread upon the sandy sea bottom.

I am saddened, for although I realize that this is not my own Fate, I understand that in some strange way, I am becoming just like him. My hair is long, long now, and floats in separate plaits around my head. In fact, when I dive deep down, it stands on end above me and flows behind my back. Sometimes it moves in waves around my eyes and I have to shake my head from side to side so I can see where I am going. I no longer touch the rocks beneath me; instead, I now hover around in a gentle and watery world. The novelty of moving into new places intrigues me and I revel in this for what seems to be a long, long time.

Then, one time, I see something up above, a bluish-green light that's surrounded in brightness like a beacon. I swim towards it and come to the place of the rocky shoreline of long long ago, when all memory stopped. The surface of the water is glossy; it is only my ripples that break its smoothness. I go to scramble on the rocks to resume an old familiar life, but then notice something that makes my heart nearly stop. For in the mirror of the lake, I see that the lower part of my body has become a large glistening fish tail with greenish scales. I still have shoulders and breasts, but they are covered in woven sea lettuce and kelp, which I pull off and throw as far as I can and watch as the pieces float away in the current. I feel the water on my barren skin and enjoy the freedom of newfound movement.

What is it I hear? Laughter. But who is laughing? I have not heard any sounds for a long, long time, for I have been living in a thick and silent world.

Then I see the Merman of Olsen's Island; he is lapped up against the rocks. When he begins to speak, I understand in a flash, in an eye's twinkle, that my life in the massive and timeless underseas will be spent escaping his reach. Instantly, I also see that back in another life, I was weak and sad for having lost The Man I Love.

But it is very different now, for whenever the waves are high and rough, my body awakens and I rise up from the depths of the sea to the water's edge. I call out the name of The Man I Love and wave my arms, for I am sure I see him there at the cabin I left so many years ago. Even the single red rose he'd given me still stands in the vase by the curtained window. I am so strong now, and I lash the waves with my tail with all my might and break the waters in a spray of silvery drops that sparkle like diamonds in the sun.

Now, what sounds do I hear? Only once, after I became a Mermaid, did I hear the ancient owl with the evil eyes, and watched as he glided on silent wings past my head, over and beyond into another world. But that was a long, long time ago. I will not hear or see the ancient owl again, for I do not belong to that world anymore.

The only sound I hear now is my own voice as I call out the name of The Man I Love. I must shout loudly, for the waves are full of whitecaps and I must be heard over their massive and constant roar.

RESPONDING PERSONALLY

1. What feelings and memories does this story evoke for you. Share them with a partner.
2. In a group, compare ideas about what makes this an unusual and intriguing story.

RESPONDING CRITICALLY

3. What is the reason for the trip to the cabin and the swim to the island? Has the narrator lost her sanity as she herself wonders at one point?
4. What rites and rituals does the narrator perform that are associated with a relationship breakup and its attendant grief?

5. In a group, decide what is the purpose of the italicized sections? What is their role in the story?
6. What is the meaning and symbolism of the sea captain and the merman? What do you think happens at the end of the story? Refer to details in the story to support your interpretation.

RESPONDING CREATIVELY

7. Compose a lyric poem entitled "The Merman of Olsen's Island."
8. Prepare two drawings of favourite episodes from the story.

PROBLEM-SOLVING/DECISION-MAKING

9. Design a brochure to help the lovelorn overcome the loss of a loved one.

"Yes, me son, tis gonna be
rough till we git h'out of
d'harbour."

Barbara Ritson
Edward's Rocks

The knock on the door came just after midnight. It was 1947 in the quiet fishing village of Musgrave Harbour, Newfoundland. No one casually ventured out at that time of night, so this was serious business.

The knock came again with more urgency, startling Olive and George from an affectionate embrace. They were snuggling in Olive's parents' sitting room, unchaperoned; something quite unorthodox given the day in which they lived. But the teenaged couple had been courting since they were twelve, and Olive's parents were quite pleased with Olive's choice of boyfriend. The old cliché "like a son" rang true for these native Newfoundlanders, and everyone anticipated an engagement announcement soon.

"Tis some late, Garge," Olive whispered. "Git the door fast, before it wakes Mom an' Pap."

George scrambled for the door, straightening his suit jacket as he went. His three-piece, blue serge suit fit handsomely on his strong frame and was a mandatory accompaniment whenever he paid a visit to Olive's home. He'd had it tailor made, and it had cost him dearly. Fifty-four dollars was more than one man could earn in two months. But it was worth it. George dressed better to visit Olive than he did to go to church. He opened the door to find his eldest brother standing on the porch.

"We're goin' out," Walt said simply. Saying no more, he ran toward the back garden that had become the shortcut home.

George watched the darkness of the night envelop his brother. He turned and closed the door. The air was damp and chilled in the kitchen where the night had attempted to steal in. George turned to Olive.

"I gots to go," he whispered, pulling Olive close to him.

Olive wrapped her arms around George's neck and hugged him tightly. She was shivering. Was it the cold air or was it a sense of foreboding? She couldn't tell. She whispered in his ear. "Don't leave me."

George relaxed his embrace just enough to look down at her. He thought she was beautiful in the lantern's soft glow. Over the past five years, he had seriously begun to think she was an angel in disguise. She was graceful and sweet with exquisite features, and he was sure there was a little of heaven's light around her soft green eyes. He looked deeply into them now.

"I'll be back t'morrow. 'Opefully we'll git a good day of 'unting in."

He pulled away reluctantly from Olive and put on his overcoat and cap. Olive watched him in the dim light. His rugged features were a mixture of heredity and the sea. His lean stature and black hair, so reminiscent of his father, joined with his most prominent facial feature, a squared off and dimpled chin, to give him an irresistible appeal. Olive's heart melted. He was so young, and yet sometimes it was hard to believe he was only seventeen. His dark brown eyes were old, filled with a wisdom that only came from hard work and sacrifice. He had been just nine years old when he quit school to help shoulder the burden of providing for his family.

Olive knew there was no use trying to talk him out of going. Fishing and hunting were in his blood. He'd been on the sea since he was old enough to walk.

George pulled Olive to him again and gave her one last kiss. He lingered, holding her close. It was hard to let her go. She was his life's sweetness.

As he opened the door he glanced back at Olive and then disappeared into the night.

George walked briskly down the lane way to the main road, and thoughts of the exhilarating task before him raced around in his head. It was June 5, and the seals had arrived at Pimming Islands. They came in just long enough to bear their young, and they'd be gone again, within a few days: Each day was crucial. Seal hunting was more than a necessity to George's family; it was survival. Although winter seemed a long way off, they all knew that if canned seal meat didn't end up neatly stocking the kitchen pantry, the winter ahead would be unbearably harsh. There was no means of refrigeration in their home and it would be almost impossible to keep fresh venison on the table. The seal pelts would bring a good price in St. John's. For a small fee, a neighbour up the next lane would clean and dry the pelts.

Pimming Islands were officially named Penguin Islands, but Pimming was easier to say and had become the local slang for the two small islands brimming with indigenous birds and seals.

Pulling his coat tighter around his body, George remembered Olive's warm embrace. How he longed to be back there now. The night air was cold and wet. He hurried on. The main road was deserted and the night black. The ocean's edge was just off to his right, only a few feet from the road. He listened, hearing the waves crashing against the shore.

D'sea's come h'in. We'll be lucky if we're not smashed upon d'rocks t'night, George thought as he plodded along. It was hard to believe that a late spring storm; one hundred miles away, could cause the harbour to be so rough. Away from shore the water was calm, but near land the undertow was strong and the ocean perilous. It would be quite a task to approach Pimming Islands safely tonight. He wondered why Father had changed his mind about going.

A couple of minutes later George tumbled into his house.

The two-story, white clapboard house housed two parents, eight children, and boasted six bedrooms. Like most homes in the area, it had no heat, no running water, and no electricity. Nevertheless, it held a prominent position within the community. The home was located in the centre of town off the main road. It sat at the end of a long lane-way gently graded upwards from the street. The house could be seen coming into the harbour and was used by the local townsfolk as a navigation marker. It was clean and cozy. His family had come a long way from the two room shanty they had all lived in a few years before. The sea had been good to them.

"I'm 'ome," George called out as he pulled off his cap and coat in the back hallway. He ducked up the back stairs and changed into his work clothes. Mother had already poured hot water in his wash bowl and it felt good to wash off the damp night air.

Within a few minutes he had made his way back down the front set of stairs into the kitchen. It was buzzing with activity, and like all homes in Musgrave Harbour, the kitchen was the heart of the house with the wood stove keeping it the warmest. It was the central gathering place where there was always a pot of tea brewing. A daybed in one corner invited weary residents to take a respite from their hard life. Tonight the kitchen bristled with excitement. The first night of the seal hunt was always exciting.

George listened intently to the lively talk at the family table. He sat next to Father while eating fried eggs, back bacon and toast. Although it was only one o'clock in the morning, Mother lovingly prepared breakfast for her husband and older sons.

"'Ows' d'sea, Garge?" Father asked, taking a bite of toast.

"It's in, Father. D'h'underground sea is rough in d'harbour. But I s'pose we'll be okay once we're h'out."

Father nodded. "We'll be fine." He spoke with authority and confidence. It helped the sons relax and enjoy their meal. The toast was especially good. Controlling the heat on the top of the wood stove was a difficult task, and more often than not only the bread's charred remains could be rescued.

"I 'ope the sea'll allow us to land at d'Pimmins," Walt offered. Walt, George's oldest brother, was already a full partner in the family's cod fishing business. Someday he, along with George and their brother Gerald would carry the business on their own.

"No problem," Father answered.

"Wat time do you tink you'll be 'ome?" Mother asked as she poured another cup of coffee into her husband's mug. She pushed a stray hair from her plump face. It had been a long day.

"Tis 'ard to tell. If we git dere in a good time, an' git a good day in, we should be 'ome after noon sometime."

"D'Steeles an' Whiteways wants t'come down when you git in fer a good meal of seal," Mother said. The annual seal hunt always brought friends and family around for days of cooking and canning and feasting.

"Okay, Mother. We'll see wat we can muster h'up."

Father pushed back his chair, indicating it was time they were on their way.

They packed light. Their bread box was filled with hard tack biscuits and water. They wore knives on their belts and were dressed warmly. They climbed into their slickers and thigh rubbers.

Around a quarter to two, George, Walt, Gerald, and their father set out. The water's edge was no more than a few hundred feet from their front door at the end of their lane way. The harbour was fretful, throwing three-foot columns of water onto the shore.

They climbed into their punt; a small rowboat they used to reach their larger fishing boat, anchored farther out in the harbour. Even when they arrived at Pimming Islands, they would still use the punt to go ashore, leaving the fishing boat anchored at a safe distance offshore. Their punt had taken on a life of its own.

"D'h'underground sea is some strong," Gerald hollered over the ocean's roar.

"Yes, me son, tis gonna be rough till we git h'out of d'harbour," George yelled back. "I 'ope d'seals are in."

"Der in," Father said, again with a confidence that only years on the sea could bring. Father knew the risks, and this was one he was willing to take.

"Still, d'h'undertow's a little strong t'night, even fer me," George shouted, but his words were lost in the crashing waves.

George usually relished some rough boating. It brought the colour to his young cheeks. But tonight the sea was ominous, and he felt uneasy. Over the years the sea had become an intimate friend of his and he knew how to determine its moods. He knew only too well how unpredictable it could be. Tonight's waves told him to take care.

The little troupe made it to their fishing boat and pulled themselves aboard, tethering the punt in tow. With the motor started, they headed out. Their route was familiar, having made the two-and-a-half miles out and six miles down shore trip dozens of times before. Usually an hour was plenty of time to reach their destination. Hopefully they'd make good time tonight.

The father and sons were silent. Everyone had their job to do and they didn't need much talking. The drone of the engine wouldn't have made chitchat easy anyway.

The ocean's frenzy eased as they left the harbour, leaving the water calm and serene. There was no hint of the turbulence they had experienced closer to shore. A light mist rolled a few inches above the water.

A slivered silver moon and innumerable stars hung in the sable sky though visibility was nil beyond the end of the boat. A three cell flashlight offered light, but was a mere speck in the expanse of murkiness before them. The mist made the horizon soupy, and they knew it would be hard to make out any landmarks to aid the journey.

George enjoyed sitting in the front of the boat, where he found himself tonight. He shone the flashlight out into the darkness. Father, sitting nearby, was in charge of navigation with the help of a compass.

The men were quiet; each left to his own thoughts. The sea was like bath water, the boat cutting through it smoothly. The motor's monotone hum made it easy to drift away. It didn't take George long to be back in Olive's embrace, rehearsing his engagement. "Twill be in der favourite place down d'shore a piece, or maybe 'ee'd be brave 'nuff t'propse in Olive's living room, or maybe ..."

Suddenly, a gasp slipped from George's throat. Without warning, something loomed up in front of them.

George saw it first. Incredibly, a wall of rock over twelve feet high jutted out of the black sea. The mist had not permitted any forewarning and the boat was almost upon the rocks. Startled, George let out a loud growl, though his lips refused to form any words. He instinctively slashed the flashlight's beams to the right, and waved it furiously, signalling a swift course change.

Father, without a sound, slammed the tiller hard. The distant storm's undertow surrounding the rocks tried to throw the boat against the cliffs. They came within inches of the rugged rockface. George reached out his arm. If he stretched, he could have touched its jagged features.

Walt was in the engine house attending to the engine. "Wat's goin' h'on?" he screamed, struggling to steady himself against the boat's sudden change of direction.

"Walt, turn the engine h'off an' weigh d'h'anchor!" Father yelled as soon as they were clear of the rocks and undertow.

Walt cut the motor and dropped the grappling hook into the water. The older brothers scrambled up to the front of the boat where George stood. The night was eerily silent. And with the motor still, the only sounds were the waves lapping at the side of the boat. They all looked at each other.

"Wat was dat?" Gerald cried, shaken.

"'Twas the inside h'of Edward's Rocks," George pointed the flashlight toward the rugged islands.

"Take d'punt an' figger h'out where we are," Father yelled, looking at George and Walt. "We shouldn't be anywhere near Edward's Rocks."

Edward's Rocks were named after a local fellow. No last names were necessary. Residents knew who Edward was. He had been killed when his boat was crushed against the rocks. If these were the rocks that belonged to Edward, George and his brothers had come within inches of joining him.

George and Walt pulled their slickers closer and climbed down into the rowboat. Maneuvering the rocks in the distant storm's undertow would command all their skill.

They moved slowly out from the fishing boat, and circled the rocks. There were three distinct peaks, clustered close together. While there were places where boats could approach her rocks on a calm night, in tonight's underground sea they were only three sharp pinnacles jutting out of the water.

"Tis Edward's Rocks h'alright." George motioned to Walt. The familiar edging on the inside of the largest cliff gave itself away.

Walt nodded, and they headed back to safety in the fishing boat.

George and Walt tethered the punt back to the fishing boat and they clamoured back aboard.

"So, wat was it?" Gerald asked.

"I was right. Tis Edward's Rocks," George confirmed.

"Edward's Rocks?" Gerald challenged, standing by the edge of the boat. "We can't be dere. Do ya realize 'ow far h'off course we'd be?"

"Over 'alf h'a mile," Father yelled, interrupting. "But Edward's Rocks are d least of our worries. We gots t'find a way t'git back h'on course."

They were in a desperate situation, for they knew all too well the dangers of being alone on the black sea, with no navigation, and a strong undertow. They had experienced the terror once before during a freak storm, when they had nearly lost their lives.

Father studied the compass perched on the seat in front of him. The insignificant light from the flashlight made the compass markings difficult to read.

"Accordin' to d'compass, we're still h'on course," Father said. "I don't h'understand it. I don't see 'ow we could be where we are. H'an' yet, 'ere we are."

He furrowed his brow and looked at his sons. The fear he felt had stolen to his eyes and the boys read it there.

Father sat down and pushed the compass gently to one side being careful not to disturb its course. He motioned his sons to come and sit with him. Before they could, the compass' needle began to move. Father watched in horror as it found a new north.

His brow furrowed deeper; and gingerly, he moved the compass back to its original position on the seat. Again the compass' needle began its search, and again another magnetic north was selected.

George looked at his father. No words were needed. They both understood. Without a word, George began to pull apart everything around him. He dumped the contents of the boxes that lay in the corner nearest them. He yanked open the drawers in the engine house. He even dragged out their lunch, shaking out the contents onto the wooden seat. Nothing was spared.

When none of their possessions gave up what he was looking for, he began to tear up the gangboards in the bottom of the boat.

"Garge, are you nuts?" Gerald yelled. "Wat are ya doin'? We gots no catch of fish t'night, an' we sure don't 'ave any worry of d'sun spoilin' dem! What are ya wantin' with d'gangboards?"

"Quiet!" Father ordered. Instinctively knowing what George was looking for; he helped rip up the floor.

Intense minutes passed. Walt and Gerald remained quiet as father and son continued to pull at the gangboards. George lifted each gangboard in the after-room of the ship, closest to where his father had been sitting. Brushing the sweat from his face, he could see a glint in the darkness of the hull, and it teased him as he wrestled to reach it. The object was wedged deep in the ship's belly and George strained every inch of his body stretching to grasp hold. He struggled to keep his footing. Wrapping his fingers around the object he yanked and tugged. Finally with one last mighty jerk George came free of the gangboards along with his new found possession. He lay sprawled out on the deck.

Picking himself up, a triumphant smile passed over his face as yelled, "'Ere tis! 'Ere tis!"

"Wat? Wat?" the brothers echoed.

George held up a small object and flung it the length of the boat, nearly grazing Gerald's head.

"Dear God, was dat an 'ammer?" Walt asked.

"Aye, an' d'reason why we're h'off course," George answered. "D'head is metal."

"But where did it come from?" Gerald demanded.

"No matter," Father shouted. "We gots a new setting on d'-compass. Pull up d'h'anchor an' let's git h'out of 'ere!"

With the motor humming, father and sons set out again, leaving Edward's Rocks behind. By three-thirty, still two full hours before daybreak, the men could vaguely make out the shoreline of the south Pimming Islands. It would be a great day of hunting. The islands were brimming with seals, and while the night's shadows still lingered with the break of a new day, forty-two pelts would be theirs.

Back in Musgrave Harbour, dawn silently crept into her bedroom. Olive, who had tossed fitfully for hours, finally settled in a relaxed sleep.

RESPONDING PERSONALLY

1. For small group discussion: This story originates from Newfoundland and is written in dialect. What are some colourful words and expressions used in the story?
2. Is the premise of the non-functioning compass plausible? Compare your ideas with those of a partner.

RESPONDING CRITICALLY

3. For paragraph response: "The characters in the story are decent, hard-working people." Use examples from the story to support this statement.
4. What is the livelihood of George's family? Is their life an easy one? Explain.
5. Describe the men's predicament and its solution.

310 : EDWARD'S ROCKS

6. What is the significance of Edward's Rocks in the story? How does that place affect the characters and the mood of the story?

RESPONDING CREATIVELY

7. Using a similar dialect, write the conversation George and Olive might have the day after the hunt.
8. Write the local newspaper's coverage of the seal hunt's strange event. Include quotations provided by George, his brothers, and his father.

PROBLEM-SOLVING/DECISION-MAKING

9. For anecdotal writing: Describe a time when you or someone you know were similarly confused, disoriented, or baffled by an odd situation. Did you solve the mystery? Explain.

Glossary of Fiction Terms

allusion

An allusion is a brief direct or indirect reference to a person, place, or event from history, literature, or mythology that the author hopes or assumes the reader will recognize. Most allusions expand on or develop a significant idea, impression, or mood in the story. The title "North End Faust" contains two allusions— one to the north end of Winnipeg, the other to the legendary figure of Faust, a magician who sold his soul to the Devil in exchange for extraordinary experience and knowledge.

antagonist

The antagonist is the major character or force that opposes the protagonist. The mother (and later, the father) in "Boys and Girls" become the narrator's antagonists.

antecedent action

This is the significant action that takes place before the story begins. The antecedent action in "The Man to Send Rain Clouds" is an old man dying just before the narrative begins.

anticlimax

An anticlimax is a sudden shift from a relatively serious or elevated mood to one more comic or trivial. The ending of "Internal Monologue on a Corner in Havana" is anticlimactic.

antihero

An antihero is a protagonist who has none of the qualities normally expected of a hero. The term also refers to a humorous take-off of the traditional hero. The characters played by Woody Allen and Rowan Atkinson (Mr. Bean) are examples of antiheroes. The narrator in "The Organized Woman Story" has none of the qualities normally associated with heroes.

atmosphere (or mood)

The atmosphere or mood is the prevailing feeling created by the story. Atmosphere usually sets up expectations in the reader about the outcome of an episode or plot. It is created by descriptive diction, imagery, and sometimes dialogue. Some teachers or critics may distinguish between the two terms by referring to the "atmosphere of a story" and the "mood created in the reader." The atmosphere of "The Lamp at Noon" is dark, sombre, and brooding. In "The Merman of Olsen's Island," the mood the writer creates is a thoughtful, pensive one.

character

The term refers to both a fictional person in a story, and the moral, dispositional, and behavioural qualities of that fictional person. The qualities of a character are generally revealed through dialogue, action, and description. Characters themselves may be classified as flat or round, stereotyped or realistic, static or dynamic. Each classification is described below. See also *foil*.

Classifications of Character
- *Flat character* is a limited, usually minor character with only one apparent quality. The policeman with the whip in "Ashes for the Wind" and Ranji in "The Poison of the Blue Rose" are undeveloped flat characters.
- *Round character* is a realistic character with several dimensions. The wife in "Another Evening at the Club" and the doctor in "Lenses" are both round characters.
- *Realistic character* is a multi-dimensional and recognizable character who has complex relationships and motivations. Some realistic characters are the mother in "A Moving Day" and Mr. Sikirski in "The Curlew's Cry."

- *Stereotyped character* is a predictable, one-dimensional character who is recognizable to the reader as "of a type," for example, the jock, the brain, the yuppie. Two stereotyped characters are Virginia, the organization worker who has mixed feelings about her job in "The Museum of Vain Endeavours," and the girl in "Love Song."
- *Dynamic character* is often the protagonist and is a character who undergoes a significant, lasting change, usually in his or her outlook on life. The narrator in "The Thunderstorm" and Sheila in "The Curlew's Cry" are dynamic characters.
- *Static character* is one who does not change in the course of the story. The beggar in "Interior Monologue on a Corner in Havana" and Charlotte's mother in "The Metaphor" are examples of static characters.

characterization

Characterization is the process through which the author reveals to the reader the qualities of a character. In short stories, the author will either reveal character directly (through author comments) and/or indirectly (through the character's speech, thoughts, or actions).

character sketch

A character sketch is a description and analysis of a character's moral, dispositional, and behavioural qualities, including specific examples and quotations from the story. When writing a character sketch, one does not normally describe the character's physical appearance or dress, though these, incidentally, may reflect symbolically the character's personality. A character sketch for Alex in "North End Faust" might read as follows:

> Alexander Markiewicz is a university psychologist who is obsessed with his isolation chamber experiments. These experiments reflect his loner personality, which can be traced back to childhood to a time when his older brother locked him for hours in a closet. Instead of expressing normal fear,

Alex feels nourished and strengthened by moments of isolation.

When he married Kathy, it appeared that he had overcome his isolation, but as the author points out, "he seemed to have embraced loneliness like a bride." Alex becomes even more detached from Kathy when they have children. He is driven instead by his determination to continue his experiments, taking great pride in his own ability to stay in the isolation chamber longer than anyone else.

His personality disintegration is foreshadowed by his increasing isolation from others, his paranoia about his colleagues, his growing anxieties about the chamber, and his bouts of disorientation and powerlessness. Finally, Alex "snaps" and retreats to his childhood world where, in desperation to complete his imagined summer cottage, he takes his life.

climax
The climax is the highest point of emotional intensity in a story. It is the major crisis in the story and usually marks the turning point in the protagonist's fortunes. The climax of "Grace Period" occurs at the end of the story with a nuclear explosion lighting up the narrator's house.

complicating incident (or complication)
The event that initiates a conflict is the complicating incident. In "The Man to Send Rain Clouds," the event that initiates the funeral is the old man's sudden, unexpected death.

confidant (or confidante)
The confidant(e) is the person with whom a character, usually the protagonist, shares his or her thoughts, feelings, and intentions. Aunt Edna is the confidante of Beth in "To Set Our House in Order."

conflict
This term refers to the struggle between opposing characters or forces, that is, the protagonist and someone or something else.

Additional conflicts, which the protagonist is not involved in, may also be found in a short story. Three common types of conflicts are as follows:

1. *Conflict between a character and his or her environment.* The environment may be nature, society, or circumstance. The street artists in "Why Don't You Carve Other Animals" are in conflict with the "urban jungle."

2. *Conflict between two characters.* This struggle may be physical, emotional, or psychological. An example of this conflict occurs between the husband and wife in "Another Evening at the Club."

3. *Conflict within a character.* In this case, the character experiences conflict in emotion and/or thought. The protagonist in "Boys and Girls" has mixed feelings about her gender identity.

contrast (or juxtaposition)

Contrast refers to a difference, especially a striking difference, between two things being compared. In this context, contrast may involve characters, situations, settings, moods, or points of view. Contrast is used in order to clarify meaning, purpose, or character, or to heighten certain moods (especially humour, horror, and suspense).

In "The Portable Phonograph," the physical, emotional, and spiritual impoverishment of the four survivors is contrasted with the intense beauty of the Debussy nocturne.

Juxtapositions are contrasts in which positioning is important, for example, when two contrasting characters are placed side-by-side in a story.

Juxtaposed characters in the fatal shooting scene in "Harrison Bergeron" include Harrison, the ballerina, and Diana Moon Glampers.

crisis

A crisis is a moment of intense conflict. The major crisis of the story is called the climax. Two crises in "Lenses" are the doctor's performing the operation and the follow-up removal of the bandages.

denouement (or resolution)

Denouement (pronounced day-NEW-mahn) is the French word for "unknotting" and refers to the unknotting of or resolution to the plot or conflict. The denouement follows the climax and constitutes part or all of the falling action. The denouement in "Another Evening at the Club" happens when the couple are getting ready to go the club at the end of the story.

dialect

Dialect is a manner of speaking or variation on a language peculiar to an individual, a people, a social class, or a geographic region. A dialect differs from the standard language of a country. Cuban words such as *paladares* are used to suggest dialect in "Internal Monologue on a Corner in Havana." Much of "Edward's Rocks" is written in Newfoundland dialect.

dialogue

Any conversation between two or more characters in a story is dialogue. The conversational exchanges of "Good morning" in "The Possibility of Evil" create a superficial atmosphere of congeniality. The dialogue between the two street artists in "Why Don't You Carve Other Animals" reveals their personalities and approaches to their crafts.

diction

Diction is the vocabulary used by a writer. For each story, the writer chooses and arranges words appropriate to his or her purpose, subject, story type, characters, and style.

dilemma

A dilemma is a situation in which a character must make a choice between two disagreeable, undesirable, or unfavourable alternatives. Posing a dilemma is one method an author can use to generate conflict and suspense in a story.

In "The Lamp at Noon," Ellen's dilemma is whether she should remain in the house and go mad, or escape into the dangerous dust storm with her baby.

dynamic character
See *character*.

epiphany
Epiphany refers to a moment of significant realization and insight experienced by the protagonist, often at the end of a story. As a literary term, epiphany originates with James Joyce, who built each short story in his *Dubliners* around what he called an epiphany. "Boys and Girls" ends with the protagonist's epiphany about her identity as a girl. "All the Troubles of the World" reveals that Multivac wants to die because it knows too much about the problems of human nature.

episode
An episode is an incident or event within the main plot of the story. Episodes can be viewed as selected portions or scenes developed in detail by the author. One episode in "The Man to Send Rain Clouds" is the visit to the priest.

escapist fiction
This refers to stories written solely to entertain the reader, thus helping the reader to escape the daily cares and problems of reality. While provoking thought on the part of the reader and providing entertainment for the reader are not mutually exclusive, the term *escapist fiction* suggests an extreme. Escapist fiction has lively melodramatic plots and stereotyped or flat characters, and it requires limited involvement on the part of the reader. Many mass-marketed science fiction, westerns, thrillers, and romances fall into the category of escapist fiction.

"Blue Boots" is close to being escapist fiction and originally appeared in a book of crime fiction.

exposition
Exposition is background information provided by the author to further the development of plot, conflict, setting, and characterization. The first three paragraphs of "The Portable Phonograph" not only describe a post-war futuristic setting, but also a mood of desolation.

falling action

The falling action is the action immediately following the climax and lasting until the end of the story. An example of falling action in "Harrison Bergeron" is when George and Hazel talk after watching their son get shot on television.

fantasy

A fantasy is a highly exaggerated or improbable story. As a rule, fantasy has fantastic events, characters, and/or settings not found in real life. "The Merman of Olsen's Island" is a fantasy about achieving peace after the breakdown of a relationship.

fiction

Fiction is any narrative which is imagined or invented. Fiction may be based on actual happenings, which can, in turn, make fiction seem realistic.

flashback

A flashback is a sudden switch in the plot from the present to the past. This device may be used to illustrate an important point or to aid in characterization. There are several flashbacks to the mother's past in "A Moving Day."

flat character

See *character*.

foil

A foil is a character whose behaviour, attitudes, and/or opinions contrast with those of the protagonist. The contrast of the foil helps the reader to understand better the character and motivation of the protagonist. Two foils are the carver and the painter in "Why Don't You Carve Other Animals."

foreshadowing

This is a device which hints or warns of events to happen later in the story. Foreshadowing prepares the reader for the climax, the denouement, and any changes in the protagonist. The young man's early history in "Love Song" foreshadows his strange death.

form
Form is a general term referring to the way in which a story is put together, its shape or structure. Form is sometimes called the "how" of a story, and includes both technique and style.

goal
See *motivation*.

hero (or heroine)
This is a protagonist of a story who possesses heroic qualities such as courage, or virtues such as honesty. The terms *hero* and *heroine* are not interchangeable with the more general term *protagonist*. The man in "The Inheritor" is a hero by virtue of his determination and superior thinking skills.

humour
Humour refers to writing that is intended to amuse the reader or provoke laughter. "Blue Boots" is a clever, humorous piece about a would-be criminal in search of a victim.

images (and imagery)
Images are concrete details and figures of speech that help the reader form vivid impressions of the subject. Imagery refers to the pattern of images in a single piece of writing. In "The Metaphor," Miss Hancock is described in images such as "fond of peasant dresses encrusted with embroidery, from which loose threads invariably dangled."

indeterminate ending
A story ending in which there is no clear outcome, result, or resolved conflict is called an indeterminate ending. "Blue Boots" ends indeterminately before a crime can be committed.

in medias res

In medias res (pronounced in MA-deas RAS) is a Latin term which refers to readers joining a story "in the middle of things." The story "Grace Period" starts abruptly in medias res with the husband watching his wife pull out of the driveway as he trims the hedge.

interpretive fiction

This term refers to stories which have meaningful, usually realistic, plots, conflicts, settings, and characters. Interpretive fiction is usually serious in tone and designed to be interpreted. It is instructive, unlike escapist fiction, which is designed chiefly for entertainment. Most of the stories in this book are examples of interpretive fiction.

irony

Irony involves contrast between two elements and, as a literary device, provides depth of meaning and impact. When irony is used, meanings tend to become unconcealed or contradictory, an effect which we call "ironic." The following are three common types of irony:

1. *Verbal irony* occurs when what a character says contrasts with what the character actually means.
2. *Dramatic irony* occurs when what a character says or believes contrasts with what the reader or other characters know to be true, based on information given to us by the author. An example of dramatic irony occurs in "The Metaphor" when Charlotte does not tell the other students that she had Miss Hancock as a teacher in junior high school.
3. *Situational irony* (or irony of situation) occurs when what finally takes place is different from what was expected or seemed appropriate. When Miss Strangeworth opens a letter to herself, the last thing she is expecting is to find that her roses have been destroyed.

juxtaposition

See *contrast*.

local colour (and regionalism)

Local colour refers to the detail in a story that is specific to a geographic region or an environment. Local colour develops the setting and atmosphere, increases reader interest, and adds authenticity by including descriptions of locale, dress, customs, dialect, and ways of thinking and feeling characteristic of local people. Regionalism refers to stories in which setting (developed with local colour) is of significance to the text and necessary to the writer's purpose.

"Ashes for the Wind" uses names, regional details, and political references to suggest a Colombian setting.

mood

See *atmosphere*.

moral

The implied lesson of a story is called the moral. Viewed in isolation, a moral is a relatively unimportant part of a story and should not be confused with theme, a far more significant element of fiction. A moral of "Choices" is that one never knows what someone is like until a crisis tests that person.

motivation (and goal)

Motivation is both what causes a character to do what he or she does and the character's aim, or goal, in taking that action. The character's temperament and circumstances determine motivation. The pursuit by the protagonist of his or her goal results in the story's conflict. Characters must have sufficient and plausible motivation in order for a reader to find the story effective. In "North End Faust," one of Alex's motivations for experimenting is to see if others can adapt to the chamber as well as he does.

narrative

Narrative is another word for "story." Narratives contain the following elements: plot, conflict, characters, setting, and point of view. Narratives may be fictional or non-fictional, and include novels, autobiographies, biographies, short stories, and anecdotes.

narrator

The narrator is the storyteller. In the case of a story told from the first person perspective, the narrator is one of the characters; in the case of a story told from the objective, omniscient, or limited omniscient points of view, the author assumes the role of narrator. The narrator in "The Poison of the Blue Rose" is an unhappily married woman.

plot

The storyline or organization of events or episodes within a story is called the plot. The conventional plot has rising action, a climax, and falling action. See also *subplot*.

point of view

The point of view is the perspective from which a story is seen or told. Point of view establishes the relationships among author, reader, and characters. The following are the three most common points of view:

1. *First-person narrative* features a character telling the story directly to the reader in the first person (that is, using "I"). This point of view tells us what the character thinks and feels from a vantage point "inside" the story, from one character's perspective. "The Organized Woman Story" and "The Merman of Olsen's Island" are first-person narratives.

2. *Limited omniscient* or third-person narrative occurs when a story is told from "outside" the characters, but from the perspective of one character. In this point of view, the characters are referred to in the third person (as "he" or "she"), and the narrator is limited to knowing the thoughts and feelings of only that one character. "Fear of the Sea" and "The Curlew's Cry" are limited omniscient narratives.

3. *Omniscient narrative* or "all-knowing" narrative tells the story with knowledge of the thoughts and feelings of more than one, or all the characters. "Ashes for the Wind" and "Harrison Bergeron" use omniscient narratives.

predicament
A predicament is a difficult problem or unpleasant situation. Predicament should not be confused with a related term, *dilemma* (see above). In "Ashes for the Wind," Juan's predicament is that he wants to stay on his farm despite eviction notices and death threats.

prose
Ordinary language or literary expression not marked by obvious rhythm or rhyme is called prose. This type of language is used in short stories, essays, and modern plays. The text you are now reading is written in prose.

protagonist
The protagonist is the main character of a story. While some protagonists may be heroes or heroines (or antiheroes and antiheroines), the term protagonist is broader and does not depend on moral judgements of the character's actions. Two protagonists are Vanessa in "To Set Our House in Order" and the poet-narrator in "The Organized Woman Story."

purpose
Purpose refers to the main effect the author hopes to achieve, for example, entertainment, thought, enlightenment, action, demonstrating something about life or human nature. Rarely does a story have only one purpose. Purpose may include theme, but should not simply be equated with the story's main idea. One purpose of "Love Story" is to pay tribute to a unique boy and his intense relationship with a girl.

realism
This term refers to any subject matter or techniques that create a true-to-life impression for the reader. Writers of realism present life "as it is" and as though the stories have simply "told themselves." In another sense, realism can also refer to stories about simple, everyday people. See also *fantasy, romance,* and *verisimilitude.*

A realistic story is "Fear of the Sea," which is about a boy's first encounter with death.

realistic character
See *character.*

regionalism
See *local colour.*

resolution
See *denouement.*

rising action
Rising action in a story consists of the incidents that precede the climax. During this stage of the story, background information is given, characters and conflicts are introduced, and suspense is built up. There may even be moments of crisis. Typically, the rising action is often longer than the falling action of a story. See also *plot.* The rising action in "The Thunderstorm" consists of the events leading up to Elijah losing his chariot wheel.

romance
Entertaining stories that contain one or more of the following characteristics—fantasy, improbability, extravagance, naiveté, love, adventure, myth—are generally called romances. "The Museum of Vain Endeavours" contains most of the above characteristics of romance.

round character
See *character.*

satire
Satire is the use of irony to ridicule an idea, a person, or a thing, often with an aim to provoke change. Satire usually targets human foibles or vices. "Harrison Bergeron" is a biting satire about egalitarianism carried to an extreme.

science fiction

Science fiction is speculative writing about the effects of technology or science on the future of human beings. While the purpose of some science fiction is purely escapist entertainment, science fiction can be written for a range of serious purposes, too. "The Portable Phonograph" is an example of science fiction.

setting

The setting is the time and place of a story. While, in some stories, setting may affect the plot, conflict, characters, and theme, in others, it can be of great significance and the main fiction element. "Fear of the Sea" is set in a Caribbean seacoast town in modern times.

short story

A short story is a brief fictional prose narrative, having one main character, a single plot, limited setting, and one main effect. Edgar Allan Poe, one of the first significant theorists and practitioners of short story writing, said that short stories:
1. can be read in one sitting, and derive their power from the fact the writer has to select details for economy and emphasis
2. have a single effect or purpose and are constructed so that every sentence from the first to the last one supports that effect
3. leave the reader with a feeling of satisfaction and finality, desiring no further completion or alternate ending
4. have their basis in truth or life-likeness.

static character

See *character*.

stereotype

A stereotype is any fixed pattern of plot or character. Stereotyped plots usually fall into the realm of escapist fiction. Stereotyped characters are familiar figures in fiction, such as the hard-boiled private investigator, the absent-minded professor, or the military officer with a stiff upper lip. See also *character*. A stereotyped plot occurs in "The Inheritor" when man triumphs over nature.

stream of consciousness

Stream of consciousness is a modern narrative technique that attempts to depict the uninterrupted flow of feelings and random thoughts of a character's mind. However, the author includes details relevant to plot, character, and theme in the apparently natural flow of thoughts and feelings. "Choices" is written in such a way as to present the random thoughts of Peggy.

style

Style is the individual manner in which an author expresses himself or herself. In fiction, style is basically determined by such grammatical and sensory aspects as diction, sentences, and images. "Choices" is written in a poetic, impressionistic style with vivid images and short, fragmented sentences.

subplot

A subplot is a minor storyline, secondary to the main plot. Subplots may be related or unrelated to the main action, but may also be a reflection of, or variation on, the main plot. Compared to novels, short stories tend to have few, brief subplots (or none) because of the brevity and density required of the short story genre. An example of a subplot in "The Metaphor" is seen in the ongoing conflict between Charlotte and her mother.

surprise ending

The sudden twist in the direction of a story, producing a resolution that surprises the reader and often the story's characters as well, is called a surprise ending. An example of a surprise ending occurs in "The Possibility of Evil" when Miss Strangeworth gets a poison pen letter announcing the destruction of her favourite roses.

suspense

Suspense is the feeling of anxiety and uncertainty experienced by the reader (and possibly characters) about the outcome of events or the protagonist's fate. In "The Lamp at Noon," both Paul and the reader are in suspense about what will happen to Ellen and the baby in their desperate flight during a dust storm.

symbol

A symbol is something that stands for or represents something else. Characters, objects, events, conflicts, and settings can all be symbolic. The museum in "The Museum of Vain Endeavours" is a symbol of human frustration and failed aspirations.

thematic statement

This is a one-sentence general statement about life or human nature that can be derived by interpreting a story's overall message. It does not mention specifics from the story (that is, specific names, settings, or events), but instead generalizes accurately and comprehensively about the story's main meaning. A thematic statement for "The Possibility of Evil" might be as follows: Evil is circular and often returns to plague the agents or perpetrators of mischief.

theme

The theme is the central idea of the story, usually implied rather than directly stated. It is a story's observation about life or human nature, and should never be confused with the moral. The theme of "Another Evening at the Club" is about how people will lie rather than admit personal error.

universality

Universality is the quality of a story that gives it relevance beyond the narrow confines of its particular characters, subject, or setting. Stories which have universality reveal human nature or common truths of life experience. Universality in a story also implies that the story could apply to most people's experience. "The Poison of the Blue Rose" is a universal story about lost true loves.

verisimilitude

Verisimilitude is a life-like quality possessed by a story as revealed through its plot, setting, conflict, and characterization. See also *realism*. "A Moving Day" has the verisimilitude of a situation in which a parent is resolving and disposing of her past.

vicarious experience

Vicarious experience refers to the reader sharing imaginatively in a character's feelings and experiences. Vicariously (literally, "acting or done for another") experiences can be had, for example, through reading travel literature. "Grace Period" takes the reader vicariously through the start of a nuclear war.

Permission Credits

Every reasonable effort has been made to acquire permission for copyright material used in this text, and to acknowledge such indebtedness accurately. Any errors or omissions called to the publisher's attention will be corrected in future printings. In particular, we would be grateful for any information regarding the copyright holders of *The Curlew's Cry* by J. Leslie Bell, and *The Inheritor* by Frank Roberts.

Love Song by Deirdre Kessler, from WATER STUDIES: NEW VOICES IN MARITIME FICTION, edited by Ian Colford, Pottersfield Press, 1998. Reprinted by permission of the author. *Grace Period* by Will Baker, from FLASH FICTION: 72 VERY SHORT STORIES edited by James and Denise Thomas, and Tom Mazuka, W.W. Norton & Co., Inc. 1992. First published in GREAT STREAM REVIEW, Vol. 1, No. 1. Copyright 1989 by Will Baker. Reprinted with permission of the author. *Blue Boots* by Carol Newhouse, from SECRET TALES OF THE ARCTIC TRAILS: STORIES OF CRIME AND ADVENTURE IN CANADA'S FAR NORTH, edited by David Skene-Martin, Simon & Pierre, 1997. Reprinted by permission of Simon & Pierre and the author. *Internal Monologue on a Corner in Havana* by Josefina de Diego. Translation © 1998 Dick Cluster. From CUBANA: CONTEMPORARY FICTION BY CUBAN WOMEN, edited by Mirta Yanez and published by Beacon Press. Reprinted by permission of Josefina de Diego and Dick Cluster. *The Museum of Vain Endeavours* by Cristina Peri Rossi, translated by Margaret Jull Costa, from THE FABER BOOK OF CONTEMPORARY LATIN AMERICAN SHORT STORIES, edited by Nick Caistor and published by Faber & Faber. Originally published as "El museo de los esfuerzos inutiliser." Copyright © 1983 by Cristina Peri Ross. Reprinted by permission of the author. *North End Faust* by Ed Kleiman from THE IMMORTALS by Ed Kleiman, NeWest Press, 1980. Reprinted by permission of the author. *Lenses* by Leah Silverman. First published in ON SPEC,

Joel T. Maki, Douglas & McIntyre, 1996. Reprinted by permission of the author. *Edward's Rocks* by Barbara Ritson from WORDSCAPE 4: MYSTERY AND SUSPENSE STORIES AND POEMS edited by Cynthia Green. Copyright © 1997 Barbara Ritson. Reprinted by permission of the author.

Photo Credits

Abbreviations: t = top; c = centre; b = bottom; l = left; r = right

p. v: (t) D. Madison/Tony Stone Images, (c) P. Samuels/Tony Stone Images, (b) C. Bissel/Tony Stone Images; p. vi: (t) D. Sanders/Masterfile, (tc) F. Siteman/Tony Stone Images, (bc) D. Sarton/Tony Stone Images, (b) G. Fitzpatrick; p. vii: (t) M. Tomalty/Masterfile, (c) J. Dole/Image Bank; p. x: D. Madison/ Tony Stone Images; p. 6: K. Brofsky/Tony Stone Images; p. 10: C. Windsor/Tony Stone Images; p. 16: P. Samuels/Tony Stone Images; p. 18: L. Resnick/Tony Stone Images; p. 40: C. Bissel/ Tony Stone Images; p. 43: B. Pieters/Masterfile; p. 50: M. Hunn/ Frederick Lewis/Archive Photos; p. 58: P. Conrath/Tony Stone Images; p. 66: D. Sanders/Masterfile; p. 70: R. Boudreau/Tony Stone Images; p. 76: G. Faint/Image Bank; p. 84: B. Nielsen; p. 102: F. Siteman/Tony Stone Images; p. 110: R. Anania/Tony Stone Images; p. 124: T. Horowitz/First Light; p. 128: D. Sarto/ Tony Stone Images; p. 140: Archive Photos; p. 152: G. Fitzpatrick; p. 154: A. Sirulnikof/First Light; p. 164: B. Nielsen; p. 176: N. Dolding/Tony Stone Images; p. 186: M. Tomalty/Masterfile; p. 188: B. Nielsen; p. 206: D. Peebles/First Light; p. 216: COMSTOCK; p. 234: J. Dole/Image Bank; p. 237: R. Welb/Tony Stone Images; p. 255: COMSTOCK/H.A. Roberts; p. 264: B. Brooks/Masterfile; p. 292: B. Nielsen; p. 300: D. Wilson/ Masterfile.